SCIENCE, TECHNOLOGY, AND RELIGIOUS IDEAS

Edited by

Mark H. Shale
Kentucky State University

George W. Shields
Kentucky State University

UNIVERSITY
PRESS OF
AMERICA

Lanham • New York • London

INSTITUTE
FOR
LIBERAL
STUDIES

Copyright © 1994 by
University Press of America®, Inc.
4720 Boston Way
Lanham, Maryland 20706

3 Henrietta Street
London WC2E 8LU England

Copublished with the
Institute for Liberal Studies

Library of Congress Cataloging-in-Publication Data

Science, technology, and religious ideas / edited by Mark H. Shale,
George W. Shields.
p.   cm.
Papers originally presented at three conferences held in 1990, 1991,
and 1992, sponsored by the Institute for Liberal Studies, Kentucky
State University.
Includes bibliographical references.
1. Religion and science – Congresses.   2. Technology – Religious
aspects – Congresses.   I. Shale, Mark H.   II. Shields, George W.
III. Kentucky State University.   Institute for Liberal Studies.
   BL241.S324   1993   291.1'75 – dc20   93-35875   CIP

ISBN 0-8191-9346-1 (cloth : alk. paper)
ISBN 0-8191-9347-X (pbk. : alk. paper)

 The paper used in this publication meets the minimum requirements of
American National Standard for Information Sciences—Permanence
of Paper for Printed Library Materials, ANSI Z39.48–1984.

CONTENTS

22 54

90566

PREFACE

While the relation between science and religion is an issue perhaps as old as the existence of such enterprises, the past two decades or so have seen extraordinary developments in the physical and biological sciences which have acutely raised new possibilities for conversation about the cognitive integrity of religion and moral values. Indeed, the literature of science-religion studies has recently burgeoned and is notable for the contributions of natural scientists as well as philosophers, theologians, and cultural historians (for a brief reading list see my essay, Note 2). It comes as no surprise then that such lively interdisciplinary ferment would reach the attention of even the popular press. As I sit writing this sentence, I am glancing at the cover of the 1992 year's end *Time* magazine, which reads, "What Does Science Tell Us About God?"

It is thus especially timely and appropriate that the Institute for Liberal Studies (hereafter ILS) at Kentucky State University publish the proceedings of its annual conference on science, technology, and religious ideas, inclusive of the years 1990, 1991, and 1992. In so doing the Institute hopes to achieve at least two aims—to make the ILS conference itself known to a wider audience and to make available a number of new essays authored by a group of promising younger as well as already accomplished senior scholars. Before introducing these essays and their organization into the volume's three parts, it might prove helpful to provide some historical background concerning Kentucky State University's Institute for Liberal Studies.

In 1982 Kentucky State University was designated the Commonwealth of Kentucky's public liberal studies university with the smallest student-faculty ratio. With this new mission came the creation of the Whitney Young College of Leadership Studies (devoted to "Great Books," the study of classical languages, and the history of science and mathematics), and the Integrative Studies Program (devoted to interdisciplinary examination of the history of culture). With the emergence of these institutions came the appointment of a faculty with strong interests in interdisciplinary conversation and scholarly research. The Institute for Liberal Studies was created to provide opportunities for conferences and other activities which are of direct interest to this interdisciplinary community of scholars.

In Fall 1988 discussions were underway regarding possible topics for an ILS conference, so I suggested to then ILS Director, Dr. Paul Ciholas (now retired), that the field of science-religion studies would be of great personal interest and likely to provide the vehicle for the kind of interdisciplinary scholarship we were attempting to foster. To our delight the concept was well-received by then President Raymond M. Burse, who graciously provided an initial budget. A conference *Proceedings* which would feature essays by noted plenary speakers and also highlight some of the scholarship of Kentucky State University's own faculty members was part of the initial plan. Fortunately, Frederick Ferré, surely one of the American deans of philosophy of technology and religion, warmly agreed to be our first plenary speaker. We were thus set for a two-day conference, held 6-7 April 1990, at the Capital Plaza Hotel in Frankfort, Kentucky, only a short distance from the University campus. Following the success of the first conference, the ILS conference committee decided to keep the announced theme of "Science, Technology, and Religious Ideas" as the continuing theme of future conferences. A second conference featured eminent Notre Dame historian and philosopher of science, Ernan McMullin, and was held 11-12 April 1991, followed by a third, featuring Stanley Jaki, held for an expanded three days on 2-4 April 1992. The ILS plans to continue the conference indefinitely into the future.

While the University's own "in-house" conference *Proceedings* are annual publications, the collection of them into a University Press of America edition has offered the possibility of a more coherent thematic organization. The eleven essays which originally appeared in the annual publications are here freshly edited and in several cases substantially revised. The essays rather neatly and naturally fall into the following thematic categories, which represent the book's first three parts, respectively: the Nature of Science, Religion, and Technology; Recent Physics and the Design Argument; and Studies in the History of Science-Religion Interaction. The essays are placed within each part according to chronological order, that is, essays at the 1990 conference precede 1991 papers which are then followed by 1992 essays.

Part I, devoted to explorations of the general nature of science, technology, religion and their relationships, begins with Professor Ferré's delightfully titled, "Christendom Goes to College" (Plenary Session, 1990). Here he presents a sweeping vision of the connections and disaffections between science, technology, and religious ideas. Ferré challenges what he sees as three "simple but wrong views" of the science-religion relation, very roughly, the view that science and religion are valid in their own domain, the view that religiously motivated attacks upon science are to be encouraged, and the view that science should set limits for whatever religious thinkers are permitted to say. Ferré goes on to suggest that the "triumphant abstractions of modern science" and their accompanying world-view may well yield to a new paradigm of ecologically inspired "post-modern science," a science more amenable to the qualitative domain of religion, art, and morality. Jacquelyn Ann Kegley's 1992 essay on "Technology as Creativity and Embodiment" echoes Ferré's post-modernist theme in a somewhat distinct but complementary fashion by arguing that technology is inherently value-laden because it resides on a continuum of human aesthetic expression which includes art, craft, and science as more or less arbitrary divisions. And Thor Hall's 1990 paper on Michael Polanyi's "fiduciary" critique of Kant's separation of the domains of "fact" and "value" provides one mode of underpinning for Ferré's and Kegley's shared view that science and value cannot be sharply separated without serious difficulties. A contrasting voice is heard from Professor Jaki (Plenary Session, 1992), who calls for more forthrightness and intellectual honesty on the part of both scientists and religionists. In his view, science and religion are distinctive domains and recognition of this distinctiveness is necessary for resolving what he envisions as the "identity crisis" of science and religion. Finally, my colleague Ronald Mawby moves the discussion in a rather different but intriguing direction. He calls our attention to the apparent fecundity of "paraconsistent strategies" in science and religion, strategies as found, say, in quantum electrodynamics, or portions of Newton's calculus procedure, or in the orthodox doctrine of the Trinity, which reject the usual canons of logical consistency in standard logic. Mawby argues that such paraconsistent strategies are rational provided that they issue in significant intellectual advance.

Part II, concerned with the recent notion of "fine-tuning" in cosmological physics and its possible implications for a theistic design argument, begins with my own 1990 contribution on "The Wider Design Argument and the New Physics." Focusing on physicist Paul Davies' discussion of theism and theistic arguments in his *God and the New Physics*, I argue that the prospects for a theistic design model of the universe are stronger in the light of the new cosmological picture than Davies seems to suggest, and I offer some particular logico-philosophical objections to a number of non-theistic metaphysical scenarios adumbrated by Davies. Professor Dennis Temple's 1991 essay, "The New Design Argument: What Does It Prove?," complements my own effort by unpacking the logic of "why explanations" and by suggesting that, in the light of this logic, the creator hypothesis is simple and direct when compared to many-universe theories. Ernan McMullin's "Fine-Tuning the Universe?" (Plenary Session, 1991) presents an historical review of scientific inquiry into origins, including recent anthropic cosmology, and in course makes a case for his view that recent cosmology should be taken as a signal to enlarge theological horizons, not to underpin a new natural theology with apologetic intent.

Part III re-examines some important moments in the history of science-religion interaction. Co-editor and colleague Mark Shale's 1991 address on "William McDougall and the Reaction Against Victorian Scientific Naturalism" begins the series with an inquiry into McDougall's struggle against reductionist models of mind having currency in the Victorian hey-day of T.

H. Huxley and C. H. Lewes. This is followed by historian Ron Levy's 1992 examination of the status of Reformation "Theological Voluntarism" in the thought of the great experimentalist Robert Boyle and by philosopher Edward Schoen's 1992 revisitation of Galileo's challenge to tradition. Professor Schoen argues that it was Galileo's rejection of the prevailing method of deduction from necessary First Principles and his bold coupling of observation, analogy, and prediction that was genuinely revolutionary. Each of these historical studies, I submit, throws some new light on their subjects.

The volume is completed by a comprehensive catalogue of descriptions of conference papers given over the past three years. Since the departmental and institutional affiliation of each author is given, it will then be possible for scholars interested in particular research topics to correspond or seek copies of papers.

Acknowledgements

In closing, I must acknowledge the support and hard work of a number of individuals. First of all, a sustained word of thanks to Paul Ciholas, to whom the co-editors warmly dedicate this book. A graduate of the University of Paris and Ph.D. recipient from the University of Strasbourg, Dr. Ciholas came to Kentucky State after teaching history of ideas in the undergraduate honors program at the University of Kentucky. Professor of Integrative Studies and the original Director of the Institute for Liberal Studies, Dr. Ciholas played a leading role in the implementation of programs designed to fulfill the University's mission as a unique liberal studies institution. His energy and vision were part and parcel of the success of the initial conference and indeed the very life of the Institute itself. Secondly, acknowledgement is due the current ILS Director, Dr. George Weick. His enthusiastic support, editorial advice, and careful reading of portions of the manuscript were greatly appreciated. Mark Shale, my co-editor, deserves credit for the long hours spent reviewing the essays, making stylistic improvements, and communicating suggestions to the contributors. Yet perhaps the greatest debt of gratitude is owed to Mrs. Nancy Brooks, ILS Administrative Secretary. Not only did she expertly type the manuscript, but she performed countless detailed tasks during all three conferences with much efficiency and professionalism. A special word of thanks goes to Dr. Mark Garrison, Professor of Psychology at Kentucky State, who offered both expert technical assistance in preparation of the manuscript and sound editorial advice.

Several administrators at Kentucky State have been strongly supportive and have graciously provided financial resources for ILS conference activities. They truly deserve our thanks. I have mentioned former President Burse, but the support has continued firmly under former President John Wolfe and under the current leadership of Dr. Mary L. Smith, who addressed conferees at a 1992 conference dinner. I should also mention Dr. Lester Newman, Dean of the College of Arts and Sciences, and Dr. William Pollard, Dean of the Whitney Young College, who served as co-directors of the ILS during the 1991 conference.

Finally, a word of thanks to the many faculty members at Kentucky State University who very competently served as moderators of paper sessions. It has indeed been a privilege to serve with a group of colleagues who are not only highly collegial, but are among some of the most intellectually talented persons I have encountered anywhere.

GEORGE W. SHIELDS
KENTUCKY STATE UNIVERSITY

PART I

THE NATURE OF SCIENCE, TECHNOLOGY AND RELIGION

CHRISTENDOM GOES TO COLLEGE[1]

FREDERICK FERRÉ

I begin with a true story about the experience of a fourteen-year-old immigrant boy from Sweden, living in Minnesota on a farm in 1922. He was at an impressionable stage of early adolescence, the deeply religious son of an extremely conservative Swedish Baptist preacher. The boy had immigrated all alone to America the year before and was now busily learning English, doing farm work to cover his room and board, studying at a local academy by day, and attending frequent Swedish religious services in the evenings.

One evening, a subject that had been simmering in that religious farming community came to a boil in a sermon. The preacher had seen the shiny spikes of faithlessness spreading from farmhouse to farmhouse, from barn to hayloft and silo. "Enough!" he shouted: the use of lightning rods to attempt to deflect the wrath of God was sheerest sin. The boy listened with fascination as the preacher demonstrated that attempts to shield lives and property from lightning in this world would be requited with fire—everlasting fire—in the next. Thunderbolts were God's to hurl, not man's to deflect. The fires of hell, deep under the earth on which the congregation now sat and quaked, were even then being stoked for those who insisted on rising in rebellion against God's will by installing newfangled lightning rods. Amen.

My father, Nels Ferré—for it was he who was the adolescent Swedish boy listening to the sermon and discussing it earnestly for months thereafter—had at that time no doubts about hellfire. His father had preached on it often enough. But something did not ring quite true even then. Could God's will be truly foiled by a steel rod and a grounding wire? Was it really wrong to try to protect family and livestock from the storms that swept in from the prairies with such seemingly undiscriminating force? Was God really directing the thunderbolts? Should he believe that the God Jesus called our 'Father in Heaven' really would punish farmers for taking whatever meager technological precautions might be available?

In due course the young Nels entered Boston University and continued to learn and to question. In physics he learned what generates electricity in the turbulent, supercharged atmosphere of the interior of thunder cells, and he learned about the impersonal conditions that influence lightning strokes

3

on their jagged paths of least resistance to the discharge of electrical potentials. In geology he learned theories about the interior of the earth, none of which included chambers in which Satan might eternally be torturing sinners. He was in a dilemma. The ideas of science were too logically structured, too tightly tied to vast domains of tangible evidence, for him to discard or ignore them; but these ideas were not compatible with the religious ideas of his father or of the Minnesota farm community. He could not abandon his heartfelt religious faith—indeed, in time he himself became a clergyman and a prominent theologian—but he was required by intellectual honesty to resolve his dilemma by modifying his religious ideas in the light of the findings of science.

1. The Learning Pains of Christendom

In this story we have a good parable for what happened more generally in response to science within our modern Western civilization. We all know the epic drama, but it is worth review, since it is the starting-point for all of us. Once upon a time, the most sophisticated and responsible thinkers of their age had religious ideas that were very much like those of my teen-age father before he went to college. Those religious ideas included an image of the Earth as at the center of the physical universe, an Earth surrounded by the visible heavenly bodies (which were thought to be made of material entirely different from the vulgar stuff of the Earth); these bodies themselves were pictured as embraced by Heaven itself, the dwelling of angels, God, and the redeemed, above the highest and most ethereal spheres. Below the crust on which we live was Hell. This universe was not believed to be very old. The best calculations were that four thousand and four years before the birth of Christ, God had created all this out of nothing in six magnificent days, during which the ancestors of all human beings, Adam and Eve, were brought directly and specially into being and given dominion over all the rest of creation.

Then, gradually, Christendom went to college. One of the earliest "professors" was Nicholas Copernicus, whom Martin Luther called, "the fool" (*der Narr*) for wanting to turn everything upside down, to displace Earth from its center of attention. But if Copernicus could be dismissed as a daffy old eccentric, the really radical challenger of religious ideas was his disciple, Galileo, who added empirical proof, aided by technological instrumentation in the form of his newfangled telescope. Through it, the moon could be seen as having mountains that cast shadows, suggesting that heavenly bodies were made up of matter—dirt and rocks—as vulgar as the stuff we sit on here. Likewise, Jupiter could be seen as another planet with its own moons, which fit with Copernicus's theory; and Venus could be seen to have phases, just like our moon—all of which fit the new theory too well to be dismissed, as Luther had recommended. The new ideas were fought, of course. The battle surged back and forth. But in the end the vast majority of religious people found, as my father did in college, that their religious ideas could survive and even improve from rethinking in view of the solid findings of science.

This explains why, in the middle of the twentieth century, when that great atheologian, Nikita Khrushchev, proclaimed that Uri Gagarin, the first Soviet cosmonaut, had finally "disproved" Christianity by going around in the heavens without once encountering God or the angels, his claims were met with mere amusement from religious believers. Modern religious people had by then so firmly modified their religious ideas, now to include the Copernican Revolution, that Khrushchev's blustering was no threat at all. Most religious believers found nothing theologically damaging, either, in our American expeditions to the moon, even though they brought back samples of rock and dust that would have driven Galileo's critics to frenzies of rebuttal.

It is extremely important to our topic to notice that this can happen. It has happened over and over again. Religious ideas have had to accommodate the age of the earth being stretched by science from roughly four thousand years to roughly four billion years before Christ, and, embraced by that million-fold increase, these ideas have had to make room for a geological understanding of our planet that has nothing to do with Hell, and with vast biological evolutionary changes that do not cohere with stories of the special creation of a literal Adam and Eve.

Some continue to fight, of course, and the battlefront surges back and forth over specific issues. But the essential point of my allegory—and of this story of the parallel experience of Christendom at the hands of its great science "professors" like Copernicus, Galileo, Lyell, Darwin, and Freud—is that religious ideas are not condemned to be static in the face of science. Over and over again, scientific findings challenge religious ideas; but, with equal regularity, religious believers find ways of refining their ideas to maintain what they then can affirm as no less adequate—perhaps more adequate—to the essentials of faith. Science has forced major changes in religious ideas, but to date science has not come close to eradicating religion, even from among the most highly educated groups of modern society. The more intelligent the believers, and the better educated, the more capable they are of dealing with scientific challenges on the level of intellectual content. There are intellectual strategies, forged over the centuries, to deal with such intellectual threats.

Threats to religion, however, are by no means always intellectual ones. This is one of the greatest significances of technology for our topic, quite apart from science. Remember the alarm of my father's Swedish preacher at the spread of lightning rods among his rural flock. Technology puts power into human hands. Consider the simple lightning rod as symbol for human empowerment. It is a pretty good symbol for science-led technology: First, it is based on at least partial human understanding of what is going on in nature—lightning recognized experimentally (thanks to Benjamin Franklin) as electricity tending to arc across the potential between cloud and ground—and, second, while it may not work all the time, such technology attempts to channel vast forces according to our interests. It gives us something intelligent to do about cosmic forces, perceived as natural phenomena, rather than leaving us absolutely helpless and dependent on them.

But Friedrich Schleiermacher (1768-1834), who is often called the father of modern theology, defined religion itself as "the feeling of absolute dependence." What could be a more direct challenge to religion, so understood, than implements of human empowerment, designed to reduce our state and feelings of dependence? To the extent that our feelings of dependence are reduced by technology, it would seem that religious *attitudes* are undermined, even though religious *ideas* may not be directly challenged. This would seem to hold true for any technology; but if modern, science-based technology is more and more empowering, directly in proportion to the increasing penetration of scientific understanding into the natural order on which we depend, then science poses another indirect threat to religion, not so much through its theory as through its application.

Long before the age of scientific technology, important religious strands within the Jewish and Christian tradition were deeply suspicious of the attitudes of human mastery represented by crafts and inventions. This perennial suspicion is dug deep into the biblical tradition. We find it vividly in the story of the Tower of Babel. There human technologocial prowess is depicted as a challenge to God. The tower, which was to have its "top in the heavens" (Genesis 11:4), was just a sample of what human beings could do if they should remain united on a technical project:

> And the Lord said, "Behold, they are one people, and they have all one language, and this is only the beginning of what they will do; and nothing that they propose to do will now be impossible for them" (Genesis 11:6).

Such prowess was clearly not permissible, so self-evidently wrong that no reason is thought necessary to be given for its impermissibility. More generally, the technologies of civilization itself—the word *"civil"* in "civilization" coming from the Latin for "city"—are deeply suspect in the early stories of the scripture. Who, after all, is responsible for the first city? It was the major artifact of the murderous Cain.

Then Cain went away from the presence of the Lord, and dwelt in the Land of Nod, east of Eden . . . and he built a city, and called the name of the city after the name of his son, Enoch (Genesis 4:16-17).

Thus civilization itself bears the mark of Cain. The theme of the wicked city—Sodom, Nineveh, Babylon—runs like a deep organ tone through the biblical saga. We are situated by these stories just outside the urban technological enterprise, positioned with the viewpoint of a suspicious desert nomad looking askance at the corruption brought about by too much ease and by too much fancy know-how.

Now, however, practical know-how is instructed by theoretical science, and civilization is incomparably "fancier" than in early biblical days. The whole thrust of modern technological society has been to take charge of the universe, to assert human mastery over all things, and to struggle out from under oppressive feelings of dependence. There has never been a civilization less ready to accept dependence on anything. We dam the course of mighty rivers, we leap over distances by our airplanes and satellite dishes, we light up the night in our cities, we defy the cold and heat in our hermetically sealed buildings, we force the land to give forth food in unprecedented abundance, we create new species at will for our convenience or amusement, we hold death at bay with organ transplants and dream of cheating death altogether with cryogenic resurrections into future ages of still higher technologies. If the essence of religion is to be found in feelings of absolute dependence, there has never been a less religious civilization, in practice if not in profession, than our own.

Perhaps, however, real, functioning religion is to be measured, not in degrees of dependence-feelings but in what might be called our absolute commitments. That is, if, instead of judging by Schleiermacher's standard of "absolute dependence," we considered the religiousness of civilization in light of Tillich's "ultimate concern," ours might turn out, paradoxically, to be one of the great ages of faith. It has not been a faith based on feelings of dependence but on commitment to independence. Our modern society has been shaped by unlimited faith in ourselves, particularly in our capacity *to know* by the methods of modern science and our ability *to control* the world by embodying that scientific knowledge in our technologies.

Paradoxically, the typically modern worship of absolute independence, its world picture drawn in cool formulae of science and its ultimate concerns expressed in warm commitments to technological progress, has by the very immensity of its own triumphs brought modern civilization to a dawning awareness of limits that were always there, and has roused feelings, again, of utter dependence. The language of apocalypse is again being heard and increasingly heeded. Nuclear winter remains one realistic hell, whose jaws will gape for us, despite the end of the Cold War, as long as the means of atomic holocaust remain in existence and our increasingly fragmented globe is ruled by political units expressing collective selfishness, hatred, and fear. Another apocalyptic scenario, as we all know, flows from the destruction, by human technologies, of the protective ozone layer high in the atmosphere, without which all life as we know it could be endangered. The damage may already be irreversible, with the consequences of past releases of chlorofluorocarbons, those already in the environment, still working their way in the atmosphere. Or, perhaps, the apocalypse of vast, uncontrollable climate changes awaits us, with warming or cooling effects that may force evacuation of coastal cities and completely change the zones of arable land. Or, speaking of land, perhaps the erosion of land and the poisoning of water, worldwide, has already carried us over the brink at which long-term food supply for the earth's growing human population becomes unsustainable and the gaunt Horseman of famine will ride among us as never before. Or, might another apocalyptic Horseman, a plague of unprecedented proportions, against which we have no natural defenses, sweep us away as a result of our unwise injection of genetically engineered organisms into the biosphere?

This cheerless litany could go on and on. I recite an abbreviated version only to remind us all of the new sense of limits to which we as a civilization have been brought by the characteristic triumphs of modern technology. One of our greatest scientific and technological achievements was in the discovery and splitting of the atom. But that way we see nuclear nemesis. Our air conditioning and our automobiles are among our most typical artifacts. But those are among the more prominent causes of ozone depletion and climate change, respectively. The productivity of modern agribusiness has been one of our proudest boasts. But ruin of land and loss of genetic diversity looms that way. Biotechnology is one of the newest flowerings of our civilization. But unknown hazards lurk and the public remains fearful. As a civilization we are rapidly discovering that to make human empowerment through technology our ultimate concern is to worship an idol that does not finally have the power to save. Such technolatry[2] is being exposed in our time as folly. We are being forced instead to learn the appropriateness of attitudes of dependence on the powers that "limit and bear down on us"[3]; we are being required to learn the urgency of policies of interdependence with other humans, other species, and the earth.

2. Rebuilding a Positive Relationship

If we are truly in a mood, at last, to consider these things, what shall—or should—be the contributions of science, technology, and religious ideas to the new world that needs to emerge from the modern? What should each contribute to a chastened "postmodern" scientific, technological and religious civilization that has learned to live with limits and to blend personal responsibility with the acceptance of mutual dependence?

Rebuilding a positive relationship between technology and religious ideas should start with the recognition that religion has a still more complex relationship to technology than we have seen so far. One side of the relation is, as we have seen, well symbolized by suspicion of lightning rods. Christian doubts about technological faith are old and deep.[4] But there is another side of the relation to technology that rests on something else we have also noticed: namely, the ancient sense that the human species is somehow special, with unique powers and unique responsibilities. That sense is symbolized in the story of Adam and Eve, as we noticed earlier, by their depiction as being specially created and being given dominion over the rest of creation.

Much depends upon how the elements of that story are taken. In an age of scientific knowledge, the story of Adam and Eve cannot be interpreted literally by religious persons who care about intellectual integrity, but the story loses none of its spiritual depth on that account. What does it mean to have a sense that the human species is in some ultimately important way unique, set apart from everything else in our known universe? What does it mean to have a sense that nature, in some very fundamental way, is "ours"? More important yet: is it *right* to have this sense and to act on it?

Taken pridefully, the story of special human creation coupled with the doctrine of human dominion can encourage disregard for the natural environment and a rapacious policy toward the earth. This has doubtless been one of the sad legacies of one interpretation of the religious ideas found in the Genesis story. A huge literature debating this question has been generated in the years since Lynn White's scathing indictment of Christianity's "heavy burden of guilt" for the present environmental crisis, appeared more than two decades ago.[5] Arrogant anthropocentrism, a domineering attitude toward other species and the resources of our planet, are possible lessons to be taken from a selective reading of these scriptures. Even though such lessons are unbalanced distortions of the full Jewish and Christian approaches to the human place in nature, we must not forget that basic and important religious ideas encourage human empowerment even as other religious ideas warn against its spiritual perils.

Both sides are important and true. The human species, though fully part of nature (as symbolized by Adam's being fashioned out of "dust from the ground" [Genesis 2:7]), is also unique within known creation because of our powers of awareness, reflection, and anticipation. We are indeed "special" as the only animals who, as far as we know, can in any major way conceptualize the natural order in which we find ourselves (as symbolized by Adam "giving names" to all the creatures [Genesis 2:19-20]). We are also "special" as the only animals who, as best we can discover, can deliberately alter nature according to our long-range plans and by means of our purposefully designed implements. In those apparently unique powers we are godlike, relative to all other parts of nature. In that sense we see ourselves functioning in the image of God.

The religious legitimization of human powers of intervention in nature is an important theme to develop in the current debate over the shaping of the postmodern world. The modern world has bequeathed huge practical problems to the next generation, insoluble without new technologies of the most sophisticated sort. It is fortunate that spiritual wholeness need not necessarily be in conflict with technological inventiveness as such.

On the other hand, our fateful powers create for our species, uniquely in the known universe, the moral imperative to invent and intervene *responsibly*. So far as we know, none of our fellow creatures are blest—or saddled—with moral responsibility. If beavers build a dam that blocks a stream and destroys a primal forest, they carry no burden of guilt. If we humans decide to do the same thing, we must stand answerable for our actions. It seems unfair! But that is the glorious agony of our human condition. We have the powers of remembering our past and contemplating our future; we can anticipate (and, with science, increasingly accurately predict) the consequences of our actions; we can deliberate about conflicting principles of right and wrong; we can (and sometimes do) restrain our heedless impulses for the sake of greater long-run good and/or for the sake of justice in the distribution of the good we seek.

Here religious restraints against unbridled human empowerment work to keep us in balance. Our interventions into nature are not to be taken without a healthy sense of moral accountability. The creation is "good." Our special powers within it give us special opportunities to name and nurture it, to make a garden, but as stewards of the higher, wider good, we are not morally free to pillage and destroy. The pressing human task of creating a postmodern global garden, with wildness too, preserved in it, will need both the encouragement and the restraint of these religious ideas.

But are these basic religious ideas compatible with the best in science? Are these ideas not only *needed* and *beautiful*, but also open to belief as *true* without the sacrifice of intellectual integrity? As my questioning father's son, I too must finally ask these questions of truth. We have seen that conflicts between religious ideas and science often have been resolved by the gradual untangling of religious ideas from unacceptable factual claims. Are there new potential conflicts here, in fundamental religious ideas about human *freedom and responsibility*, and in key religious ideas about the *wider goodness of creation*, from which science will force us to retreat?

This is a complex question, on the unpacking of which I have spent much of my career. Before answering it, it seems to me that there are three simple, but wrong, positions that need to be set aside. The first of these is the popular dodge that holds, in effect, that scientific and religious ideas are each fine in their own domain, but have nothing logically to do with one another. On this conflict-avoiding proposal, religion and science constitute different "language games," structured by incommensurable logics and insulated from one another like island universes in empty intergalactic space. On first appearance this seems an urbane and comfortable position, but it suffers from two fatal defects. First, in real human life there are no hermetic barriers between interests and activities. Consequently, our ideas overlap and crisscross in countless ways. Settling for separate logics would be settling for permanent fragmentation, not only in language but also in thought and life. A second defect in this position is that it fails to account for the historical facts of conflict between religious and scientific ideas. Copernicus, Galileo, and Darwin knew that their ideas would clash with accepted religious ideas, and of course they did clash. The agonies of conflict, including those within my young father's mind, were not simply based on the misconstrual of the logics of scientific and religious discourse. They were not pseudo-conflicts. And yet, as we have seen, the blazes of conflict can and do die down, leaving the landscape changed but healthy. Religious ideas, refined in these fires, can be revised and improved without essential damage to what motivates religion. This shows that the island-universe theory of conflict-avoidance, though wrong about the total independence of science and religion, has something important to contribute to the answer to our question. The logics of science and religion, though not completely out of relation to one another, are significantly different in function. One, science, is especially concerned for accurate description of empirical regularities and their coherent understanding. The other, religion, is especially concerned for adequate focus of valuations and their relation to living within the context of ultimate reality. Both care about how things are; that is their unavoidable point of contact—and conflict. But each approaches from a different primary concern.

A second wrong position, to which many today are still tempted, is the view that religion can and should challenge specific scientific ideas, like the age of the earth or the evolutionary account of the origins of human life, on the basis of particular doctrines or dogmas. If the danger of the first proposal lies in fragmentation, the danger of this second is fanaticism. Frontal assault on the empirically fortified positions of science by the children of faith is suicide of reason. In the long run, such self-blinded assaults on confirmable fact will earn contempt and isolation for faith, too.

The third wrong position, one that by default might seem the only one left, is the view that science by right rules religious ideas, that influence between science and religion flows only one way—from science to reli-gion—and that whatever scientists say should therefore be meekly accepted by religious thinkers as the ground and horizon for whatever else they might be permitted to say. This view tends to forget history and thus to distort the logic of science. Historically, science has grown and flourished only within a larger worldview that permitted and nourished it. What we now call science could not have emerged in a world dominated by the religious conviction, for example, that empirical experience is systematically illusory, fundamentally irregular, or impenetrable by mind. That the world of experience is real, regular, and important enough to spend a lifetime studying—these are not themselves scientific ideas, but supply the metaphysical and valuational ground needed for scientific ideas to germinate and survive.[6] As fundamental expressions of what is taken to be most real and most important, these are religious ideas functioning as super-paradigms, or ontological models,[7] to allow for the possibility of science. In the absence of these supportive ideas, or in the presence of incompatible religious ideas, scientific work would wilt. The flow of influence from religion to science, therefore, has been not merely important but literally constitutive for science.

Logical consequences for present and future relations between religious and scientific ideas follow from these historical facts. We must of course be careful not to misstate what these consequences are. It does not follow that scientific ideas must literally agree with ancient religious stories, or that theological doctrines based on interpretations of these stories (in the absence of scientific information) are entitled to contradict scientific reports of empirical regularities or well-established ideas that theoretically extend our mental vision far beyond the empirical data. But it does follow that issues of the *intelligibility, lawfulness, and importance* of the world are vital and relevant to what science is and shall be. Thus where religious ideas themselves rest on profound experiential grounds that bear on those fundamental matters, those ideas, too, are logically entitled to be heard in the debate over the adequacy of scientific ideas in depicting and shaping this still far-from-understood world in which we all find ourselves thinking and living.

Let us get back down to cases. The present discussion of the mutual relationships of scientific and religious ideas was prompted by worry about whether religious ideas, like the "goodness of creation" and the "moral responsibility of human agents," which may be beautiful and may even be needed to contribute to the nurturing of a better world, are in the end compatible with science. A skeptical answer would not be surprising. Modern science, after all, was founded in a spasm of revulsion against the value-laden science of Aristotle in which qualitative considerations dominated quantitative ones and in which purpose, known as "final causation," was an essential element. Galileo and his followers successfully reversed both features of pre-modern science in the great revolution that founded modernity. Thus, if modern scientific ideas were to be radically abstracted from qualitative features of the world, like colors, harmonies, textures, and the like, and instead focused on the formal, quantitative aspects of things, how much more remote and alien would scientific ideas need to become from issues like the "goodness of creation"! And if modern science were to exclude all notions of teleology from the world, where would notions of "morally responsible free human agency" fit? Indeed, they do not fit within paradigmatic modern science. The great, constitutive abstractions of modern science which have shaped our view of the world and guided the development of our technologies, magnify the quantitative and work to persuade us that the qualitative dimensions of human experience are, in principle, properly reducible to mind-dependent properties of quantifiable energy functions. And in the study of mind, so conceived, for some hyper-modern thinkers there remains no conceptual place for "folk psychological"[8] terms like "freely chosen purpose"[9] or "morally responsible agency."

These are the same triumphant abstractions that have given us the technologies of quantification: bigger, faster, more efficient—above all more powerful and profitable. In the modern civilization shaped by this worldview, the "bottom line" becomes the fundamental criterion of significance. What counts is the countable; the resulting ugliness of rusting automobile graveyards moldering between endless rows of filling stations, fast food joints, and neon, is, after all, "only the mind-dependent product of secondary qualities." Ideals of social justice, harmony with nature, are "just" ideals, alien and negligible within the formulae of the modern scientific world picture. They do not compute.

If this is so, then modern science and its associated technologies need the challenge of religious ideas. The funded human experience of freedom and purpose, as well as the importance of morality, beauty, and the holy, needs to count, too, in the critique and construction of frameworks for thought and life. All thinking, of course, requires abstraction, but some abstractions are more remote from life and experience than others. The more remote an abstraction is, the more powerful it becomes, for some purposes, since it can include more. This power to abstract has been the genius of modern science. But the more remote abstractions become, the more richness of specific content they must exclude and ignore. Sometimes in that richness there are elements that can be omitted from careful consideration only at great peril.

The science of ecology has taught such a lesson. Study of the interactions of organisms and chemicals in a tank of water—even a very large tank—may seriously mislead us, for example, about these interactions in the incomparably richer environment of a natural river system. Other lessons have been taught by the new, "subversive science"[10] of ecology, as well. To take a second example, it is fruitless and self-defeating to omit the natural teleological tendencies of organisms when studying the stability of systems.

For a third example, it is hard or impossible to get along without qualitative concepts like "health" and "equilibrium" to which quantitative methods contribute but can neither define or exhaust. And, for a fourth example, unlike the paradigmatic modern sciences, human involvement in what is studied by ecology cannot be excluded from the full picture. Here we have the makings of a new, postmodern paradigm for science: a sophisticated science using all the modern tools of quantification and analysis, but using them in the context of less remote abstractions open to qualitative richness, and using them fundamentlaly in the service of systematic understanding of prior existing, interactive wholes; a science hospitable to recognition of purpose and value in nature; a science by its scope and inclusiveness non-alienating between nature and humanity, the known and the knower.

It may be mere coincidence that there is currently a triple convergence: (a) our need for new technologies to shape a postmodern world, (b) traditional ideas and values supported by religious ideas of purpose and value in the creation, and (c) the framework ideas of the new science of ecology. They converge, however, at a moment in history when many are beginning to recognize that the magnificent abstractions of modern science have all along been too simple to hold the answers to what the world is like, and that the time for another revolution—perhaps as profound as the revolution that brought in the modern world—is upon us. Religious ideas change, mellow, are refined and burnished in the fires of controversy with science. Scientific ideas, too, are subject to change, sometimes to deep change. In recent centuries we have observed most of these changes in science to result from unsolved anomalies and other internal scientific challenges, but it may now be time when profound reforms in science will rise from reexamining what I earlier called its super-paradigms, from accepting external aid from religious ideas, as well as from recognizing nagging internal anomalies. The example of subversive sciences, like ecology, will help. Whatever happens, science, technology, and religious ideas—though no longer expressed in the simple terms of hellfire or lightning rods—will be intimately entwined in the shaping of our future.

NOTES

[1]An earlier version of this paper was presented at the 1990 ILS Conference as "On Hellfire and Lightning Rods: Science, Technology, and Religious Ideas." A very similar version appears in Dr. Ferré's *Hellfire and Lightning Rods: Liberating Science, Technology, and Religion for the Future*, published in 1993 by Orbis Books.

[2]See Chapter 11, "Demythologizing Technolatry," in my *Hellfire and Lightning Rods: Liberating Science, Technology, and Religion for the Future* (Orbis Books, 1993).

[3]James Gustafson, *Ethics from a Theocentric Perspective* Volume One, *Theology and Ethics* (University of Chicago Press, 1981).

[4]See *Hellfire and Lightning Rods*, Ch. 4.

[5]Lynn White, Jr., "The Historical Roots of Our Ecologic Crisis," *Science* 45 (March 10, 1967).

[6]Alfred North Whitehead, *Science and the Modern World* (Macmillan, 1925). See especially Ch. 1, "The Origins of Modern Science."

[7]Thomas S. Kuhn, *The Structure of Scientific Revolutions*, second edition (University of Chicago Press, 1970) "Postscript—1969," p. 184.

[8]See Paul Churchland, *Matter and Consciousness*, second edition (MIT Press, 1988).

[9]B. F. Skinner, *Beyond Freedom and Dignity* (Alfred A. Knopf, 1971).

[10]Paul Shepard and Daniel McKinley, eds., *The Subversive Science: Essays Toward an Ecology of Man* (Houghton Mifflin Company, 1969).

MICHAEL POLANYI'S CRITIQUE OF CRITICISM:
PERSONAL KNOWLEDGE AS KEY TO THE POST-CRITICAL CORRELATION OF SCIENCES AND HUMANITIES

THOR HALL

Introduction

This paper is designed to highlight Michael Polanyi's unique contributions to the development of a post-modern epistemology—one that is capable of combining strictly scientific and broadly humanistic perspectives in a wholistic and integrative view of human knowledge. Polanyi's contributions can be summarized as follows:

1) Polanyi presents what is perhaps the strongest challenge yet to the positivistic objectivism of the so-called scientific point of view developed in the nineteenth and twentieth centuries—and he does so on the basis of long-standing involvements in the modern scientific community.

2) Polanyi presents at the same time an equally strong challenge to the subjectivistic individualism of modern existentialist perspectives—and again his criticism is offered from a standpoint that has deep affinities with the existentialist point of view.

3) Going to the very roots of the epistemological problem, Polanyi develops a perspective that transcends the traditional dichotomy of subject and object, and its consequences, the extremes of solipsism and positivism. His key to avoiding both these epistemological dead ends is a unique brand of phenomenological inquiry into *human noesis*, namely, what he calls "personal knowledge."

4) Polanyi's project—his so-called "fiduciary program"—constitutes an important correction to Kant's critiques and represents a proposal for the development of a post-critical (post-modern) understanding that points the way to a wholistic theory of knowledge, scientific *and* humanistic, and an integrative ontology that can serve as basis for new and creative interactions between the sciences and the humanities, between reason and faith.

1. Polanyi and Kant's Critique of Doubt

Obviously, anyone who desires to do epistemology in the modern era will have to come to terms with the Kantian critiques of reason. Polanyi is no exception, although his direct references to Kant are rather few and far between. There is reason to believe, in fact, that he was not all that well acquainted with Kant. Yet he understands the Kantian perspective very well.

In *Personal Knowledge*,[1] Polanyi refers to Kant in two different contexts: first in a chapter entitled "The Critique of Doubt," then in a sub-section of a chapter on "Commitment" entitled "Evasion of Commitment." (There is a third reference in the latter part of the book, but this is simply concerned to point out that what Polanyi calls "the typical device of modern intellectual prevarication", namely, the technique of making light of knowledge which we hold to be true but which cannot be accounted for by way of critical criteria, disparaging it while yet continuing to use it, was first systematized by Kant by way of his reference to so-called "regulative principles"—a process which Polanyi has already analyzed in the chapter on "Commitment." We can therefore ignore this latter reference here.)

In the chapter on "Critique of Doubt," Polanyi says that his own resolve to make philosophy the declaration of his own ultimate beliefs would be undermined if he did not square accounts with a certain kind of prejudice inherited from philosophical criticism (p. 269). This prejudice is described as the tendency to take for granted that the acceptance of unproved beliefs is the broad road to darkness, while truth is approached by the straight and narrow path of doubt. Originated by Descartes, this perspective was formalized by Kant when he said that in mathematics there is no room for "mere opinion," but only for "real knowledge," and that short of possessing this knowledge we must refrain from all judgement (ibid.). The method of doubt is described as the logical corollary of objectivism. Hume had seen the difficulty of pursuing such consistent skepticism—at times abandoning it when he found he could not honestly follow his conclusions. But Kant made the distinction between critical doubt and personal belief absolute. In what Polanyi describes as "a superhuman effort" to clean up the situation exposed by Hume, Kant proceeded to root out the causes of such disturbances, hoping to establish an indubitable and incontestable estate of reason. So strong is the influence of this tradition that the modern mind has forever after felt that "to accept a belief by yielding to a voluntary impulse, be it my own or that of others placed in a position of authority, is felt to be a surrender of reason" (p. 271). As Kant warned:

Reason must in all its undertakings subject itself to criticism; should
it limit freedom of criticism by any prohibitions, it must harm itself,

drawing upon itself a damaging suspicion. No thing is so important through its usefulness, nothing so sacred, that it may be exempted from this searching examination, *which knows no respect for persons*. Reason, depends on this freedom for its very existence (quoted by Polanyi, p. 271f, italics added).

What Polanyi does with this warning is first to heed it—and precisely, as Kant said, with no respect for persons, least of all Kant. He shows so little respect for him, in fact, as to submit the Kantian method of critical doubt to precisely the kind of analysis that Kant himself called for. What happens is that by way of the critical analysis of doubt Polanyi discovers that not even here is the personal element—the element of commitment or of tacit assertion—at any point absent. The process of doubting any explicit statement is shown, in fact, to imply "an attempt to *deny* the belief expressed in the statement, in favor of other beliefs which are not doubted for the time being" (p. 272, italics added).

Polanyi's analysis runs like this: Suppose someone says "I believe **p**," to which I answer "I doubt **p**." This may be taken in two ways—either that I contradict **p**, which means, "I believe not-**p**," or that I object to the assertion of **p** as true, which is to say "I believe **p** is not proven." In the first case, that of *contradictory doubt*, the logical equivalence of the affirmation and the contradiction is obvious: the difference between making a positive statement and the denial of a positive statement is simply a matter of wording. In the second case, that of *agnostic doubt*, the matter is somewhat more complex, in that it may imply either a temporary doubt ("I believe **p** is not proven") or a final doubt ("I believe **p** cannot be proven"). In either case, however, the agnostic suspension of belief has itself a fiduciary content—it implies the acceptance of certain beliefs concerning the possibilities of proof, or as Polanyi expresses it, "the acceptance of some not strictly indubitable (or proven) framework within which **p** can be said to be proven or not proven, provable or not provable" (p. 274). Applied to Kantian doubt, this means that in the final analysis Kant's own demand that we must abstain from all acts of judgment unless we *know* (as in the case of pure mathematics), agnostic doubt itself becomes an impossibility (p. 273f). Of course, Kant could not himself acknowledge this contradiction, since he considered the foundations of mathematics—including the axioms of Euclid—as indubitable, as given *a priori*. This opinion has nevertheless since been proved mistaken.

In sum, as Polanyi sees it,

Objectivism has totally falsified our conception of truth, by exalting what we can know and prove, while covering up with ambiguous utterances all that we know and *cannot* prove, even though the latter knowledge underlies, and must ultimately set its seal to, all that we *can* prove (p. 286).

Thus, in the end, "since the skeptic does not consider it rational to doubt what he himself believes, the advocacy of 'rational doubt' is merely the skeptic's way of advocating his own beliefs" (p. 298).

2. Polanyi on Kant and the Objectivist Dilemma

Polanyi's second reference to Kant comes in his discussion of what he calls "the objectivist dilemma," namely, the existence of an insoluble conflict (insoluble, that is, on the presuppositions of the subject/object dichotomy) between the demand for an impersonal truth which drives one to commit himself or herself (p. 304). Hume's oscillation between a skepticism which admittedly lacked conviction and a conviction which dared not consciously acknowledge its own acts is a typical consequence of this dilemma. In Polanyi's view, the dilemma is built into the correspondence theory of truth itself. Bertrand Russell used to express the theory as follows: truth is the coincidence of one's personal belief and the actual facts. Yet within Russell's perspective, as Polanyi sees it, there is no possibility for showing how this coincidence can ever happen. The two are by definition mutually exclusive.

It is this dilemma that Kant sought to overcome, at least as far as mathematics (especially geometry) is concerned, namely, by deducing the basic concepts of mathematics as *a priori* categories or "forms of experience" (pp. 306f). Since the end of the nineteenth century, however, references to such *a priori* categories have become less and less tenable in philosophy. An alternative line in Kant's philosophy has gained credence instead, namely, his doctrine of "regulative principles" (this is Fredrick Waisman's terminology. According to this line, Kant recommended that certain generalizations, for example the teleological aptness of living organisms, should be considered *as if* they were true, even without assuming that they are in fact true. As Polanyi looks at this procedure, however, he finds that Kant does not say that we should entertain such generalizations as true even though we know them to be false; Kant's recommendation is rather based on the tacit assumption that the generalizations are in fact true. Thus Kant managed to include a fiduciary commitment without once confessing that it is upheld by way of personal judgment.

Interestingly, Polanyi finds the same procedure at work whenever modern science describes scientific truth as mere "working hypotheses" or "interpretative policies"—this represents the generalization of Kant's "regulative principles" to all of science (p. 306). A scientist would never use as hypothesis a theory which he believed to be false; such procedures, medieval to their core, were already rejected by Kepler. Moreover, the suggestion that all scientific theories are tentative, since scientists are presumably always ready to modify their conclusions in the face of new evidence, is considered by Polanyi to be irrelevant to the issue strictly speaking. It does not change the fiduciary character of the hypothesis; the operational principle is still the same.

In short, then, the Kantian doctrine of "regulative principles," and the concept of science which springs from it, are nothing but an attempt *to act on a belief* while denying, disguising, or otherwise minimizing the fact that we are actually holding such a belief. To Polanyi, this kind of philosophy is dishonest and contradictory: it secedes from the commitment situation as regards the beliefs held within it, but it remains committed to the same beliefs in acknowledging their factual content as true (p. 304). It is therefore a philosophy that cannot face up to its actual intellectual commitments (p. 308).

3. Polanyi's Alternative to Kantian Criticism

We have exhausted Polanyi's direct references to Kant. But this analysis does not conclude the interaction between Polanyi's philosophy and that of Kant. Polanyi's philosophy offers, namely, a constructive alternative to Kant, a post-critical Kantian criticism. To see this we shall have to enlarge our perspectives somewhat and reflect more generally on the epistemological issues between them.

Anyone who knows anything at all about Kant recognizes that he took as his starting point the assumption of a chasm that separates the realm of fact and the realm of value. Kant produced critiques of both realms, the first in *Critique of Pure Reason*, the second in *Critique of Practical Reason*. In the first context Kant presents his theory of knowledge, his epistemology; in the second, his theory of ethics, his axiology. In separating the two critiques, Kant creates the impression that knowledge has nothing to do with value—that it has to do instead with objective-factual truth, a realm governed by fixed principles, rules, or logical formalisms, as distinct from the subjective beliefs which are nothing but expressions of value judgments, personal opinions, even passions. In Kantian epistemology the realm of the personal is an embarrassment.

Not so for Polanyi. His starting point is the simple assumption that it is *a person* who knows, and that personal judgments (tacit or explicit) therefore enter into all empirical awareness. One simply cannot produce a reasonable epistemology in complete disjunction from axiological consider-ations without seriously distorting the phenomenon of knowledge itself.

As a consequence of Polanyi's orientation to the person who knows, the knower, it is clear that Kant's fact/value dichotomy must be discarded. So, in fact, must the subject/object dichotomy, which underlies it. But with this Polanyi has taken on the trickiest problem in philosophy—Descartes' problem, Hume's problem, Kant's problem. It is the problem handed down as a legacy through the generations of Western philosophy and thought to be as inevitable as philosophy itself, namely, the diastasis of the knower and the known. Descartes sought to solve the puzzle by logical fiat: the subject knows only the subject, but from the starting point of indubitable subjective certainties (the cogito) one can proceed to deduce the knowledge of everything else, including God. Hume was rather more honest about it: he acknowledge that the knower cannot, on the supposition of the subject/object dichotomy, strictly speaking "know" who knows—the subject cannot become an object to itself. Kant chose a different approach: he developed a concept of the self as a "model experience," a semi-mechanical subject that is simply something that knows.

Now, the Kantian concept of the human self or subject is, of course, more complicated than that. It does include the notion of "regulative principles," to which we have referred already, as well as the so-called "oberste Prinzip alles Erkenntnis," and with it the transcendental unity of all perception. The "model experiencer" is thus a rather complex thing—though not so complex as to include the active, creative, or evaluative input of a dynamic mind. The Kantian experiencer is a spectator, located over-against the objects observed in an unambiguous way—as a static contemplator who receives knowledge impersonally, much like a computer.

We must note, of course, that Kant's computer-type self, the subject as an experiencing machine, is the concept he develops in his first critique. In the second critique he develops a different model altogether, namely, the moral agent, the self as a person who make decisions, identifies basic categories, and formulates maxims for action that can be universalized as moral principles. But for Kant, the two should never meet.

This is precisely the notion that Polanyi challenges. His magnum opus, *Personal Knowledge*, stands, in a sense, as his attempt to rewrite Kant's first critique in the light of the second. Knowledge is now not something subjects receive; *persons* know, and persons *know*—that is, they are the active agents of knowledge. Knowledge is not composed of data, facts, mechanical experiences; rather, all knowledge is inquiry, a quest for meaning and sense. And in the quest are involved action, decision, commitment, belief. There is no distinction between the decision "to be or not to be" and what mathematicians are doing. Both involve commitments as to the nature of reality and the meaning of life.

4. Personal Knowledge as Key to the Correlation of Science and Faith

As the differences between Kant and Polanyi are becoming clearer, we begin to discover the profile of a new, post-critical, wholistic and integrative theory of knowledge that is uniquely equipped to form the framework for new forms of interaction between the sciences and the humanities, between reason and religious faith. The key is the dynamic knower, the *person*.

As long as the human self was interpreted as a static experiencer, a reactor, not as an actor, the knower was considered a subject rather than a person. Kant did of course admit that subjects can *have* beliefs, they *hold* them. Moreover, while Kant sees human imagination as a faculty, Polanyi takes the imagination to be the active capacity of mind to create order out of chaos. This, then, is the essential difference between the Kantian "model experiencer" and Polanyi's "personal knower": knowledge, according to Kant, is an impersonal thing, a picture of reality produced as by a camera designed to record things by way of three-dimensional categories; according to Polanyi, on the other hand, it is a heuristic process, a function of how human beings look at things. Meaning is always a product of imagination, and imagination is always an expression of personal creativity, of appraisal, value judgment, commitment, and passion.

Now, when we finally come to reflect on what Polanyi's perspectives can come to mean for the restructuring of the relationship between science and faith—that relationship which was badly broken under the impact of Kantian criticism and its consequence, i.e., positivistic objectivism and subjectivistic existentialism—we must be careful to distinguish between the sorts of correlations which would be warranted by Polanyian perspectives and those which would be illegitimate. As an example, Polanyi's emphasis on the fiduciary character of science may sound rather similar to the apologetic attempts by certain religionists to point out that, since both science and religion are based on belief, science is not essentially different from religion and religion is not essentially less viable as a form of knowledge than science. That is, the apologists claim that the hypotheses based on religious faith are no less viable than the hypotheses that lie at the roots of scientific investigations. On its face, such a statement might seem legitimate in the light of a superficial reading of Polanyi's theory of knowledge, but it is clearly *not* legitimate if it persists in ignoring the basic differences that are there between the human awareness of physical and ordinary realities and the human awareness of spiritual and transcendent "realities." The fact that science and religion are both fiduciary forms of knowledge does not warrant seeing science as a form of religion, or religion as a form of science. They are both forms of knowledge, certainly, and we are all, as persons, involved in both. But this does *not* warrant the claim that science and religious faith are *the same enterprises.*

But what then, exactly, is the correlation of science and religious faith that is warranted by Polanyian perspectives and viable on the basis of the principle of "personal knowledge"?

I have for some time now worked on the basis of an epistemological model that both *integrates* the various forms of knowledge and *distinguishes* between them in terms of their different functions and character. This model allows us to see human awareness wholistically, as a single whole, a sphere of human knowing that operates in terms of the personal dynamics (the active role of the human self and mind) that Polanyi has pointed to, but it allows us also to make distinctions within this wholistic structure between various "dimensions of awareness" in terms of their difference in function and in presuppositions. The model can be pictured as a sphere, an inclusive atmosphere (the full extent of human awareness). However, within it—each dimension sharing the fiduciary character of all human knowledge—are a number of concentric subspheres, identifiable dimensions of human awareness, such as scientific awareness, aesthetic awareness, ethical awareness, and religious awareness (perhaps also metaphysical speculation, transcendent imagination, dreams, etc., that is, dimensions of awareness that explore and to some extent probe beyond the acknowledged limits of human awareness). This wholistic, integrated, but differentiated model signifies that *the same epistemological dynamic* is at work throughout the structure of human awareness, and at the same time that there is within human awareness a number of distinct and different types of awareness which must be distinguished without being separated, and integrated without being mixed or confused.

I stated that the different dimensions or spheres of awareness are distinguishable in terms of their various functions and presuppositions. In closing, let me briefly outline the differences in function and presuppositions between four of these dimensions of awareness—the "basic four," if you will, namely, science or technology, aesthetics or art, ethics, and religion.

Science is that dimension of human awareness which focuses on phenomena for purposes of *investigating*, obtaining information and developing an understanding of what things are and how they work (the so-called "facts"). Technology takes this scientific knowledge a step or two further and develops processes, instruments and machines that at times *duplicate* the phenomena we have learned about and have come to understand by way of science, making them manageable and controllable, and at times creatively *superseding* these phenomena and producing new ones. The presupposition for the entire enterprise, both of science and technology, is that this form of knowledge is "common," shared, obtainable by acknowledged and uniform methodology and measurements. The aim of science is *probable truth*; of technology, *technical skills*.

Aesthetic awareness, on the other hand, focuses on phenomena for a different purpose. Here the driving interest is not the investigation of facts, but the *appreciative relationship* to every phenomenon. The artist is one who looks at phenomena from a perspective peculiar to himself or herself, appraising them and describing them as only he or she sees them, and creating artifacts which express that individual's particular taste or sense of beauty or form or color or sound or movement, thus seeking to trigger the same—or some other—sense of appreciation in those who encounter these artifacts. The presupposition here is not so much a common perspective or a single methodology, a normative principle of aesthetic awareness, but simply the validity of "the appreciative relationship," of our likes and dislikes, our tastes and sense of style. Art aims at expressing and soliciting *thoughtful feelings and feelingful thoughts*.

Ethical awareness, in the third place, is different again. This dimension of awareness functions by way of *evaluation* of phenomena, as judgment and decision-making relative to what is good and what is bad, *in* them or *about* them, as well as in our own relationship *to* them. The presupposition underlying ethical awareness is that all of us have a sense of what is right and wrong—though not necessarily the same sense. Individuals differ, societies and cultures vary, but a standard of judgment, an imperative of some kind exists in every person and every context. We should probably give more thought to the exploration of human values and the endeavor to develop "categorical imperatives"—concepts of personal and social responsibility—that we can all accept and respect. In the meantime, all that can be presupposed is the validity of human ethical evaluation when it aims to determine what is good and right.

Religious awareness, finally, is not like science, investigating facts; not like aesthetic awareness, sensing and expressing appreciation; and not like ethics, representing the moral "ought." Religious awareness focuses on discovering and responding to what may be termed *"the ultimate meaning"* of all particular events. Religious awareness functions by way of *interpretation*, and its interpretations are the expressions of certain perspectives. These perspectives are informed by various assumptions—again the presupposition is not that there exists only one absolute and normative perspective, but simply that the perspectives that exist and are operative are absolute and normative for those who hold them. That is also the sense in which religious awareness represents "ultimate meaning": not that a certain faith system is ultimate *in se*, but that *all* faith systems that inform religious interpretation have the character of ultimacy for those who follow them.

The four dimensions of human awareness that I have described here are all integral to the human self and the human mind. And they are interactive, but they are not the same. Each operates in its own manner, on its own presuppositions, for its own purposes, and within its own context. Mixing them, tearing them out of their contexts and transferring them to other contexts, does nothing but confuse the picture of human knowing, human feeling, human acting, and human faith. Keeping them distinct and yet interactive, and being ourselves involved in all dimensions of human awareness, is the road that leads from the wholistic-personalistic epistemology of Polanyi to the kind of complex, multifaceted but integrated system of human knowing that can apply both on the level of personal knowledge and in the relationship between the sciences and the humanities.

NOTES

[1]All references are to M. Polanyi, *Personal Knowledge* (Harper & Row, 1958).

SCIENCE AND RELIGION IN IDENTITY CRISIS

STANLEY L. JAKI

Three hundred or so years ago not a few scientists spoke of science and religion as united in a holy alliance. Two hundred years later theologians could do little about the warfare in which science and religion appeared to be locked forever. Today, many theologians and some scientists speak of the mutual integration of science and religion, these two paramount forces in human life.

From both sides all too often mere generalities rather than tangible specifics are offered. This may already indicate a lack of simultaneous competence in both fields. Actually, those generalities suggest that an identity crisis may be enveloping both science and religion, and to an extent far greater than one may suspect.

The religious side of that crisis is easier to diagnose by a mere look at programs of instruction offered in most departments of religion and religious studies, as well as divinity schools and theological faculties. Actual exposure to what goes on in those places can readily bring into focus a feature typical of most of them. Whenever a question is posed, only a multiplicity of answers is tolerated. Even the slightest effort to cut through that multiplicity, within which contradictory stances too are acceptable, is frowned upon as judgmental. The result is the rise of that church where, to paraphrase a remark of Chesterton, each communicant is sharing the other's unbelief.

A biting portrayal of this pathetic situation was given less than a year ago in a book, *The Search for God at Harvard*, written by Ari L. Goldman, religion reporter for the *New York Times*. It may not have been a sound idea at all on Mr. Goldman's part to spend a full year at Harvard Divinity School to search for God there. Actually, the true target of Mr. Goldman's search was not so much God as some experience about Him. Such a search could, of course, have ended, even if successful, only in mistaking God's identity for some religious experience with no real identity.

Indeed the variety of religious experiences, to which Mr. Goldman found himself exposed in that prestigious divinity school, seemed to serve the purpose of concealing their true identity. Nothing has indeed changed there since that legendary guru about religion as "experienced," William James, had come up with his own theory about the varieties of religious experience.

Had Mr. Goldman thought of William James at Harvard he would not have been forced to identify the Christian religious experience as "the most elusive experience" of his early days in the "Div School," as it is called there in a quasi-affectionate tone: "If, for example, there was a mention in class of the divinity of Jesus, the lecturer would offer an apology to the non-Christians in the room." No wonder Mr. Goldman found shattered his expectation to encounter some religious experience which he could have identified as "old-type Christian piety." This piety has always been rooted in clearly identifiable dogmas, but the Div School's atmosphere was "religious relativity." There "religious truth did not seem to exist" at all.[1] What Mr. Goldman could not find in the classrooms of the Div School, he failed to find in its imposing Chapel. Whether during the daily Noon service, which he faithfully attended, or whenever he peeked into the Chapel in going to classes, he "never saw anyone on his or her knees." At most, he saw "someone sitting there meditating," but this did not happen frequently.[2]

Clearly, the Div School at Harvard did not advance a whit beyond the state of affairs which was searingly portrayed a generation ago in *God and Man at Yale*. Of course, that searing portrayal was possible only because its author, W. Buckley, offered an evaluation in terms of definite values, or standards. Whether these are called dogmas or not, should seem irrelevant. They could just as well be called fishnets. If Mr. Goldman had one, it was his visceral attachment to orthodox Jewish practices which he never cared to put on clearly definable intellectual foundations.

This is why he was torn about Roman Catholicism. On the one hand he felt deeply attracted to the Mass. On the other hand he could not warm up to dogmatic Catholicism. It is difficult to decide whether he deplored the present status of Catholicism, as he perceived it. Although he seemed to be upset over the Catholic Church's loss of moral authority within society, he was ambivalent about its cause, "the internecine struggles over authority with Rome and the anti-abortion cause."[3]

Only if one is wholly unfamiliar with the long-standing uncertainty of Congregationalists about their own identity, can one voice surprise over the utterly elusive identity of religion at a Divinity School and University with Congregationalist roots. The doctrinal atmosphere at Harvard Divinity School reminded Mr. Goldman of that nutshell summary of liberal Protestantism which H. R. Niebuhr had given half a century ago: "A God without wrath brought men without sin into a kingdom without judgment through the ministrations of a Christ without a cross."[4] Such a religion could not be distinguished from Mr. Goldman's Judaism, except for his attachment to ritual laws. In all those denominations, one can freely wear the p.c. (politically correct) badge, this most effective sedative against the pressing need for true identification.

A p.c. religion will have no problem being integrated with science, though the relation may not amount to more than a convenient cohabitation that can be initiated, acted out, terminated, resumed, and reinterpreted on short notice. Cohabitation is always a dissimulation of the true identity of a rapport, an identity crisis in short. The religious side of that cohabitation can only function as religious syncretism. Thus no real difference will be claimed between nature worship and a worship steeped in that supernatural which is a Creator free to create or not to create what is called Nature writ large, that is, a universe.

Within that syncretism every form of religion can be accommodated. There polytheism, with its worship of idols, will not appear too distant even from a worship that forbids the making of graven images of God. And when God and nature are fused to the extent in which this is done in pantheism, not only one's religion cannot be identified, but even one's true identity diminishes to the vanishing point. In no form of pantheism has there ever been a place for that personal immortality which alone makes one's identity (and one's religion) meaningful and raises it above the lowlands of mere estheticism.

Syncretism, or the abolition of true identity, certainly foments heavy reliance on verbalism which is in view, for instance, when pantheism is promoted in the guise of panentheism. Syncretism, or religion's identity crisis, may be couched in such noble words as ecumenism, global consciousness, and moral rearmament, to say nothing of such dubious labels as Gaia and New Age.

The so-called "mere Christianity," first proposed around 1675 by William Baxter, a Puritan divine tired of religious controversies,[5] was a symptom of identity crisis. The symptom resurfaced when in 1943 C. S. Lewis resurrected Baxter's idea in a book, *Mere Christianity*, which made religious history for the latter half of this century of ours. C. S. Lewis could offer but his gut-feeling as to what "mere Christianity" was when he said he meant by Christian faith that "which is what it is and was what it was long before I was born and whether I like it or not."[6] No more clarity was shed on the subject by his equally elusive definition of Christian belief as the one "that has been common to nearly all Christians at all times."[7]

This is not to suggest that C. S. Lewis was not aware of the problem of leaving out of "mere Christianity" all items smacking of controversy in order to focus attention on items non-controversial. But were there such items or tenets? No less importantly, even if there were some, could they be discoursed upon for any length of time without bringing up matters not only controversial but also pivotal for the articulation and defense of points commonly held by almost all?

That almost complete unanimity evaporates like the morning mist once one raises the question whether "mere" Christianity implied miracles.

Without talking of miracles in *Mere Christianity*, C. S. Lewis held miracles to be an integral part of the Christian proposition. Otherwise he would not have defended the possibility, as well as the reality, of miracles against Humeans, erstwhile and modern.[8] Yet, many Christians, who hold high a Christianity restricted to its mere basics refuse to face up to non-biblical miracles that are much closer to us and far easier to investigate. Nor do they see that agnosticism about post-Biblical miracles is destructive of faith in biblical miracles as well.[9] Still other Christians prefer not to speak of miracles precisely because they want to integrate science and religion, though on terms dictated by the interpretation of science given by most scientists who have no use for miracles at all.

Some defenders of biblical miracles grant them only because they take the space-time of relativity and the indeterminacy of quantum mechanics for a scientific possibility of miracles. They do not realize that in doing so they do away with miracles as well as with the physics of relativity which is based on the strict continuity of the physical and for which time is, as Einstein once memorably admitted, a mere parameter of measurements.[10] It seems that they are not sure of themselves and of the grounds, not at all scientific but deeply philosophical, on the basis of which alone one can confidently speak of miracles, and do so with a healthy disregard for science.

It is not even certain that today Christians are unanimous in their belief in creation out of nothing and in time. Christians are a motley lot in their interpretation of Genesis 1. Stances vary from taking it for the relic of preliterary legends to interpreting it in a grimly literalist sense as this is done in creation science.[11] Typically, proponents of creation science make much, as if to cover their own uncertainties, of the uncertainty of various scientific conclusions and of the uncertainty of scientists about them.

Last but not least, there is Christianity's central belief: redemption in Christ. Newborn Christians all too often do not want to hear about the conceptual certainties of dogmatic definitions achieved in the great christological debates of the early Church. Even within the proverbially dogmatic Catholic Church, discourses can be heard about Christ that can only prompt any consistent thinker to part with belief in Christ as the only begotten Son of God. Quite recently an Anglican bishopric was awarded to the Regius professor of divinity at Oxford whose scholarly reputation rests on a programmatic rehabilitation of Arius.[12]

Even Arius held Christ in a much higher esteem than the Roman Catholic authors of two recent lives of Christ. According to one of them, who protests his Roman Catholic orthodoxy, Jesus may have been a celibate, but he certainly had real brothers and sisters. But that author's religious identity becomes sublimated when he argues that although historic scholarship can prove only that Jesus was a peasant Jew, his divinity can be had on faith.[13] He seems to be blissfully unaware of the historic fact that this dichotomy between historic or "scientific" evidence and faith has been a chief source of depriving all too many Christian professions of faith of the identity they should have manifested. The very identity of Christ is indeed in widespread doubt among Christian theologians who lend receptive ears to some "experts" on the Qumran scrolls that Christianity in its earliest form contained nothing essentially new that Judaism at that time did not contain.[14]

The systematic leveling of Christ to very low human levels is, of course, part of the carefully cultivated uncertainty about sin. Genuine Christian awareness of the reality and seriousness of sin has now for decades been under a mounting pressure to align itself with "new" perceptions about sin. Such is the view that sin is a psychological infirmity; the other consists in not perceiving sin at all. For fashionable thinking there are only so many patterns of behavior. Consequently, any behavior, once it becomes a pattern, that is, once it is acted out by a statistically significant number of people, can claim social acceptance. From there it is but a short step to claims for legal protection and moral respectability as if legal were equivalent to moral.[15]

Christian (and Jewish) awareness seems to have come a long way from the injunction given in the book of Exodus: "You shall not repeat a false report . . . Neither shall you allege the example of the many as an excuse for doing wrong" (Ex. 23:1-12). Too many Christians seem to be worlds removed from those forebears of theirs who accepted cheerfully the truth of the words: "You will be under pressure in this world," because "no disciple is greater than his master." Christian theologians are few and far between with a style that would retain a touch of Tertullian's incisiveness: "Christ said, 'I am the truth.' He did not say, 'I am the custom'."[16] Far many more are those theologians whose "reasonings" illustrate Edmund Burke's acid remark: "Custom reconciles us to everything."[17]

Speaking of Exodus is as good a reason as any to say a few words about the disarray in which Jews of our times find themselves concerning their religion. Varieties of opinion range from literally militant Zionism to no religion at all. I wonder whether Christians, who firmly believe in the personal immortality of their souls and in subsequent resurrection, would find much resonance among Jews, except for the most orthodox. Cultural conservatism, very popular among American Jews, is not enough. It does not by itself lead beyond this life on earth to an otherworldly compensation for cruel deprivations suffered in this life. That there can be no such compensation was the gist of Norman Podhoretz's objection after I had spoken in Moscow, in June 1989, before a meeting sponsored by the Soviet Academy of Sciences and Moscow University on belief in the existence of God as supported by science. In that speech I also referred to that belief as the only ground on which one can think of an eventual compensation for tragedies whose number, in this life, is far more than legion. And yet I was speaking only of the hundreds of millions of innocent sufferers without saying a word about those not a few who never suffer in this life any punishment for horrible crimes.[18]

About two other religions, Islam and Buddhism, both increasingly popular in the West, a few remarks should suffice in their possible relation to science. Behind the Islamic religious revival lies a feature hardly ever noted by Western observers. Owing to the demands of technologization, Islamic lands now have to provide scientific education on a large scale. This in turn confronts their people with the challenges of empiricism, rationalism, and positivism. The result is a turmoil, for the moment still largely under the surface, but a turmoil which the Islamic clergy seems to perceive in its real magnitude. There will be a replay, but on a much more dramatic form, of the famed medieval debate between the Muslims who are genuine mystics and rationalists who are Muslims only in name.

A millennium ago, leading Muslim mystics such as al-Ashari and al-Ghazali, held that reference to the laws of nature was a blasphemy against Allah's omnipotence. The leading Muslim rationalists, such as Ibn-Sina (Avicenna) and Ibn-Rushd (Averroes), held that the truly enlightened Muslim can hold the idea of triple truth: The lowest truth, or the truth of catechism, was for the populace; the middle level was for the imams, repeating the Koran; the highest form of truth, the truth of science, was the privilege of the enlightened. These, however, were to keep that third truth to themselves, lest they suffer the consequences.[19] The medieval Muslim world could not find a middle ground, such as the one worked out by the great scholastics shortly afterwards, concerning faith and reason. Whether modern Muslim intellectuals can work out a satisfactory balance, remains to be seen. But they had better recognize that an identity crisis is looming large over their heads, a crisis fueled by science, or rather by the impossibility to live today for more than a few minutes without taking advantage of this or that scientific tool.

As to Buddhism, its numerous varieties may in themselves suggest a chronic identity crisis. Such a crisis has plagued many of those young people in the West prior to their embracing Buddhism as a religion. At any rate, in its classical method, aimed at giving an escape from the self, Buddhism can hardly escape the suspicion that it offers a cure for identity crisis by depriving the self of its identity. In fact, in all great philosophical presentations of Buddhism, including its amalgamation with Confucianism and Taoism, a central place is occupied by the denial of what is known in Western logic as the principle of identity and non-contradiction.[20] No wonder that Buddhism received a very sympathetic consideration by those who see in the Copenhagen interpretation of quantum mechanics the highest form of enlightenment because it has on it the seal of a science which too many take for the ultimate in science. To make matters culturally far worse, Niels Bohr lent his full scientific prestige to establish the principle of complementarity as a philosophy that would give better guidance in life than religion ever could.[21]

An integral part of that interpretation is the principle of complementarity. Dime a dozen are the books and articles, written by theologians and scientists, and at times together, in which one finds it registered with great satisfaction that science and religion are complementary like the particle and wave aspects of matter.[22] This claim certainly deserves some scrutiny even within the perspective of this lecture. The claim leaves in studied indefiniteness the religion in question. A moderately careful reading of the philosophical works of Bohr, Schrödinger, Max Born, and Heisenberg should easily reveal a conviction common to all of them. They would protest as a man against the claim that the principle of complementarity entitles one to make a rational plea for immortality, to say nothing of revelation, miracles, resurrection, and a judgment pertaining to an eternal reward or eternal punishment.[23] The principle of complementarity tolerates only a religion which is reduced to that sheer estheticism where one is faced with ever shifting moods, styles, and with a perennial craving for fulfillment that never comes.

But the principle of complementarity, as taken for a philosophical and religious panacea, or cure-all, leaves even science, that is, the science of quantum mechanics, in an identity crisis. A priceless glimpse of this was provided by no less an insider than the late Professor Dirac. It tells something of the measure of that identity crisis that what Dirac said in the broadest scientific daylight, the Jerusalem Centennial Einstein Conference in 1979, has been studiedly ignored by the scientific establishment, and by its chief ally, or perhaps millstone around its neck, the establishment known as the philosophers and historians of science. Dirac said nothing less at that Conference than that quantum mechanics, as it stands today, would have to be reformulated along the lines of strict predictability as demanded by Einstein: "I think that it is very likely, or at any rate quite possible that in the long run Einstein will turn out to be correct even though for the time being physicists have to accept the Bohr probability interpretation—especially if they have examinations in front of them."[24]

Clearly, this is not the kind of diagnosis which its subjects would sedulously recall to themselves, let alone to their students. Ostriches love to bury their heads in the sand lest they should be forced to face the true identity of their predicament. This is precisely what the champions of the Copenhagen interpretation of quantum mechanics did with respect to its most considered appraisal by J. S. Bell (of "Bell's theorem" fame). On the one hand, they have not ceased to recall his famed theorem which they took for the final proof that ultimately everything is haphazard. Yet all he did was to show that quantum statistics is more successful than classical statistics in coping with a certain kind of coincidence in radioactive emission. Two years later, on finding subtle illogicalities in the "reduction of wave packets," a pivotal issue in theoretical quantum mechanics, he felt impelled to conclude that quantum mechanics "carries in itself its seeds of destruction."[25] Physicists, and philosophers of physics, still have to pay adequate attention to this much more profound conclusion of Bell. When they bring it up, they usually display that touch of nervousness which transpires from K. Gottfried's very polite rebuttal of Bell's claim.[26] Theologians, who continue integrating their field with quantum mechanics, should pay heed. Unwittingly, they may promote their own self-destruction, the ultimate form of identity crisis.

Much has been said about the identity crisis that had beset physics toward the end of the nineteenth century. Much less are aired the early traces of that crisis. There is much more than meets the eye in an apparently innocent facet of Newton's *Principia*. It contains not a single paragraph on the philosophico-methodological questions raised by the fact that he had written not merely a *Principia*, in itself a grave word, but a *Philosophiae naturalis principia mathematica*. One would in vain interrogate Newton as to what he meant by nature, by philosophy, and even by mathematics.

Newton may not even have been absolutely sure of himself as a physicist. Otherwise, he would not have spent precious hours in erasing from his manuscripts references to Descartes, lest posterity should suspect that he owed anything to the Frenchman. No wonder. Cartesians in France greeted the *Principia*, with the remark that for all its fine qualities, it was not physics.[27] What was it? It certainly was not a mechanistic physics insofar as this means mechanistic models of which the *Principia* was conspicuously void. Only some time later were those models grafted, and in large numbers, on the mathematics of the *Principia* which ushered in the age of infinitesimal calculus.

Although a rigorous proof of the "limit" did not come until the early nineteenth century, Newton's infinitesimal calculus stood for a blissful state of total certainty, with no trace of identity crisis. The next scientifically momentous book, with the word *Principia* in its title, was published in 1910, under the title, *Principia mathematica*.[28] It did not contain a retraction by its co-author, Bertrand Russell, concerning his earlier description of mathematics "as the subject in which we never know what we are talking about, nor whether what we are saying is true."[29] Later, Bertrand Russell qualified his agnosticism about mathematics only to the extent of saying that physics is "mathematical not because we know so much about the physical world, but because we know so little; it is only its mathematical properties that we can discover."[30]

This warning of Bertrand Russell's should be ample food for thought for those who cultivate other branches of physical science, especially the various branches of life-sciences.   Being the most exact among all empirical investigations, physics is eagerly imitated by other empirical sciences. Their cultivators may suffer some identity crisis owing to their being overshadowed by their glamorous big brother, big physics. This remark, if pondered by them, may bring back to their senses various cultivators of the humanities.   Whenever psychologists, sociologists, or historians try to imitate physics, and there are quite a few among them, they merely reveal symptoms of identity crisis.[31]

This is even truer of philosophers, to say nothing of theologians. The program of a so-called scientific philosophy is a fairly old fad that had such prominent devotees as Descartes, Hobbes, Hume, Kant, and Comte, and produced long discredited systems of philosophy. The fad of a "scientific" theology is rather new. It produced lengthy treatises about the theology of the world, without a paragraph in them about that world which is the universe.[32] One could also refer to books with "insight" and "method" in their titles, though with no clear guidance in their contents as to what qualifies for insight and in what true method consists.[33] If only such theologians aimed at nothing more than offering a well-argued rational discourse! Neither philosophy nor theology is or can be a science in which physics is one, but both should be eminently rational, that is, well-reasoned instead of being submerged into endless chains of vague metaphors and new-fangled buzzwords.

Seeing their own field as a discourse that demands utmost attention to clarity and consistency, theologians would discover a curious thing about science and scientists, and in particular about physics. Until about a hundred years ago, physicists could be seen from the outside as safely entrenched in their certainties. James Clerk Maxwell well characterized that state of affairs when in 1870 he described the Royal Society as "the company of those men who aspiring to noble ends . . . have risen above the regions of storms into a clearer atmosphere, where there is no misrepresentation of opinion, nor ambiguity of expression, but where one mind comes into close contact with another at the point where both approach nearest to the truth."[34]

A quarter of a century later, Maxwell's electromagnetic theory appeared to have a truth content which resembled Nicolas of Cusa's definition of the universe: its center everywhere, its circumference nowhere. For this is the unintended gist of Hertz's famed remark: "Maxwell's theory is Maxwell's equations."[35] In other words, nobody really knew what was the true identity of those equations and that theory. Hertz's definition implied that circularity which bespoke of identity crisis. Today, in this age of string-theory, zero-point oscillations, embryo universes and what not, it is even more difficult to specify the identity relation of each and every part of very successful physical theories with physical reality.

But the true identity crisis of science lies elsewhere. This is not to suggest that in empirical sciences, even outside physics, one could not find momentous traces of identity crisis even today. Evolutionary biology still has to come to terms with two rude jolts that knocked many of its cultivators out of their blissful self-consciousness. One was the realization, quite recently, that the theory of the origin of life as proposed by S. L. Miller in 1952 cannot cope with the high temperatures which certainly prevailed on the primitive earth three to four billion years ago.[36] The other is the evidence of major catastrophes to which the earth is exposed every 26 million or so years and some of which result in substantial extinctions of all living forms.[37] The identity crisis that resulted from this is well exemplified by the so-called theory of punctuated equilibrium of evolutionary development. At a national gathering of its devotees the level of consistency was such as to prompt one participant to remark that he would find more intellectual honesty at a national gathering of second-hand car dealers.[38]

The real source of identity crisis in science today does not lie with its internal problems of which it would very likely never run out. Who can give assurance that future decades and centuries hold no surprising discoveries, totally unimaginable today? The real source of that identity crisis lies in the fact that scientists have, to a considerable degree, ceased being the official spokesmen of what science is about. The image of science as entertained by society at large, and even within academic circles, is now determined as much, if not more, by what philosophers and historians of science, and mere science writers, state about science.

The change should seem enormous. A hundred or so years ago, relatively little was written about the philosophy of science. Authors of such books were either philosophers with very little training in science, and scientists with as little familiarity with philosophy. William Whewell, in the 1830s, was the first prominent scientist to write a serious book on the philosophy of science, and he was not imitated until Ernst Mach, Pierre Duhem, and Henri Poincare came along around 1900 or so.

From the 1920s there was a rapid increase in the number of prominent scientists who wrote books on the philosophy of science. To speak only of physicists one may recall the names of James Jeans, Eddington, Bohr, Born, De Broglie, Margenau, Whittaker, Schrödinger, Heisenberg and, more recently, Feynman. But the books that really formed the image about science were written by philosophers, at times with proper training in physics, though at times with no such training; Moritz Schlick was not a physicist, nor was Karl Popper, nor Hans Reichenbach, nor Herbert Feigl. While Thomas Kuhn had full training in physics, this was not true of Lakatos and Feyerabend. Yet it was these who imposed on our culture the view that science is intrinsically uncertain about itself. What can such an uncertainty breed if not an identity crisis and a chronic one?

No major articles on science, contributed by philosophers of science to major encyclopedias, would give a fair certainty as to what science really is. There are still some grim inductivists around, as well as some dreamy-eyed Platonizers. Classical positivists, in the style of Auguste Comte, are few and far between, but the number of Machists is great, though not of those Machists who take consistently their master's sensationism which ultimately led Mach to embrace Buddhism.[39] Most would endorse some form of the idea of science as based on the hypothetico-deductive model. Yet, divergences of opinion abound as soon as one comes to the art of forming hypotheses and to the legitimacy of deductions. With the exception of Duhem, who was a realist and held high common sense as the only consistent starting point,[40] they would have only scorn for T. H. Huxley's famous definition of science as "trained and organized common sense."[41]

Many philosophers of science offer explanations of science that border on being nonsensical. Such is the case when science is taken for an exercise in falsification. But, if all that science can do is falsify conclusions, not only the identity of its conclusions is at stake but its very own identity as well. Such should seem an inevitable conclusion unless one is denied the liberty to see the contradictory character of the claim: only such statements have truth-content that are falsifiable, though this truth is immune to the test of being falsifiable.[42] If science is a series of images, of themata, of research programs,[43] what will assure that they fuse into one image, one thema, one program that can be safely identified? That the idea of science as an anarchical enterprise[44] has found devotees may be symptomatic of the identity crisis that breeds anarchists, intellectual and other. That science has also been spoken of as a game, very clever of course, is characteristic of recent decades when too many young academics had it too well and lost sight not only of the identity of their subject but very often of their own self-identity as responsible human beings.

Intellectually very treacherous is the case when science is identified with a big word that everybody uses and nobody defines. Apart from this, it should be obvious that if science is a never-ending chain of revolutions, this very proposition is its own refutation, because the proposition is offered as not being subject to the kind of change which is revolution understood as radical upheaval. Or should we let some philosophers of science have it both ways, namely, to bank heavily on big words and be cagey about what they mean by them? Those who speak constantly of scientific revolutions should come clean whether they mean more than what is implied in the French phrase, "plus ca change, plus ca reste la meme chose," which is possibly the best account of all political revolutions.

The phrase has a hardly ever noted philosophical profundity. That depth was covered up when that great apostle of scientific revolutions, T. S. Kuhn, reversed his revolutionary tracks and invoked the principle of essential tension[45] as if metaphysics could be reinstated through the back door. And even by allowing metaphysics back to the stage, Kuhn granted it no more than the role of a mere co-actor, if not an inept complement to the fascinating game of science with quantities.

Yet metaphysics is the very stage which any intellectual performance needs for its being acted out. Even the very word metaphysics indicates that it is not supposed to be something juxtaposed. In that case Aristotle would have called it paraphysics and left it aside as something no more worth considering than paralogisms. Aristotle would have felt sympathy for that French phrase. All his philosophy rested on his coming to grips with the problem of identity through change as the safeguard of the sanity of human intellect.

It is also the safeguard of the sanity of science. Only if changes are such as to leave somehow intact the sameness of things undergoing change, does one have a ground to speak of science with no identity crisis. For science deals with things in motion or change and has a major stake in the possibility that its observations and conclusions transcend the truth of the moment.

Working scientists would fully sympathize. They are also the ones who somehow sense that all the sophisticated assertions about science in much of modern philosophy of science can but foment and promote the malaise which is perceived as the identity crisis of science. It is that malaise which is resented by working scientists who time and again put studies on the history of science on the X-rated lists.[46] History has always been the favorite hunting ground of sceptics and scoffers. They make most of the keen observation of Chesterton that history is so rich in data that one can make "a case for any course of improvement or retrogression."[47]

The identity crisis of science, insofar as it is not turned into an ideology by philosophers and historians of science and by scientists who in their old age wax philosophical, is far less serious than it may appear. The reason for this lies in Bertrand Russell's second remark quoted above. The remark calls attention to a radical limitation of science, of physics in particular. The science of physics knows both enormously much and enormously little about the material world because it can only know its quantitative properties. Science becomes involved in an identity crisis only when it ignores its own method or when it lets philosophers, eager to promote their agnosticism and subjectivism, take over as the spokesmen for science.

Whereas the cure for the identity crisis of science should seem relatively simple, the cure for the identity crisis in religion is a far more serious matter. At any rate, any theologian who speaks about the relation of science and religion should first come clean as to what religion he stands for. The philosopher must do the same and take the consequences. It seems to me that the art of camouflage, to say nothing of mere chameleonship, is not exempt from the commandment that forbid lies. Identity crisis can have its cure only in total commitment to the words: truth will make you free. One indeed must first identify and remove a vast heap of debris in order to see the very complex and nuanced truth about the relation of religion and science and about their ongoing interaction.

Interaction makes sense only between two distinct items, factors, or entities. Distinctness in turn can be manifold. Some forms of it impose themselves, some others can make impatient the proverbial system makers who are hell bent on fusing everything into everything and set the stage for intellectual infernos. Chafe as they may, the fundamental domain of is, or plain existence, to say nothing of the all-important domain of should, or the domain of unitary knowledge, insofar as it means a one-track knowledge, belongs to the domain of Utopia on earth, which is not the domain of angels.

The only kind of unitary knowledge about which man can profitably speculate is the knowledge of angels. Unfortunately, latter-day theologians are most reluctant to face up to that topic. Yet by discussing it they would be able to tell modern men (who since Descartes have been trying to play the angel[48]), that mere man must implement his cognitive life in terms of mutually irreducible conceptual domains.

To put it in a perhaps facetious, perhaps slightly blasphemous, but certainly blunt way: domains that God had kept separate for man, man should not try to join together into one single domain. The resulting realm will not be a synthesis, not even a fusion, but a confusion which is all too evident in the manifold symptoms of the real and perceived identity crisis which for some time has been plaguing science as well as religion. I have spoken so much about diagnosis, relatively little about remedies, and almost not at all about a healthy state, because an effective cure heavily depends on making the diagnosis as full and realistic as possible.

NOTES

[1]A. L. Goldman, *The Search for God at Harvard* (Random House, 1991), p. 43.

[2]Ibid., p. 44.

[3]Ibid., p. 276.

[4]As always, here too, the vacuum had to be filled: "For the golden harps of the saints it [liberal Christianity] substituted radios, for angelic wings concrete highways and high-powered cars, and heavenly rest was now called leisure." H. Richard Niebuhr, *The Kingdom of God in America* (Willett, Clark and Company, 1937), p. 196. That was, of course, before the commercially "golden" age of TV and VCR, to say nothing of "grass" and psychedelic religion, had come about.

[5]Baxter's "mere religion" was a platform which already to Baxter's more perceptive contemporaries appeared as one that "might be subscribed by a Papist or a Socinian." See article, "Baxter, Richard," in *Encyclopedia Britannica*, 1991 edition.

[6]C. S. Lewis, *Mere Christianity* (Macmillan, 1952), p. vii.

[7]Quoted in M. Nelson, "C.S. Lewis, Gone but Hardly Forgotten," *New York Times*, Nov. 22, 1988, p. 27.

[8]C. S. Lewis, *Miracles: A Preliminary Study* (Geoffrey Bles, 1947).

[9]See my book, *Miracles and Physics* (Christendom Press, 1989).

[10]Einstein did so under questioning from Bergson, at the Sorbonne, in April, 1922. See *Bulletin de la Societe francaise de philosophie* 17 (1922): 107.

[11]This subject is discussed in my forthcoming book, *Genesis 1 through the Ages*, the enlarged text of eight lectures I delivered in New York City, under the sponsorship of Wethersfield Institute, in late April and early May, 1992.

[12]R. Williams, *Arius: Heresy and Tradition* (Darton Longman and Todd, 1987).

[13]J. P. Meier, *A Marginal Jew* (Doubleday, 1991). The other book, *The Historical Jesus* (Collins, 1991), was written by J. D. Crossan.

[14]One wonders what is to be gained on the Jewish side by the claim, most memorably made in this century by Rabbi J. Klausner, that all ethical and religious tenets of the Gospels occur in early Jewish writings. Whatever the identity crisis that should be logically generated by such a claim, it makes it impossible to identify Judaism as a universal religion. This is what Klausner unwittingly admitted, in addition to destroying his claim that Jesus had offered nothing new in the way of ethics and religion, as he wrote: "Jesus came and thrust aside all the requirements of the national life. . . . In their

stead he set up nothing but an ethico-religious system bound up with his conception of the Godhead." *Jesus of Nazareth: His Life, Times and Teaching*, trans. from the original Hebrew by H. Danby (Macmillan, 1926), p. 390. But if one's conception of the Godhead has nothing to do with one's religious and ethical tenets, what is their source? One's national or racial affiliation?

[15]A topic further discussed in my article, "Patterns versus Principles: The Pseudoscientific Roots of Law's Debacle," to be published in *Notre Dame Law Review*.

[16]L. Tertullian, *De virginibus velandis*, cap. 1. It was with this phrase that Saint Turibius, the famed Archbishop of Lima (1538-1606), countered gold-hungry conquistadors, who tried to justify their evil ways by invoking "tradition." See *Butler's Lives of Saints* (P.J. Kenedy and Sons, 1962), vol. 2, p. 167. The phrase is fully applicable to many captains of capitalism and neo-capitalism.

[17]E. Burke, *A Philosophical Inquiry into the Origin of Our Ideas of the Sublime and Beautiful* (Harper and Brothers, 1844), pt. IV, sec. xviii, p. 185.

[18]"Sushchestvnet li Sozdatel?" in *Obshchestvennye nauki Akademiia nauk SSSR* [Moscow] 6 (1990): 170-180.

[19]For details see ch. 9, "Delay in Detour," in my book, *Science and Creation: From Eternal Cycles to an Oscillating Universe*, 2nd ed. (Scottish Academic Press, 1987).

[20]As can be seen in such programmatic identification of quantum mechanics with Eastern philosophies as F. Capra's *The Tao of Physics* first published in 1975. For a list of unsparing criticisms of Capra's claims, see E. R. Scerri, "Eastern Mysticism and the Alleged Parallels with Physics," *American Journal of Physics* 57 (1989): 687-92.

[21]For his exact words, recorded by a confidant of his, see my book, *God and the Cosmologists* (Scottish Academic Press, 1989), p. 221.

[22]For instance, J. Honner, "Unity-in-Difference: Karl Rahner and Niels Bohr," *Theological Studies* 46 (1985): 480-505.

[23]Recent major biographies of Schrödinger, Dirac, and Heisenberg are particularly telling in this respect.

[24]As reported by R. Resnick, a participant at that Conference, in his "Misconceptions about Einstein: His Work and His Views," *Journal of Chemical Education* **52** (1980): 860.

[25]J. S. Bell, "The Moral Aspect of Quantum Mechanics" (1966); reprinted in J. S. Bell, *Speakable and Unspeakable in Quantum Mechanics* (Cambridge University Press, 1988), p. 27.

[26]K. Gottfried, "Does Quantum Mechanics Carry the Seeds of Its Own Destruction?" *Physics World* **4** (1991): 34-40. Professor Gottfried discussed the same in a lecture given on February 27th, this year, at Rockefeller University.

[27]Thus the anonymous reviewer of the *Principia*, who wrote for the prestigious *Journal des Scavans*, coupled his praise of Newton's work as "most perfect mechanics that we can imagine" with the wish that he would crown it by giving "us a physics as exact as the mechanics." See E. J. Aiton, *The Vortex Theory of Planetary Motion* (Macdonald, 1972), p. 114.

[28]By A. N. Whitehead and B. Russell, of course.

[29]B. Russell, "Recent Work on the Principles of Mechanics," *The International Monthly* **4** (1901): 84.

[30]B. Russell, *Philosophy* (Norton, 1927), p. 157.

[31]Something akin to the pathological may be on hand when a prominent historian of the antecedents of the American Civil War claims that nothing would be really known about its true reason until the full voting record of the Congress, from the previous thirty years, had been evaluated by a computer. For further details see my forthcoming article, "History of Science and Science in History," in *Thought*.

[32]This is particularly true of the so-called transcendental Thomists. For details, see my Pere Marquette Lecture 1992, *Universe and Creed* (Marquette University Press, 1992).

[33]I am, of course, referring to B. Lonergan.

[34]J. C. Maxwell, "Introductory Lecture on Experimental Physics" in *The Scientific Papers of James Clerk Maxwell*, ed. W.D. Niven (Cambridge University Press, 1890), vol. 2, p. 252.

[35]H. Hertz, *Electric Waves*, trans. D. E. Jones (1893; Dover, 1962), p. 21.

[36]In fact, as shown by N. R. Pace, "Origins of Life: Facing up to Physical Setting," *Cell* (May 17, 1991): 531-33, the mere presence of water could be destructive of the process adovcated by Miller. See also the report by M. W. Browne about Pace's paper in the *New York Times*, June 18, 1991, section C1.

[37]The first systematic study is the article by D. M. Raup and J. J. Sepkoski Jr., "Periodicity of Extinctions in the Geologic Past," *Proceedings of the National Academy of Sciences* **81** (1984): 801-05.

[38]Reported in *Newsweek* April 8, 1985, p. 80.

[39]For details, see ch. 8, "Mach and Buddhism," in J. T. Blackmore, *Ernst Mach: His Life, Work, and Influence* (University of California Press, 1972).

[40]For further details, see my work, *Uneasy Genius: The Life and Work of Pierre Duhem* (Martinus Nijhoff, 1984), p. 321.

[41]T. H. Huxley, "On the Educational Value of the Natural History Sciences" (1854), in his *Science and Education: Essays* (Macmillan, 1899), p. 45.

[42]The inconsistency echoes the one contained in Comte's memorable dictum: Everything is relative and this is the only absolute truth.

[43]Views promoted by Holton, Lakatos, Elkana and others. For details, see my Gifford Lectures, *The Road of Science and the Ways to God* (University of Chicago Press, 1978), pp. 235-36.

[44]Much food for thought is contained in the very titles of some of P. Feyerabend's books, such as *Against Method: Outline of an Anarchistic Theory of Knowledge*, rev. ed. (Verso, 1988) and *Farewell to Reason* (Verso, 1987). Curiously, he failed to note that any argumentation in support of anarchy has to be non anarchical in order to make sense.

[45]Tellingly, in his *The Essential Tension* (University of Chicago Press, 1977), T. S. Kuhn failed to explain what he meant by metaphysics or even by essence. The book may indeed produce no small tension in any reader of it appreciative of logic.

[46]See S. C. Brush, "Should the History of Science Be Rated X?" *Science* **183** (1974): 1164-72.

[47]G. K. Chesterton, *All Things Considered* (John Lane, 1909), p. 221.

[48]For details, see ch. 1, "Fallen Angel," in my book, *Angels, Apes and Men* (Sherwood Sugden, 1983).

Technology as Creativity and Embodiment:

A New Critical View

Jacquelyn Ann K. Kegley

Technology has been villified and exalted; cast as a mere neutral instrumentality or feared as an autonomous force which overrides all traditions and values and molds human societies and beings quite against their wills. Technology is, in fact, a very complex phenomenon and among the many things that it is, it is both a fundamental mode of human creativity and of human embodiment. Looking at technology in this way allows us to re-explore the relationship between art, craft, technology, and science. Placing technology on a continuum of human creativity allows us to view technological production as a multifaceted human activity involving aesthetic motivations and creative drive as well as practical, economic, and political intentionalities. This approach opposes any notion of technological determinism and any claims that technology is an autonomous force which overrides all tradition and values, molding human beings and societies against their wills. Choice is involved in technological decision-making and humans cannot cop out of responsibility for technological creations. As a form of human creativity, technology, as science and art, is fully a cultural and social product, both reflective of and a commentary on its time, place and society. Because it is a social/cultural product, technology demands more conscious attention to allow us to be critical of and to change social aims, trends, and technological directions. By being self-conscious and critical of our technological creating we can possibly discern more flexibility of response to technology as well as design better fitness of technology to human users.

Viewing technology as a mode of human embodiment, in addition, will allow us to see technological choice as a choice we make about what humans are and can become. Technology defines both creator and user as "human types." Awareness of this fact refocuses our moral analyses of technology from questions of consequences on people and their societies to questions of choices for people and their societies. Viewing technology as a form of human creativity, indeed, makes evident that it is human creators who are in fact in charge of the direction and substance of technology. To stress the element of human control in technological creation, however, is not to deny that our technological products, although our creations, also do mold both us and our choices. But by recognizing technology as a mode of human creativity as well as human embodiment we can open up the real possibility of a radical redesigning of technology; a redirection and reconstruction of technology into a significant means for liberating humanity and nature and producing a more free and fulfilling society.

We begin, then, with the claim that technology is a fundamental form of human creativity, lying on a continuum along with other forms of human creativity such as the fine arts, craft, and science. Such a view, however, goes against the received wisdom view, originating with the Greeks and reinforced in philosophy of technology, philosophy of science, and aesthetics, which carefully distinguishes science, the fine arts, craft, and technology. This view also invokes a hierarchy of value which places higher value on science as an embodiment of theoretical wisdom and less value on the fine arts as imitative of nature. Craft and technology, the so-called productive skills, are given much less value and are placed close to the much devalued labor or toil.[1] The pursuit of art and of science are considered ends-in-themselves; they are activities to be pursued for themselves and not as means to other ends. Science seeks truth and the fine arts pursue beauty. Art, for example, is to be approached with an aesthetic attitude, i.e., one which is fully and completely open to the experience of the art object and which is disinterested in outside and extrinsic concerns. Art, it is claimed, provides its own fulfillment both for artist and for the perceiver of the art work. Technology, in contrast, is viewed as concerned with utility, efficiency, and practical matters. It is means-oriented, engaging in problem solving and its products are for practical use and only secondarily, if at all, for enjoyment or contemplation.

Technology, it is argued, is a radically different pursuit than art. Technology certainly is not seen to have intrinsic value and technology and art are understood almost as contradictory endeavors. Thus, those of this viewpoint would oppose the use by artists of technology in their work, e.g., such as in kinetic or computer art. These persons would also be shocked at the notion that computers might produce original works of art and they certainly would not even contemplate calling such productions "creative."

Attempts to radically distinguish, categorize, and differentially evaluate science, craft, the fine arts, and technology, I believe, are just further examples of the seemingly endless attempts to reduce and compartmentalize human activity. Can we really believe that the early individual who modeled clay into a fertility figurine was merely a technologist seeking a definite purpose? In addition to assisting fertility, the creation of this figurine also surely involved the aesthetic impulse to create an object of beauty as well as scientific curiosity in seeking to understand the properties of the material at hand. Art objects can have a multiplicity of uses and meanings. For example, we see some art works as criticizing society and stimulating political re-evaluation. Technological objects also have a multiplicity of purposes, although this is not often highlighted nor in the consciousness of many persons. A prime example of this is the clock. It was invented for religious purposes but it has come to serve social and cultural purposes while also becoming an object of beauty and of aesthetic appreciation. The notion of a continuum of technology, science, craft, and the fine arts, I believe, not only allows us to deal more adequately with this multiple aspect of many technological objects, but it also makes sense of aesthetic impulse in science, e.g., in the search for simplicity and for harmony in theory and in the universe. It allows us to see the scientist as "creative" and theories as involving "novelty" and creative advance. It also is in consonance with similar points of view about continuum in human activities that have been developed in other areas such as feminist approaches to epistemology.[2]

In fact, this continuum-based approach was first articulated in 1970 by Cyril Stanley Smith, metallurgist and historian of science and technology, in an article entitled, "Art, Technology, and Science: Notes on Their Historical Interaction.[3]" Smith discusses numerous historical examples of ways in which art and technology have been intimately connected. On the basis of this evidence, he asserts:

> Over and over again scientifically important properties of matter and technologically important ways of making and using them have been discovered or developed in an environment which suggests the dominance of aesthetic motivation.

Thus, for example, the planting of flowers in Neanderthal graves for enjoyment came before the development of agricultural technology for food supply. The first use of ceramics and metals occurs in decorative objects. Copper dress ornaments preceded the use of copper for weapons. Smith places the aesthetic impulse as crucial to the human species. He writes:

> Paradoxically, man's capacity for aesthetic enjoyment may have been his most practical characteristic, for it is at the root of his discovery of the world about him and it makes him want to live. It may even have made man himself, for to elaborate a remark of the poet Nabokov, it seems likely that verbal language . . . was simply a refinement of the form-appreciating capabilities first made manifest in singing and dancing.[4]

Smith's highlighting of the aesthetic impulse lends support to my idea of a continuum of human creative activity along which art, technology, craft and science are somewhat arbitrarily placed. Craft activity, since the beginning of human history, has always had its aesthetic elements—the beautifully decorated pottery and other implements of various civilizations testify to that. We speak of craftsmen as having a "feeling" for materials and we know that craftsmen sought to improve their skill not only by making swords sharper and more useful, but also in trying to make them more beautiful.

Many craft works now appear in museums of art and, of course, contemporary artists have been insistent on breaking down the barriers between art and life. Octavio Paz, commenting on contemporary crafts, celebrates crafts as a bulwark against what he sees as two dehumanining aspects of modern life which he calls the "cult of art" and the "cult of the useful." The former cult regards works of art as isolated objects fitted primarily for contemplation for its own sake, while the latter cult labels products of technology as objects whose form is dictated solely by function. Craftwork, says Paz, returns us to a world in which beauty and usefulness are fused, and, in doing so, it mediates between the two modes of dehumanization.[5] Paz's thesis is interesting, and it helps to highlight the traditional attempt to dichotomize technology and the arts. These cults dehumanize because they falsely divide into absolutes the continuum of human creative activity.

Such a continuum makes sense, in fact, of architecture, which is considered both a form of art and of technology. Architects work with space, form, and matter, as do other artists, and artistic genius clearly shines forth from such technological achievements as the Greek Parthenon and the Medieval cathedrals. The great architect, Le Corbusier, once commented that his aim in a building was to "create poetry." And in line with our concept of the continuum of human creativity, Le Corbusier also asserted that "a house is a machine for living in." John Dewey makes an even more provocative suggestion when he notes that houses are "continually created as they are lived in."[6]

Machines, agreed upon technological products, have been celebrated by many artists, including those of the Futurist movement, and machines have been embodied in work of art such as the paintings of Turner and the poetry of Walt Whitman.[7] Steam locomotives, for example, have been described as "drama and spectacle and poetry rolled into one" and as "a sublime demonstration of man's partnership with the creation."[8]

Engineering too is a form of art. Thus, Florman tells us that at the heart of engineering lies existential joy.[9] Engineers work with order and design and, like artists, have a feel for materials and the visual satisfaction of knowing that "if a job looks right, it is right."[10] The term "artist-engineer" appeared in the Renaissance when individuals such as Leonardo da Vinci engaged in both art and engineering, but it also has been applied to more contemporary engineers such as Robert Malliart and F. W. Lancaster, builder of automobiles.[11]

Our shortsightedness and neglect of the aesthetic and creative elements of technology, I believe, play a crucial role in two erroneous notions about technology: that technology is a neutral, value-free instrumentality and that it is an inexplicable, autonomous force that cannot be restrained. The latter idea is captured in the concept of the "technological imperative," often described as the lure of ever pushing forward to greater feats of technical complexity and performance. A good example of this imperative is the Manhattan Project in which nuclear scientists continued to pursue the development of the atomic bomb even though their goal of defeating Hitler had already been achieved. They felt pushed to work day and night to complete the "Gadget" and they felt a tremendous sense of "satisfaction" and "completion" at the first atomic explosion at Trinity. Many of these same scientists, upon hearing about Hiroshima, said, "Thank God, it worked." These scientists were taken up with the urge to complete the project and with the sense of fulfillment that completion would provide, just as an artist is often consumed with the process of completing a work of art. Herbert York uses the term "technological exuberance" to describe this lure toward completion of a technological process. He believes that this lure provides part of the explanation for the fact that nuclear scientists in the U.S. have often pushed the development of nuclear weapons far beyond the requirements of a rational defense policy.[12]

Again, such behavior as this is often explained by the notion that technological progress is "autonomous" and "irresistible." These scientists are seen as taken over by a blind, uncontrollable power which dictates that whatever is feasible must be tried. Arnold Pacey is absolutely correct to call this an evasion.[13] John Kenneth Galbraith gives York's "technological exuberance" the name, "technological virtuosity," but this drive could just as well be called the "creative drive," the sheer joy any creator takes in the creative process and in the final achievement. Elements of aesthetic experience are also involved, namely, pride in one's skill and mastery of the material. It is a drive linked to one's internal motivation. Thus Pacey believes that it is much more correct to account for the behavior of technologists driven by technology in terms of a drive from within and not a drive from without. In addition Pacey sees elements in this technological drive here of the single-minded commitment of Ahab in his pursuit of the White Whale as well as the desire for the human being to master an elemental force. This human impulse, argues Pacey, is rooted in non-economic "virtuosity values," and such an impulse, he believes, explains why high technology often goes far beyond anything that can be profitable or can make political sense. It certainly explains the stereotype of the "mad" inventor. Pacey notes that "research, invention and design, like poetry and painting and other creative activities, tend to become compulsive. They take on purposes of their own, separate from economic and military goals.[14]

Recognition of the creative impulse in technology allows us, as we have seen, to label the "technology-as-neutral" outlook as wrong. Technology involves creative values and emotions and these surely influence technological development and products as they do artistic creation and works. To ignore this is to have a faulty and dangerous view of technological decision making. To understand more clearly how technological development and decision-making take place, it would be advantageous to acknowledge that there are a variety of human motivations at work in such development. Certainly function and/or profit are primary ones in many cases, but this is not always so, as the case of the nuclear scientists illustrates. Technological virtuosity, professional pride, and technological arrogance have been evident throughout the history of technology. An example of this, eloquently described in William Golding's novel, *The Spire*, occurred in the Middle Ages when architects, bishops, and towns sought to produce the biggest, highest, and best cathedral. The result was the collapse of the cathedral at Beauvais.[15] The cathedrals involved technical, aesthetic, and religious motivation. They did not involve the profit motivation, although economic motivation may have been involved in the role of the cathedrals in displaying the wealth of the towns or the cloth merchants who financed them. Technological virtuosity and pride may also explain the pursuit today of certain sophisticated medical technological procedures which seem unrelated either to medical benefit or profit.

Acknowledging multiple human motivations in technological development, in addition to giving credence to the notion of a complex and multifarious human nature, also allows us to become much more aware of the social and political motivations often involved in such development which can even override profit considerations. In his book, *The Whale and the Reactor*, Langdon Winner cites two excellent examples of this type of motivational force. The engineer, Robert Moses built many public works, especially highways and bridges. Those he built favored the use of automobiles over the development of mass transit. For example, overpasses were constructed to discourage buses on these parkways. Robert Caro, biographer of Moses, has provided evidence that these technological decisions on Moses' part were the result of social class bias and racial prejudice; with no public transit poor people and blacks were kept off Moses' roadways.[16] The second illustration Winner provides of the dominance of social-political motivation in technological development is the decision in the 1880's by Cyrus McCormick to install pneumatic molding machines in his reaper manufacturing plant in Chicago. These machines were neither more efficient or cost-saving and they were abandoned in three years. Their main function was to destroy the union by weeding out the trouble makers in it who happened to be skilled workers. The machines installed by McCormick could be manned by unskilled laborers.[17]

Viewing technology as a product of human creativity, involving aesthetic motivations as well as others, particularly social and political ones, allows us to be more critical and discerning about technology and its direction. In the area of fine arts, there is a well-developed body of critical theory concerning aesthetic and artistic value judgments. Sheer creativity does not necessarily win approval in the art world. Why, then, should this be the case in the technological world? A more developed critical theory for technology seems most appropriate. The prevalent assessment mode for technology is cost-benefit analysis. Such a methodology focuses, however, primarily on the presumed consequences of technological development. A more informed evaluative process would examine the variety of values and motivations involved in proposed technological developments. Such a critical approach would allow better assessment of the possible directions of a technology and more informed judgments about the actual consequences of particular technological products. It would allow us to see aspects of technology hitherto ignored. Winner, for example, argues that technological artifacts have inherent political tendencies, i.e., they suggest particular types of social-political relationships. Nuclear power plants, for example, because of security needs, tend toward hierarchical, authoritarian organization.[18] Further, Winner's discussion of Robert Moses shows that reliance on automobiles rather than public transit, as we have seen, tends to favor the more affluent in a society. Acknowledging human motivations and responsibility in creating technology may encourage us to make more alert and informed judgments about technology. We hopefully would be able to draw the line between products involving admirable artistic and innovative impulses from those deriving from the arrogance of an individual or a collective of beings on a personal ego trip. Innovative impulse could be balanced with responsibility; social bias and racial prejudice could be identified and dealt with.

Seeing technology as a form of human creativity also suggests other avenues of exploration which I shall only briefly mention. In the arts, creativity has manifested itself in multifarious forms. This should also be true of technology, yet our understanding and study of technology tends to focus on only certain aspects of technology, e.g., those associated with machines, mathematics, the "hard sciences," the harnessing of power, and with the so-called advanced, industrialized nations. This is a form of reductionism, for these associations represent only one aspect of technology.

Recently we have begun to reconstruct a new history of technology which takes into account the technological contributions of women, of various races, cultures and civilizations, including those contributions of the so-called "less advanced" societies. This history demonstrates that technological creativity, like artistic creativity, has taken many forms of human creativity, including those labeled "intuitive" or holistic," forms often ignored in the past because they were associated with "feminine" or "primitive" modes of producing. Further, this history opens the door to the exploration of alternative modes of technological problem-solving other than those associated with the hard-sciences and linear thinking. Such an exploration might well lead to more "human-friendly," "user-friendly," "nature-friendly," technological products. For example, in her sociological study of computer users, Sherry Turkle discusses two modes of computer mastery.[19] "Hard mastery" involves control and structured linear planning while "soft mastery" involves "interaction and negotiation." The latter mode of technological mastery Turkle likens to "bricolage," the term used by Levi-Strauss to describe the science of pre-literate societies, the science of the "concrete."

Turkle and her colleague, Seymour Papert, in an article, "Epistemological Pluralism: Styles and Voices Within the Computer Culture," see the computer as an expressive medium that different people can make use of in their own way. However, programmers, educators, and businesspeople, who represent the power structures in our culture, are forcing programming styles and computer uses into the "hard mastery" mold. The use of the computer is being dictated not entirely by the nature of the machine, but more by the social systems in which the machine operates. We have already discussed the social and political motivations that can be involved in technological development. This may be another example, but since computer technological development is, in a sense, in a relative stage of infancy, we can still apply a more alert, informed and critical mode of analysis to its further development.

Stressing, as we have thus far, the notion of technology as a creative product involving aesthetic as well as other motivational forces, it should be no surprise, therefore, that we should applaud the rise of a sociology of technology which stresses the social shaping of technology.[20] Technology is shaped by social interests—economic, class, national, and gender interests. Thomas Kuhn, numerous philosophers of science, as well as feminist critiques of science have already pretty well convinced us that science is socially shaped.[21] Arguing for a continuum of human creativity which includes scientific activity as creativity, should this not be the case? Feminist critiques of science argue for epistemological pluralism in science. Feminist critiques of technology in identifying the gendered character of technology also argue for pluralism in technological problem solving. The correspondence between men and machines is neither essential nor immutable and, therefore, the potential exists for technology's transformation.[22]

In his book, *Critical Theory of Technology*, Andrew Feenberg poses the question: "Can technology be designed to better serve its creators?"[23] My answer is: "Surely, why not." If technology is a product of human creativity, it should be malleable to the wishes of its creators. However, the history of technology, at least in its dominant construction, does provide evidence of the existence of some degree of technological imperative. The history of technology, unlike the history of art, seems not to display hospitableness to technological pluralism nor a deep critical spirit. Technological products, like works of art, can be deeply reflective of their culture and time, but, unlike works of art, are rarely critical and/or satirical commentaries on the follies of the time. Alfred North Whitehead argued, in fact, that one of the maxims of the practical intelligence exemplified in technology is "if it isn't broken, don't fix it." Technical orientations, Whitehead said, are indifferent or hostile to criticism.[24] However, this need not be the case. As we have argued, there is a long tradition of art criticism and there could be developed a strong tradition of technology criticism.

The development of a critical mode is likely, for the history of technology, like the history of science, is being reexamined and rewritten to portray a more pluralistic, more human, history. As we become more aware of technology as a form of social knowledge, practice and products, and as we become more cognizant of the gendered and class-shaped nature of technology, we can begin the major reconstruction envisioned by Feenberg. As we continue to explore the continuum of human creativity, the more we realize, with Feenberg, that "concretization, vocation, aesthetic investment, and collegiality" are not extrinsic to the nature of technology but rather intrinsic to complex human activity. Different directions and paths of technical development are possible even without diminishing the "productive efficiency" deemed so crucial to western capitalistic societies.

Further, in bemoaning the fact that the U.S. is falling behind in technological development in comparison to other nations, we have rightly focused on the educational system. However, we continue to be single-minded in this regard by concerning ourselves only with science and math education. This is surely a much needed focus, but another equally needed focus is to provide the educational conditions which foster innovation and creativity as well as self-consciousness about human motivational factors. There is more to technological development than skills in mathematics and science and the desire for profit.

Our reexamination of technology and its refocusing is both a possible task and an imperative one. Technology is a fundamental form of human creativity, but it is also a mode of human embodiment. It, indeed, may be understood as an essential part of our very humanity. We are *homo faber*, a technology creator and thus achieve much of our embodiment and presence in the world through technological creation. José Ortega y Gasset identifies technology as a "system of activities through which man endeavors to realize the extranatural program that is himself."[25] Technological choices, then, are choices about what it means to be human and what humans can become.

The human is a technological being and it then should be no surprise that technology has been part of the history of humankind from almost the beginning. Don Ihde, philosopher and phenomenologist, has discussed in detail how humans "from immemorial time and across the diversity of cultures [have] been technologically embedded." Even those societies most like the Garden of Eden still have been in some part technological. For example, the Stone Age Tasaday culture, discovered in 1972 in Mindanao in the Philippines, used fire, food preparation techniques, sluices, traps, axes, and temperature control devices. Thus, although non-human animals utilize prototechnologies including clubs to kill other smaller animals, humans are, as Ortega suggests, *homo faber*, technological beings.[26]

And, in fact, it is the case that humans were technological beings long before they were people of science. Ihde, as well as others, has traced the development and interactions of science and technology and this history suggests that science is a much later development and that technology has spurred scientific discovery and theoretical advance. This makes somewhat suspect the over-evaluation of science and theoretical knowledge in judging human endeavors and progress. Ihde, in fact, has cogently demonstrated that the instrumentations on which modern science is so heavily dependent are forms of human embodiment and extension of body, e.g., sight and hearing through microscopes and visual and audio telescopes. This leads him to conclude rightly, I believe, that *"there is a significant sense in which technology may be seen as both ontologically and historically prior to science."*[27]

Our technology has been a crucial component of our human existence, a tool for experiencing and surviving in the world. There is a clear sense in which we use our bodies and bodily senses as "tools" to accomplish specific ends. Bodily and self-extension is a prime goal of technological production, e.g., cosmetics, musical instruments, and instrumental extensions of sight, hearing, and mobility. And these technological products not only extend self and body; they become in a real sense a part of our bodies. Eyeglasses and contact lens extend our sight, while also becoming part of our bodily presence. Hearing aids, various prostheses, and artificial body parts and aids are similar in this regard. Further, humans began early in their history to increase technologically the range and pace of their mobility. This continues today with space and supersonic plane travel. Douglas Browning, in an article entitled "Some Meanings of the Automobile," has captured succintly the way in which humans become embodied in their automobiles. He describes the automobile as a "suit of clothes." It is our "traffic habit," our "highway gear." The automobile becomes "impersonated," serving both as a tool and a garment and we become "automobiled human beings."[28]

We are technologically embodied beings. Technology reflects and is human reality; human intelligence, or lack thereof, and human values are incarnate in our technologies. We, therefore, need to be much more conscious of technology as human embodiment and to study what it reveals about us. Ihde has provided us with a series of analytical tools for this in terms of a set of patterns of human-technology relationships. These include: (a) the embodiment relationships, e.g., (I-technology)—world; (b) the hermeneutic relationships, e.g., I—(technology-world); (c) the alerity relationships, e.g., Human-technology—(world); and the background relationships, e.g., technology in the background of human activity or in serving as a technological cocoon—heating and cooling units or recreational vehicles.[29]

From Ihde's extensive analysis of these relationships, the following conclusions can be drawn. First, technology is never neutral, mere instrumentality; it *always affects the way humans perceive, understand, and act.* The telescope, for example, dramatically transforms human perception. It magnifies and radically changes our sense of distance and size. Seeing the craters on the moon through a telescope, we are under the impression that they are "very near." We forget the great distance separating us from what we are seeing and we forget that we have only a visual experience of the objects. We are having, from the standpoint of ordinary sensory experience, a distorted and mono-dimensional view of these craters. The telescope also has led to dramatic changes in our understanding of the world. It was Galileo's observations through the telescope that partly verified for him the validity of the Copernican view of the universe. The microscope and the cloud chamber have revealed new aspects of reality and thus have also led to profound changes in our understanding of that reality. And, technology certainly changes human action. The bumper-sticker slogan, "Guns don't kill, people do," is dead wrong. A human-with-a-gun provides a very different relational experience than a human-without-a-gun.

A second observation to be drawn from Ihde's analysis is that humans, in relationship with technology, must be aware of a double aspect of such a relationship, namely, that technologies both reveal and excite and conceal and mislead. As indicated above, when a telescope reveals craters on the moon it is truly amazing, but we forget that we are only seeing one aspect of those craters, namely, the visual, and we forget the great distance involved in our viewing. Amazed at what scientific instruments reveal, we forget that they give us only a single and partial dimension of reality, e.g., genes, atoms, or brain processes, and not the whole of that reality. We grow excited at hearing via telephone our friend in Buffalo, but are unconscious of the fact that we really have not "reached out and touched" him and are not reading his mood with our full perceptual equipment. We may thus be mislead about his actual state, e.g., depressed, angry, or bored.

Overwhelmed with the feel in our body of the tremendous power and speed of our automobile, we are oblivious to the terrible destruction this tool can bring about.

In probing human-technology relationships, Ihde has also revealed the double desire we have with regard to technology, namely, to have fully transparent, embodied technology and the power of transformation that it gives, e.g., bionic eyes and limbs. Involved is a continual drive to extend human capacities to see and hear farther and to travel faster and farther. Involved also is our fascination with and fantasy about automated machines which we want to turn into "another" being, e.g., Hal of *2001* or Data of *Star Trek: The Next Generation.* These desires and fantasies need to be made conscious so they can be critically explored. What is humanness? What is machinness? Is there any crucial difference or is this the age of "vital machines," in which the biological and mechanical will be merged? Is survival a goal sought without limit even if it means numerous transplanted organs, artificial or natural? Is brain transplant and humanoid creation the next proper stage of technological development? Should artificial intelligence technology seek a Hal or Data as a goal in reality rather than in fiction?

Technological progress has brought with it a tremendous *decision burden.* And, since we are the creators of technology, we cannot pass off the burden of decision. In spite of what some would claim, we have been playing the "creator role" all along, creating and remaking reality to our image and liking. Much of our world today is a man-made world. We are surrounded by things of our own making and we even ingest more and more human created substances. Further, today because of genetic and reproductive technology, we are being placed in an even more preeminent creative role. We can choose to start life by foregoing birth control; we can, through in vitro fertilization and sperm, egg, and embyro donation, decide about the existence, number and kind of people who will be part of our future. And, incidentally, we can also decide about the existence of other life forms whether they be the Harvard mouse, blue roses or cows who produce fat-free milk. Not only are we making decisions about life, but also we can now, in many senses, choose our death. The whole movement of "assisted suicide" and durable powers of attorney for health care requires us to ponder, in a truly existential sense, our death. This, of course, also asks us to ponder, individually and collectively, questions of the value of existence and what it really means to be human.

This brings us to fundamental and profound ethical and theological questions. David Heyd, in his book, *Genethics,* argues that the morality of "creating" people, i.e., deciding on their existence, number, and kind, requires us to transcend the limits of traditional ethical theory. It certainly requires us to refocus our ethical analysis from concentrating on the implications of technology *on* human beings to ethical decisions *for* human beings. It also is imperative that we address the "playing God" issue. There are strong voices in our society against technological developments, especially in the reproductive area, on the grounds that such technology is "unnatural" and involves us in "playing God." My view is that technology is a natural, creative activity of human beings, arising out of their very natures. Further, I am in agreement with those scholars like Norris Clark who see technology as helping to develop the human being in the image of God the creator, namely, continuing the creative process.[30]

It is also human nature to fall into *hubris* and to engage in excessive and incautious uses of technology. We humans have used and changed nature since the beginning of time, but we need to use nature with care. How we use nature, how we develop our technology, displays our humanity, or lack thereof. One would assume that, as technology creators and as technologically embodied, we would want to "play God" in a rational manner with an attitude of cosmic modesty. Since technology is a product of our creativity, we the creators must make the choice. Not to choose is itself a choice.

NOTES

[1]Larry Hickman, *Philosophy, Technology and Human Affairs* (Ibis Press, 1990), pp. 100ff.

[2]Sandra Harding and Merrill B. Hintikka, eds., *Discovering Reality: Feminist Perspectives on Epistemology, Metaphysics, Method and Philosophy of Science* (D. Reidel, 1989).

[3]Cyril Stanley Smith, "Art, Technology and Science: Notes on Their Historical Interaction," *Technology and Culture* 2 (1970).

[4]Ibid., p. 498.

[5]Octavio Paz, "In Praise of Hands," *Contemporary Crafts of the World*, trans. Helen T. Lane (World Crafts Council, 1974).

[6]Larry Hickman, *John Dewey's Pragmatic Technology* (Indiana University Press, 1990), p. 77.

[7]Kenneth Hopkins, ed., *The Poetry of Railways* (Leslie Frewin, 1966).

[8]Jack Burton, *Transport of Delight* (SCM Press, 1976), pp. 49-50.

⁹Samuel Florman, *The Existential Pleasures of Engineering* (St. Martin's Press, 1976), p. 10.

¹⁰Arnold Pacey, *The Culture of Technology* (MIT Press, 1991), p. 83.

¹¹David P. Billington, *Robert Malliart's Bridges* (Princeton University Press, 1979); P. W. Kingsford, F. W. *Lancaster: The Life of an Engineer* (Edward Arnold, 1960).

¹²Herbert York, *The Advisors: Oppenheimer, Teller, and the Superbomb* (W. H. Freeman, 1976), p. 81.

¹³Pacy, *Culture*, p. 81.

¹⁴Ibid., p. 85.

¹⁵Arnold Pacey, *The Maze of Ingenuity* (MIT Press, 1976), p. 47.

¹⁶Langdon Winner, *The Whale and the Reactor: The Search for Limits in an Age of High Technology* (University of Chicago Press, 1986), pp. 22-23.

¹⁷Ibid., pp. 24-25.

¹⁸Ibid., pp. 19-39.

¹⁹Sherry Turkle, *Second Self: Computers and the Human Spirit* (Simon and Schuster, 1984).

²⁰David MacKenzie and Judy Wajcman, eds. *The Social Shaping of Technology: How the Refrigerator Got Its Hum* (Open University Press, 1990); J. Law, "Review Article: The Structure of Sociotechnical Engineering," *The Sociological Review* 35 (1987): 404-425.

²¹Thomas Kuhn, *The Structure of Scientific Revolutions*, 2d ed. (University of Chicago Press, 1970); Anthony O'Hear, *An Introduction to Philosophy of Science* (Oxford University Press, 1990); Larry Laudan, *Science and Values* (University of California Press, 1984); Patrick Suppes, "The Plurality of Science," in P. D. Asquith and I. Hacking, eds. *Philosophy of Science Association*, vol. 2 (1978); Sandra Harding, *The Science Question in Feminism* (Cornell University Press, 1986); E. Fox Keller, *Reflections on Gender and Science* (Yale University Press, 1985); Nancy Tauna, ed. *Feminism and Science* (Indiana University Press, 1989).

[22]Judy Wajcman, *Feminism Confronts Technology* (Penn State University Press, 1991).

[23]Andrew Feenberg, *Critical Theory of Technology* (Oxford University Press, 1991).

[24]Frederick Ferre, *Philosophy of Technology* (Prentice-Hall, 1988), p. 83.

[25]José Ortega y Gasset, "Thoughts on Technology," in Carl Mitchum and Robert Machey, eds., *Philosophy and Technology* (The Free Press, 1972), p. 165.

[76]Don Ihde, *Technology and the Life World* (Indiana University Press, 1990), pp. 13-14, 20.

[27]Don Ihde, *Existential Technics* (State University of New York Press, 1983), p. 25.

[28]Douglas Browning, "Some Meanings of the Automobile," in Larry A. Hickman, *Technology and Human Affairs* (McGraw Hill, 1990), p. 62.

[29]Ihde, *Technology*, pp. 72-123.

[30]Norris Clarke, "Technology and Man: A Christian Vision," in Carl F. Stover, ed. *The Technological Order* (Wayne State University Press, 1963); Frederick Ferré, *Philosophy of Technology* (Prentice-Hall, 1988), pp. 104-107.

WHEN INCONSISTENCIES THREATEN:

PARACONSISTENT STRATEGIES IN SCIENCE AND RELIGION

RONALD MAWBY

Is it ever rational to use an inconsistent theory? Standard logic says no. I believe the better answer is yes. Explaining this answer is what I undertake here.[1]

Let me begin by saying why this question matters. Often the best scientific and religious accounts we have are inconsistent, and I do not mean just that they are inconsistent with each other. I mean that sometimes the best scientific theories we have are internally inconsistent, and sometimes the best religious doctrines we have are internally inconsistent. What are we to do in such situations? Standard logic tells us that we must eliminate all inconsistency. Historical experience tells us that sometimes we do not know how to remove theoretical inconsistency without giving up a theory altogether. We face a dilemma: either renounce theory, or renounce logic. I think that with a different view of the logic of inconsistency, we might escape from this dilemma.

The shape of the paper is this. First, I explain why standard logic must reject inconsistent theories. Then I give examples of scientific and religious theories that are both valuable and inconsistent. Next I describe some nonstandard logics, called paraconsistent logics, that permit us to reason with inconsistent theories. Finally I briefly compare standard and paraconsistent strategies for dealing with inconsistency.

1. Standard Logic and Inconsistency

Why does standard logic say that it is always irrational to employ an inconsistent theory? Because in standard logic an inconsistent theory amounts to no theory at all. I will explain, in terms that are shamelessly informal. A theory, in the sense of a rational account, consists of some basic principles and the logical conclusions that follow from those principles. We may think of a theory as beginning with its explicit principles and expanding to include all the consequences of those principles. An *inconsistent* theory is one that contains a proposition and its negation. The standard logical consequences of an inconsistent theory include *everything*. That is, in standard logic, from an inconsistency everything follows. Thus an inconsistent theory will expand to include everything; it blows up. To use the technical term, standard logic is *explosive* in the presence of inconsistency.

Why should everything follow from an inconsistency? What intuition underlies explosive logical consequence? When someone says something self-contradictory, we are inclined to say, "If one were to accept *that*, one could prove anything at all."[2] If you accept an inconsistency, it seems you are in no position to reject anything. Standard logic embodies this inclination. All standard formulations of logical consequence agree, both model-theoretic[3] (couched in terms of satisfaction and truth) and proof-theoretic[4] (couched in terms of inference rules): from any inconsistency everything follows.

2. Standard Logic Makes Inconsistent Theories Worthless

This is why standard logic says that it must always be irrational to use an inconsistent theory. An inconsistent theory that includes all its standard logical consequences must contain every proposition, and that means all propositions and their negations. One inconsistency thus implies every inconsistency. With standard logic, inconsistency is not a matter of degree; it is an all or none affair. Not true, because contradictions cannot be true. Not useful, because by containing everything an inconsistency theory tells us nothing. Suppose we consider a theory as a device for answering questions. We ask of any proposition, is this proposition true? If the proposition follows from the theory, the answer should be Yes; if not, No. If we use standard logic, an inconsistent theory will always answer Yes, no matter what the question, since every proposition follows from an inconsistency. A device that answers Yes to every question is not informative. Thus an inconsistent theory amounts to no theory at all.

The standard notion of logical consequence thus determines the standard strategy for handling inconsistency. An epistemic agent committed to standard logic will think only of removing inconsistencies from his theories. Unfortunately, this strategy runs into a stubborn fact. Sometimes we do not know how to remove theoretical inconsistency without abandoning a theory altogether. I will now give three examples of theories that are at once inconsistent, valuable, and hard to render consistent.

3. Calculus in the Seventeenth Century

My first example is from seventeenth-century mathematics: the calculus as developed by Newton. Bishop Berkeley, in a wonderful polemic entitled *The Analyst*, scrutinized the logical foundations of Newton's calculus, and concluded that the calculus rested on inconsistent foundations. The core difficulty can be seen in an example. Take the problem that today we would call finding the derivative of the function $y = x^2$. Newton thinks of the independent variable x as flowing uniformly. He wants to find the fluxion, the rate of flow, of the dependent quantity x^2. Newton adds an augment to x; call it o. This makes the dependent quantity $(x+o)^2$ which expands to $x^2+2xo+o^2$. So when the augment of x is o the augment of x^2 is $2xo+o^2$. The ratio of the augments is thus 1 to $2x+o$. As Newton says, "Now let the augments come to vanish and their last ratio will be 1 to 2x. Consequently the fluxion of the quantity x is to the fluxion of the quantity x^2 as 1 to 2x."[5]

As Berkeley points out, Newton's procedure is inconsistent. He begins by assuming an augment that is not zero. From this assumption he derives his ratios. Then he negates the assumption, and supposes the augment to vanish, that is, to be zero. Yet he retains the results he obtained by the first assumption. If the augment of x is zero, the augment of x^2 is zero, and if the augment is not zero, then the fluxion is $2x+o$, not 2x. Newton's explanation is, as Berkeley says,

". . .a most inconsistent way of arguing and such as would not be allowed of in Divinity."[6]

Today, of course, we use the notion of limit and the contradiction disappears. The point, though, is this. Consistent logical foundations of the calculus were not laid until the nineteenth century, one hundred fifty years after the calculus began to be used. The great achievements of mathematical analysis and physics in the seventeenth and eighteenth century were built on an inconsistent foundation. Standard logic would tell us that we have no business using such a theory, for it is inconsistent and explosive and so no theory at all. With hindsight we can see that Newton had an insight that was sound, though his formulation was defective and inconsistent. Was it rational for him to go ahead, exploit the insight, and try to establish it on a consistent foundation? Obviously it was.

4. Quantum Electrodynamics in the 20th Century

My second example is the current physical theory called quantum electrodynamics, or QED. Here I rely on the argument from authority, because I do not know enough physics to tell the tale myself. Quantum electrodynamics has a vast range of application; it covers everything except nuclear physics and gravitation. It also has astonishing accuracy. Richard Feynman, who shared a Nobel prize for his work on QED, wrote in 1985 "at the present time I can proudly say that there is *no significant difference* between experiment and theory" and that the theory is "the jewel of physics—our proudest possession."[7] The problem with QED is that it is beset with mathematical and conceptual troubles. The theory predicts probabilities, and the meaning of probability requires that the sum of the probabilities of all alternatives be one, or unity. In QED certain calculations lead to divergent integrals and hence infinite values. Physicists have a technical trick called renormalization to avoid the infinities, but the conceptual problem remains. In his 1965 Nobel Prize acceptance speech Feynman said, referring to work done in the late 1940's:

> [a] second thing . . . was missing when I published the paper, an unresolved difficulty. . . . the calculations would give results which were not "unitary," that is, for which the sum of the probabilities of all alternatives was not unity. . . . It is lucky that I did not wait to straighten out that point, for as far as I know, nobody has yet been able to resolve this question. . . . I believe there is really no satisfactory quantum electrodynamics, but I'm not sure. . . . I believe . . . strong interactions in field theory have no solution, have no sense—they're either infinite, or, if you try to modify them, the modification destroys the unitarity. I don't think we have a completely satisfactory relativistic quantum mechanical model, even one that doesn't agree with nature, but, at least, agrees with the logic that the sum of probability of all alternatives has to be 100%. Therefore, I think that the renormalization theory is simply a way to sweep the difficulties of the divergences of electrodynamics under the rug.[8]

Feynman is not alone in his concern. Julian Schwinger, who shared in the 1965 Nobel Prize for work on QED, wrote in 1956:

> Could it not be that the divergences—apparent symptoms of malignancy—are only spurious byproducts of an invalid expansion . . . and that renormalization, which can change no physical implication of the theory, simply rectifies this mathematical error? This hope disappears on recognizing that the observational basis of quantum electrodynamics is self-contradictory.[9]
> . . . We conclude that a convergent theory cannot be formulated consistently within the framework of present space-time concepts. To limit the magnitude of interactions while retaining the customary coordinate description is contradictory . . . .[10]

Paul Dirac, one of the founders of quantum theory, also agrees. Dirac in 1975 wrote:

> Our present quantum theory is very good, provided we do not try to push it too far. . . . When we do try to push it . . . we get equations which do not have sensible solutions. We have our interactions always leading to infinites. This question has bothered physicists for 40 years, and they have not made any very substantial progress. It is because of these difficulties that I feel that the foundations of quantum mechanics have not yet been correctly established.[11]
>
> . . . most physicists . . . say: "Quantum electrodynamics is a good theory, and we do not have to worry about it any more." I must say that I am very dissatisfied with the situation, because this so-called "good theory" does involve neglecting infinites which appear in its equations, neglecting them in an arbitrary way. This is just not sensible mathematics. Sensible mathematics involved neglecting a quantity when it turns out to be small—not neglecting it just because it is infinitely great and you do not want it.[12]

Dirac does say that quantum electrodynamics can be made consistent with itself, at the price of making it inconsistent with the theory of relativity.

To sum up, three Nobel laureates hold that quantum electrodynamics is logically flawed. Yet, as Feynman said, it is the jewel of physics. The situation resembles that of the calculus. Quantum electrodynamics has an insight that we cannot yet formulate consistently. It would be crazy to reject the theory, but we do not know how to remove its inconsistency. We use an inconsistent theory, and I think we are rational to do so.

5. Early Christian Doctrines of Trinity and Incarnation

My third example concerns the early Christian doctrines of the Trinity and Incarnation. Let us return to Bishop Berkeley for a moment. The full title of his essay is "The Analyst or, a discourse addressed to an infidel mathematician wherein it is examined whether the object, principles, and inferences of the modern analysis are more distinctly conceived, or more evidently deduced, than religious mysteries and points of faith." We may ask ourselves, conversely, whether the Christian faith of the good Bishop is freer of contradictions than the science that he examines.

In *The History of Heresy*, David Christie-Murray notes that Christianity, an offspring of monotheistic Judaism, had to formulate a doctrine of the Trinity, and that its orthodox statements, as expressed for example in the

Athanasian creed, are "at first sight not so much paradoxes as downright contradictions."[13] I suspect one could write a history of Christian heresy in which heresy is seen as a way to resolve paradoxes in the orthodox doctrine. For the orthodox doctrine is that God is three *and* one, and Jesus Christ is human and divine. How might we make sense of this doctrine?

Consider this possibility. Suppose that God is one, and that the Father's first and finest creation was the Son. The Son was involved in all further creation, and the Spirit is the joint product of the Father and Son. This account keeps strict monotheism, and it justifies the language of Father and Son. However, it is heretical (the Arian heresy). Orthodoxy maintains that Son and Spirit are co-equal with the Father.

How can God be one and three? Consider this possibility. Just as a fire might be bright, orange, and hot, so may the One God have three distinct names or aspects or modes. In particular the One God may show himself to us in three relations as Creator, Redeemer, and Comforter. In this sense God may be said to be one and three. This doctrine (Modal Monarchianism) resolves the paradox of the Trinity. It too is heretical. Orthodoxy maintains that God must be really and instrinsically three, not merely nominally or extrinsically three.

Turn now to the doctrine of Christ. How can we understand Jesus Christ to be both human and divine? Suppose that Jesus was born an ordinary man. After his baptism a divine Spirit dwelt in him. The Spirit was the Christ, a power from God. Thus Jesus is a human being with a divine power. In this sense he was both human and divine. This doctrine (Dynamic Monarchianism) is heretical. Orthodoxy maintains that Jesus has a Divine personality, not just an impersonal Divine power.

Assume next that a human being is composed of body and spirit. Suppose Jesus had a human body and the spirit of God the Son. This teaching (Apollinarianism) resolves the paradox by a distinction. Jesus was human in respect of body, divine in respect of spirit. It too is heretical. Orthodoxy maintains that Christ was fully human and fully divine.

Suppose then that in Jesus Christ two persons were joined together: God the Son and the man Jesus. The man was the dwelling place of the Word. Jesus the man was born of Mary and Jesus the man died on the Cross. This doctrine finds in Christ a fully human and a fully divine person, who are in moral union. It is the Nestorian heresy. Orthodoxy maintains that Jesus Christ was one person, not two.

Suppose then that Jesus was one. He was of one nature only, his humanity being absorbed and taken up into his divinity. His humanity then would be unlike ours, as his is made divine. This doctrine (Monophysitism) too is heretical. Orthodoxy maintains that Jesus Christ is two natures in one person.

Each of the heresies I have mentioned is, I think, easier to conceive than the orthodox doctrine. Is orthodoxy just another name for the stubborn refusal to accept any intelligible formulation? I would suggest, very tentatively, that this is not so. Orthodoxy sets itself to account for what it takes as revelations of Divinity. The truth of certain books of Scripture, the efficacy of certain forms of worship, and the felt power of grace and faith are taken by orthodoxy as authentic revelations of ultimate reality. Orthodoxy refuses to discard any of that revelation, even if it cannot hold it together consistently, because it deems it impious and irrational to reject any portion of revealed insight. Heresy, from the viewpoint of orthodoxy, neglects some part of the revelation. Thus, for example, Christ must be both fully human and fully divine, because only then can the revealed truth of the salvation of the whole human being, body and soul, be made good. Heretical Christologies cannot account for salvation.

Orthodoxy maintains that if the formulation of the collected revelation is inconsistent, well, it is still the best we can do. The creed points to truth, even if its statement is inconsistent. The Catholic position is that, in the end, faith does not conflict with reason, though in this life we may never see clearly how this is so. The situation is not so very different from that in science. Dirac may use quantum electrodynamics to make predictions, while acknowledging that the theory as formulated is not sensible mathematics. He accepts the best formulation that he can get, as an interim measure until a better insight can be attained. I think this is a rational epistemic strategy.

6. Paraconsistent Logics and Inconsistency

Am I saying, then, that it is rational to be illogical? Not exactly. I think it is rational to employ an alternative logic when the presuppositions of standard logic are not met. Let me explain. On the one hand, logic may be thought of as a branch of mathematics. The logician proves theorems, theorems that might be applied outside mathematical logic. On the other hand, logic may be thought of as a reasoning tool, a canon for evaluating inferences. Now logic as a reasoning tool may use logic as a branch of mathematics. The formal validity of an inference, as shown in mathematical logic, can serve as criterion for the cogency of some reasoning. But if logic is to be a tool, it must fit the situations in which it is used. Standard logic is not useful in many inferential situations, because standard logic is explosive in the presence of inconsistency, and many inferential situations harbor inconsistencies. But there are alternatives to standard logic that are sound mathematically and useful for evaluating inferences in inconsistent reasoning situations. These logics are called paraconsistent logics. Their defining feature is that they are not explosive in the presence of inconsistency. In paraconsistent logic, it is not the case that everything follows from any inconsistency.

What are the motivations behind paraconsistent logics? One is that logic should be a universal reasoning tool, and hence should be applicable in all reasoning situations. And in some situations we must reason with inconsistent information. Standard logic considers reasoning situations ontologically. Since reality does not contradict itself, neither does any situation considered in standard logic. Paraconsistent logics consider reasoning situations epistemically. Although no actual state of affairs contradicts itself, we often reason from information that is contradictory. For example, Dirac may say that our information in regard to QED is inconsistent. We have evidence *for* QED because of its predictive accuracy, and evidence *against* QED because it is not sensible mathematics. Standard logic says, "If you accept an inconsistency, you should accept anything." Paraconsistent logic says, Why should inconsistent evidence lead to a psychotic break? If we have evidence for one contradiction, it *does not follow* that we have evidence for every contradiction. One contradiction need have no logical relation to another. Some paraconsistent logics incorporate the principle that relevance between premises and conclusion is necessary for logical consequence. This principle keeps the logic from exploding, for since a single contradiction is not relevant to every proposition, it cannot entail every proposition.

Paraconsistent logics can be given precise mathematical expression. There are a number of such logics, and each can be worked out formally in a number of ways.[14] As mathematical logics they have the same status as standard logic. The question is whether they ever should be used as tools to evaluate inferences. I think they should, and that in some cases they are better tools than standard logic. In particular they are better tools with which to reason from inconsistent theories.

Paraconsistent logical consequence permits the inconsistency of a theory to be a matter of degree. Consistency then resembles other dimensions of theory evaluation such as explanatory power, range, precision, and simplicity. All these dimensions permit distinctions of degree. Inconsistency is a flaw in a theory, but not necessarily a fatal flaw.[15] If a theory has enough other virtues we may retain it even if it is inconsistent. Paraconsistent logics thus support the idea that it may be rational to use inconsistent theories.

7. Paraconsistent Epistemic Strategies

I have said that standard logic suggests an epistemic strategy when contradictions threaten us, namely, remove the contradiction. Paraconsistent logics also suggest epistemic strategies in the face of contradiction. I will explore two such strategies: separation and containment.[16]

The separation strategy tells us to divide an inconsistent theory into consistent sub-theories, and reason only within the sub-theories. This is really the old strategy of making a distinction to avoid self-contradiction. If we find an inconsistency we make a distinction to separate the theory into two. We never reason from an inconsistency. We establish local consistency, and refuse to adopt any perspective from which we can see the global inconsistency. The strategy is to live successively in consistent worlds, worlds which collectively are inconsistent.

I think this is what most of us do most of the time. Recent work by formal logicians may thus justify our normal epistemic practice. The separation strategy is easy to adopt. Mental sloth embodies it. To keep conflicting beliefs apart, simply do not try to integrate them. Many people resolve conflicts between science and religion in this way. Science is what they believe during the week; religion is what they believe on Sunday. Science concerns natural phenomena; religion concerns spiritual values. Science is a matter for argument and evidence; religion is a matter of tradition and faith. Science on this view cannot conflict with religion, nor can it support it, for they have nothing in common, neither topic nor aim nor method. Someone who is both religious and scientific is, like the Nestorian Christ, two persons in one being.

Logically I think separation is fine. Epistemically I find it very unsatisfying. Amid all the diversity in our world there is an underlying unity, something that makes it all one world. The separation approach systematically neglects this unity. Further, by forbidding us to notice global inconsistencies, it gives us no incentive to resolve them. Thus it seems to me to settle too easily into inconsistency.

The containment strategy insists that we have one world. Inconsistencies in our theories do not spread everywhere; they are contained because we use paraconsistent logic. In the short term we use inconsistent theories if their virtues have enough weight to overbalance their inconsistency. In the long term we seek theories that are consistent. This strategy is, I think, expressed by Dirac, who admits the value of quantum electrodynamics yet will not admit that we do not have to worry about it any more.

I prefer the containment strategy. On this view inconsistency is not a logical disaster, to be avoided at any cost, nor is it something to ignore or feel easy about. An inconsistent theory cannot be true, but it can be useful.

8. A Word About Inconsistency and Error

Before I finish I want to warn against a mis-impression. You may think I am saying "Inconsistencies are fine, no problem, all our best theories seem to be inconsistent anyway, so why bother about a little contradiction?" One paraconsistent logician reports that he wondered if he should publish his work, for fear that the "rat-bag fringe" would seize upon it as a license for irrationality. I am not sure what the phrase "rat-bag fringe" refers to, but it certainly has the right *sound* about it. I too am fearful. One sees so much irrationality, so many bad arguments, so much self-contradiction, that it feels indecent to say out loud that some contradictions should be tolerated. Yet that is my position. The scientific theories I have mentioned are great intellectual achievements, whatever their flaws. We do right to employ them. But while they are inconsistent they cannot be the last word. I am not a Christian, and so I cannot speak out of my own convictions about the value of that creed, but people I respect think that Christianity gives them the best available insight into the human condition. These large theories seem to me to be very far from simple mistakes. Yet the principle of difference is, I confess, not perfectly clear. I wish to distinguish inconsistencies due to sheer error from those that give glimpses of further truths. But in practice this distinction can be hard to make.

Conclusion: Paraconsistent Strategies and Intellectual Advance

I will finish with a brief remark on strategies for handling inconsistency. A perfect theory would be at once fully logically consistent and fully adequate to our experience.[17] We often find that accounts that are more consistent are less adequate to the full range of our experience, and accounts that are more adequate to our experience are less consistent. We often must choose between a narrower, more coherent account and a wider, less coherent account. For every imperfect account we can imagine a strategy to improve it. The question becomes, Which strategy is more likely to lead to intellectual progress?

Standard logic tells us to clear our theories of inconsistency. Standard logic has such a horror of being infected by a contradiction that it counsels sterilization, even if the result is an intellectual desert. Paraconsistent strategies need worry less about the spread of inconsistency. The separation strategy prunes inconsistent theories into consistent sub-theories. It keeps the sub-theories from polluting (or pollinating) each other. The containment strategy posits that cross-fertilization is the best way to advance our understanding. New ideas are more likely to sprout from the jungle of experience than a logical desert. Contradictions will not spread, because we use paraconsistent logic. We bear with inconsistency in hopes that it will bear a finer fruit.

In conclusion, paraconsistent strategies provide a rationale for using inconsistent theories on the way to intellectual advance. As Kant says in another connection, "when the arguments of reason are allowed to oppose one another in unrestricted freedom, something advantageous, and likely to aid in the correction of our judgments, will always accrue, though it may not be what we set out to find."[18]

NOTES

[1] I thank Catherine Clement and Robert Mitchell for helpful comments on earlier drafts of this paper.

[2] An interpretation of a propositional language, in the model-theoretic sense, is an assignment of truth values to every formula in the language. A theory is a (proper or improper) subset of the formulas of the language. A model of a theory is an interpretation that assigns every formula in the theory the value "true." A set of premises S has a formula P as a logical consequence just in case every model of S is also a model of P. That is, P is a logical consequence of S if there is no model of S that is not also a model of P. In standard logic, an inconsistent theory has no model at all. Thus an inconsistent theory will have no model with any further property, such as that of failing to assign "true" to any formula in the language. Hence an inconsistent theory has as a logical consequence every formula in the language.

[3] Three inference rules are sufficient to derive an arbitrary formula from any inconsistency. The rule of Adjunction allows us, from arbitrary formulas X, Y, to derive X-and-Y. The rule of Addition allows, from an arbitrary formula X, to derive X-or-Y. The rule of Disjunctive Syllogism allows, from an arbitrary formula of form (X-or-Y)-and-(not-X), to derive Y. Suppose we are given a premise set S+ {P, not-P}. From P we derive P-or-Q, by Addition. From P-or-not-Q, not-P we derive (P-or-Q)-and-(not-P), by Adjunction. Then by Disjunctive Syllogism we derive Q. Since at the Addition step we could have added any formula in the language, the above derivation steps can be used to derive every formula in the language.

[4] The proof-theory of a paraconsistent logic must in effect deny the unrestricted validity of either Adjunction, Addition, or Disjunctive Syllogism. Non-adjunctive logics deny the former, sociative logics, which are relevant

logics in the broad sense, deny one of the latter two. It is important to note that significant philosophical differences exist in the paraconsistent logic community. The epistemic interpretation of inconsistency given above is not universally accepted; some writers believe in true contradictions, i.e., that some inconsistencies are ontological.

[5]Isaac Newton, "On the Quadrature of Curves [1704]," in D. J. Whiteside, ed., *The Mathematical Papers of Isaac Newton, VIII (1697-1722)* (Cambridge, 1981), p. 129.

[6]George Berkeley, *The Analyst* in A. C. Fraser, ed. *The Works of George Berkeley*, vol. 3, 1734 ed. (Clarendon Press, 1901), pp. 26-27.

[7]R. P. Feynman, *QED: The Strange Theory of Light and Matter* (Princeton University Press, 1985), pp. 7-8.

[8]R. P. Feynman, "The Development of the Space-Time View of Quantum Electrodynamics" in *Nobel Lectures: Physics 1963-1990* (Elsevier, 1965), pp. 175-176.

[9]J. Schwinger, ed., *Selected Papers on Quantum Electrodynamics* (Dover, 1958), p. xv.

[10]Ibid., p. 16.

[11]P. A. M. Dirac, *Directions in Physics* (Wiley, 1978), p. 20.

[12]Ibid., pp. 36-37.

[13]D. Christie-Murray, *A History of Heresy* (Oxford University Press, 1976), p. 38.

[14]N. Rescher and R. Brandom, *The Logic of Inconsistency* (Rowman and Littlefield, 1979); G. Priest, R. Routley, and J. Norman, eds., *Paraconsistent Logic: Essays on the Inconsistent* (Philosophia, 1989); A. R. Anderson and N. D. Belnap, *Entailment: The Logic of Relevance and Necessity*, vol. 1 (Princeton University Press, 1975); A. R. Anderson, N. D. Belnap, and J. M. Dunn, *Entailment: The Logic of Relevance and Necessity*, vol. 2 (Princeton University Press, 1992); R. Routley, R. K. Meyer, V. Plumwood, and R. T. Brady, *Relevant Logics and Their Rivals* (Ridgeview, 1982).

[15]Rescher and Brandom, *Logic of Inconsistency*.

[16]The separation strategy is suggested by non-adjunctive logics; the containment strategy is suggested by sociative logics, i.e., relevant logics in the broad sense.

[17]A. N. Whitehead, *Process and Reality* (Free Press/Macmillan, 1929).

[18]I. Kant, *Critique of Pure Reason*, trans. N. K. Smith, 1781 ed. (Macmillan, 1929), p. 449.

PART II

RECENT PHYSICS AND THE DESIGN ARGUMENT

THE WIDER DESIGN ARGUMENT AND THE NEW PHYSICS:

RUMINATIONS ON THE THOUGHT OF P. C. W. DAVIES

GEORGE W. SHIELDS

Introduction[1]

Extraordinary developments in the field of physical cosmology have recently prompted a number of works by physicists which directly address some of the most profound and time-honored issues of philosophy and religious thought.[2] One of the most comprehensive, lucid, and accessible of these works is *God and the New Physics* by the celebrated British physicist P. C. W. Davies. A unifying theme of Davies' work is that the "new physics," i.e., the path of inquiry followed from the time of Einstein's papers on general relativity to the recent cosmological work of such luminaries as Roger Penrose, Stephen Hawking and John Wheeler, seems to have blurred the traditional distinction between physics and metaphysics and/or theology. In effect, in order for physicists to advance their own theoretical programmes, they are being compelled to attempt to answer questions which were previously viewed as the property of metaphysicians and theologians. Accordingly, Professor Davies considers the "real scholarly value" of his book to be presentation of "very recent work on cosmology [which has not] previously come to the attention of philosophers and theologians" (*GNP* viii).

It is to be noticed, however, that professional philosophy and theology have undergone their own revolutions in the twentieth century. In fact, philosophical theology—the attempt at rational discourse about God's existence and nature—has witnessed a remarkable renaissance in the past two decades or so. In particular, two "movements" within this discipline have gained marked attention: analytical philosophical theology (which employs the tools of modern analytical philosophy and formal logic) and process philosophical theology (which draws upon the systematic metaphysical writings of principally A. N. Whitehead and Charles Hartshorne). Since Davies is committed to what is, in my view, the commendable project of understanding the world "in all of its many aspects—reductionist and holist, mathematical and poetical, through forces, fields, and particles as well as through good and evil" (*GNP* 229), then he will surely welcome critical examination of his work from philosophers trained in the analytical tradition and aware of non-traditional as well as traditional metaphysical models. It is the purpose of this essay to make a beginning at that critical examination; not, of course, with a view toward producing definitive results, but toward producing a tentative yet plausible *Gedankenexperiment* which might provoke further conversation between physicist and philosophical theologian.

The essence of my *Gedankenexperiment* is the following thesis: All cosmological models, including those articulated by Davies, fall under the scope of the proposition, "Either the natural universe is logically necessary or it is not."[3] Now, it appears to me that there are a number of severe logico-philosophical difficulties with those cosmological models (e.g., the Hartle-Hawking Universal wave function programme as employed by Barrow and Tipler, see *ACP*), which maintain that the natural universe is logically necessary. Most of these difficulties attend the commitment to determinism and the Many-Worlds interpretation of quantum mechanics which is part and parcel of current logically necessary universe models. This seeming to be the case, we are left with models which maintain that the natural universe is not logically necessary. However, these models carry with them (sometimes quite subtly) what might be called the "metaphysical problem of contingency," which by its very nature cannot be resolved by appealing to properly physical explanations. (As R. G. Swinburne would have it,[4] the "the problem of contingency" is "too big" for properly physical explanations to handle.) Moreover, the recently emerging picture of a cosmos which is "fine-tuned" for the evolution of life at the most fundamental levels raises the intriguing possibility of new intellectual life for some version of an argument from design.

I shall draw from this thought experiment the very guarded and modest conclusion that, on balance, the so-called "wider" design argument for the existence of an uncaused intelligent designer of the natural universe is less vulnerable to criticism and a more plausible account of our current picture of things than at least Davies surmises.[5]

I will organize the discussion in the following way. First, I will present a sketch of one version of the design argument as inspired in part by the writings of such philosophers as Swinburne and Hartshorne.[6] Second, I will present a critical exposition of the cosmological scenarios, and objections to the notion of design, presented by Davies in *GNP*. (I will add a brief discussion of "plasma" models as alternative to big bang models. The "plasma" cosmology is not to my knowledge mentioned by Davies, perhaps because it has attracted attention only in the past several years, post-1983.) It will be shown primarily in this second section why I think the case for the design argument ought to be at least seriously considered.

Following F. R. Tennant, I will deem the argument under discussion here as the "wider" design argument (1) in order to stress its distinctiveness from traditional "local" design arguments in the mode of, say, Aquinas' Fifth Way or Paley's *Natural Theology*, and (2) in order to stress its compatibility with (according to current orthodoxy) the non-teleological nature of such local, non-foundational sciences as biology and geology. Accordingly, teleological considerations will come into play only at the "wider" or "global" level of the large-number   coincidences or fine-tuning phenomena found in recent cosmology.

1. A Sketch of the Wider Design Argument

One very rough or casual way of putting the wider design argument is as follows:

The search for at least necessary or *sine qua non* causal explanations for the behavior of macroscopic entities seems to terminate in a simple, mathematically elegant set of most fundamental natural laws, i.e., the laws attending strong nuclear force, weak nuclear force, electromagnetism and universal gravity. Further, these laws are conjunctively coherent, perhaps even generalizable into an all-embracing super-law, and seem to be "fine-tuned" in such a way that the evolution of life is made possible. For example, Roger Penrose has calculated that big bang thrust and gravitational attraction were proportioned to one another with a high degree of precision (*GNP* 178-79). That is to say, there is a very small "margin of error" such that, if thrust was greater than this margin with respect to attraction, the result would have been a "run away" of matter-energy rendering the evolution of galaxies impossible, or, if attraction was greater than this margin with respect to thrust, the result would have been a universe of black holes, again rendering the evolution of galaxies impossible. And without the evolution of galaxies which cook up the chemical elements of carbon-based life, the evolution of carbon-based life is in turn rendered impossible. (There is in fact a wealth of examples of such "fine-tuning" which could be adduced, e.g., the delicate balance of numbers attaching to quarks responsible for proton stability or the strong matter/anti-matter asymmetry which apparently prevented a quick and violent "annihilation" of the natural universe near the early stages of emergence from the big bang event.) As Davies himself summarizes the point nicely, "it is hard to resist the impression that the present structure of the universe, apparently so sensitive to minor alterations in the numbers [numbers attaching to natural laws], has been rather carefully thought out" (*GNP* 189).

Now, the fundamental natural laws appear to carry with them indices of contingency. That is to say, the laws are quantitively definite and peculiar, one way as opposed to alternative ways. For example, dynes of gravitational force can be determined between macroscopic objects by employing the Newtonian formula m_1m_2/r^2 (or its cognate in general relativistic formulae for curved space). What is there about this formula that would make it sacrosanct or applicable to all possible worlds? Perhaps no universe containing life as we know it would be possible without a law of gravity concurrent with the Newtonian formula. But why must every possible universe contain life as we know it? There seems to be nothing *logically* incoherent about postulating a possible world in which gravitation would be quantified as m_1m_2/r^3. Thus, we have some reason to think that the laws of nature are logically contingent.

However, if a state of affairs is definite or peculiar and thus contingent, we want to know *why* it is the way it is and not some alternative way. This is the normal situation for all scientific inquiry, i.e., we seek causal explanations for contingent states of affairs. For instance, the fact that my eyes are blue rather than brown or green appropriately calls for a causal explanation, and that causal explanation—surely at least in terms of the adumbration of necessary or *sine qua non* causal conditions (rather than sufficient conditions)—can be found in a more "fundamental" state of affairs such as my particular DNA code and its interaction with the environment. But, the case of fundamental laws is not, with respect to the issue of eliciting causal explanation, essentially different from the case of having blue eyes if such laws are in fact contingent.

Yet, it would seem that if we are to offer causal explanation of apparently contingent *fundamental*[7] natural laws, we will not be able to offer an explanation in terms of natural entities, because natural entities are already constituted by fundamental natural laws. Of course, someone could respond to this by challenging the idea that the laws are in fact fundamental, and that instead the universe has an infinitely layered nomological structure such that there are an infinite number of laws explaining our so-called "fundamental" ones. But there is no positive evidence to suggest that this is the way the world is in fact, and the suggestion is extremely theoretically complicated *vis-à-vis* the current hypothesis in physics of a fundamental four-fold set of natural laws: For instance, the infinitely layered hypothesis is unverifiable in principle, and indeed if the universe is nomologically infinite, why does the history of modern physics reveal a reduction, rather than a proliferation, of the number of natural laws?

It therefore seems plausible to attribute the existence of contingent fundamental natural laws to the agency of an entity that is not itself dependent upon such laws. Further, the conjunctive coherence of the laws, and their fine-tuning for the evolution of life, strongly suggests the notion that such an entity is intelligent and thus personal. It strongly suggests intelligent or personal agency, because we are in clear possession of models of ruled behavior as a product of intelligence (for example, as in the invention of a game of chance) rather than as a product of sequences of purely random events. Granted, we are also in possession of models of ruled behavior as a product of random events (as in an evolutionary account of beavers building dams), but there are reasons to think that randomness cannot be metaphysically fundamental, and further that such examples as the evolutionary one are special cases having local, rather than global, application.

Those privy to the work of, say, chemist Illya Prigogine or mathematician J. H. Conway might object to this last assertion by pointing to models of self-organizing physical systems which appear to arise out of sequences of random events. On the basis of such models, apparently order can emerge out of "chaos" without benefit of any external agency. Design arguments lost their cutting edge by virtue of this possibility, for, in such case, how can we decide whether the world is like a self-organizing Prigogine System or the result of intelligent agency?

To make this objection more concrete, consider Conway's mathematical game called "Life," of current interest to some biologists (cited by Davies at *GNP* 227). Given a few simple rules and an arrangement of dots on a grid, computer scenarios can be produced in which emerging shapes seem to mimic behavior, e.g., intersecting lines of so-called glider shapes will produce a kind of "factory" in which a spaceship arrangement emerges at every three hundred maneuvers. The spaceship configurations are in no way antecedently planned, they just so happen to be a surprising consequence of the initial configurations of the game.

If this is meant as a forceful objection to the design argument, I think it clearly fails, as I think all suggestions about chance as the ultimate ground of order fail. The reason I am inclined to think this is because I find intuitively plausible the general principle that the concept of randomness or chance logically presupposes the concept of *fundamental* order. Consequently, the employment of Conway's mathematical game (or Prigogine self-organization) as a counter-example to the design thesis clearly begs the question. For consider: the "randomness" of the emergence of remarkable patterns itself emerges out of a fundamental order without which there could be no intelligible "gaming" at all. For instance, there are rules of formation for the sequence of dots, and the regularity of the dots and the grid itself, all of which are constants definitive of the game.

Charles Hartshorne has made the above point forcefully when discussing the similar case of Hume's "Epicurean" objection to design (*NTOT* 57):

> The old notion that "in infinite time atoms would by chance fall into all possible arrangements" was a naive begging of the question. To talk of this or that set of atoms [or this or that set of initial physical conditions] is to talk of a kind of order, not to explain that kind. The mere existence of atoms with definite character, maintaining

themselves through time and relative to one another, is already a tremendous order.

However, could not there have been an "absolute" chaos out of which some primitive constituents simply emerged acausally and then remained fixed? This suggestion is close in some ways to the so-called Free Lunch cosmology, which I discuss below, but I doubt that the idea is intelligible. Hartshorne[8] has noted that if the hypothesis of an absolute chaos were allowed—a chaos defined as "that which possesses no identity" (anything other than this definition would not properly define an *absolute* chaos)—it would be impossible to make propositional discriminations about such a "state" and this would surely lead to absurdities.

For these and still other reasons, I surmise that "cosmologies of fundamental chance" are unlikely to be sound.

But then, if any possible world must have some contingent, basic order, which is a *definitive given* (rather than a product) of that possible world, what candidates for causal explanation of such order remain if chance mechanisms for the production of order are eliminated? The only model we have in such case is that of mind deliberating (or inventing) basic order. Moreover, if we were to adopt the notion of mind as fundamental to cosmological explanation, we would incur an increase in "total explicability." This can be seen more clearly by considering an objection. An interesting objection to the argument is that postulating a divine mind at the origins of order still leaves us with arbitrary contingency (after all, what reason would a divine mind have for selecting a contingent order?). But this objection has its counter in the proposal that divine selection of a contingent world order would represent what William James called a "rationally arbitrary" decision; a decision which satisfies a general aim even though other specific decisions would have worked as well.[9] (Such a general aim could be seen as the evolution of life.) However, by definition, there can be *no* appeal to rational arbitrariness in a model which excludes mind from large-scale or cosmological explanation. Insofar a theistic design model better conforms to the principles of parsimony and least paradox.

2. Objections

Davies discusses something roughly like the argument presented here (or rather, an argument which is enfolded in the wider design argument) in chapters entitled, "Did God Create the Universe?" and "Why is There a Universe?" (*GNP* Chs. 3-4). He refers to it as the "argument from contingency" and appropriately quotes Aquinas' *secunda via* from the *Summa Theologiae* as an historical instance. He then quickly presents several stock philosophical objections, none of which seems to me, and to a number of recent philosophers of religion, to be impressive:

(i) First, there is Russell's objection, presented in his famous debate with Father Copleston,[10] that the argument commits the fallacy of composition: "Asking for a cause of the whole universe has a different logical status from asking for a cause of an individual object or event within the universe" (*GNP* 37). To use Russell's analogy, just as the fact that every human who exists has a mother does not establish that the human race has a mother, so the fact that every event has a cause does not establish that the natural universe of events has a cause. However, as I have argued elsewhere,[11] the difficulty with this objection is that the set of fundamental natural laws as *sine qua non* for all events in space-time can be properly conceived as having the same contingent logical status as the events of which they are ground, and thus such *laws* seem to beckon for a causal explanation like other contingent things. Moreover, Russell's counter-analogy does not in fact apply to all cases of part-whole relation, and consequently he needs an additional premise (or premises) to show that the concept of "cause of this natural universe" does not fall outside his counter-analogy class. A more fitting (albeit, still weak) analogy for the claims of any theistic causal argument would be: "Since every part of this painting has a uniform style [the "uniform style" of the natural universe being its fundamental laws], this painting probably has one author."

(ii) Davies wants to apply the notion of the "set of all sets"—and Russell's demonstration of its incoherence—to the natural theologian's idea of a natural universe which requires explanation. Writes Davies, "It is not clear that the universe is a *thing*, and if it is defined as a set of things it runs the risk of paradox. Such issues lie in wait for all those who attempt to argue logically for the existence of God as a cause of all things" (*GNP* 37). Now, this is quite silly as an objection to the contingency argument, for the argument simply does not assert that God is a cause of all "things," when a "thing" is being defined as a mere item for set inclusion. Rather, as I am employing the argument to help make the case for the design model, it asserts that God is a cause of all contingent, actual things in space-time (since God is cause of natural laws which are their physical ground). *This* set is hardly identical to the set of all sets, even If the cardinality of the set of actual things in space-time is infinite. (For instance, large sets of unactualized possibilia are outside the set of contingent, actual things.)

(iii) Nor is the argument trapped in self-contradiction, as Davies suggests (*GNP* 37), by claiming that God is outside the set of things requiring causal explanation. For it seems that at least the Universe Class is logically necessary,[12] and either God or the natural universe (exclusive disjunction) is the terminus of causal dependencies. But, if *fundamental* natural laws are logically contingent as they seem to be, then God as necessary existent ought to be terminus of dependencies. I add that, with Charles Hartshorne and a number of analytical philosophers (including those who have not favored theistic arguments such as Anthony Kenny[13]), I see nothing conceptually absurd in the idea that there can be *de re* necessities, and thus the idea of God as necessary existent is hardly unintelligible.

(iv) Davies notes that natural theologians might try to escape from at least some of the objections he raises by positing God as necessary existent outside the class of contingent things requiring causal explanation (*GNP* 47). But here he suggests, ". . .why can't we use the same argument to explain the universe: The universe is *necessary*, it contains within itself the reason for its own existence?" (*GNP* 47). He further suggests that there is precedent in physics for the idea of a self-explanatory physical system where causal explanations are closed in a "loop." Thus, a set A containing events E_1, E_2, E_3, E_4, each of which is contingent, may have an organic, circular relation of dependency, where E_1 gives rise to E_2, E_2 to E_3, E_3 to E_4, and E_4 to E_1. The set A could thus be explained without appeal to anything outside set A.

However, while the natural universe might turn out to be necessary for other reasons, Davies is mistaken if he is suggesting that the notion of a causal loop by itself provides a sufficient reason for holding that a universe embodying such a loop would not require explanation by something outside the loop. This is because there may be *alternative* causal loops in which case the query would appropriately arise, "Why does the natural universe embody loop set B, rather than an alternative loop set A?"

The query above leads us to consider more directly the case for the view that the natural universe is the only universe there *could* be. Davies develops this notion *vis-à-vis* the idea of God as designer or creator as follows:

> The hasty assumption that God can create any universe must be qualified by the restriction that it be logically consistent. Now if there exists only one logically consistent universe then God would effectively had no choice at all. Einstein noted: 'What I'm really interested in is whether God could have made the world in a different way; that is, whether the necessity of logical simplicity leaves any freedom at all.'

In discussing this idea it is best to consult the work of Frank Tipler and John Barrow in their monumental treatise on *The Anthropic Cosmological Principle*, for it is here that we find perhaps the most sustained development of a logically necessary universe model. Tipler and Barrow seem to acknowledge that, within the historical context of the development of physics prior to the "new" physics, natural theologians had some reason to be concerned about the problem of metaphysical contingency or "contingency in the large" (see *ACP*, Ch.2). However, the so-called Many-Worlds Interpretation of quantum mechanics suggests new possibilities. Perhaps the natural universe, understood as a super-space which includes all quantum branches of space-time, *is* the exhaustion of the set of logical possibilities for events. Further, perhaps James Hartle and Stephen Hawking have in fact found *the* mathematical key—the wave function of the universe, i.e., a path integral list of all possible histories "through which the universe could have evolved to its present quantum state" (*ACP* 105). If it can be shown that the Hartle-Hawking Universal wave function has formal properties which make it logically necessary, then there is no choice other than to say that the natural universe is that domain in which all logical possibilities will be played out. The Many-Worlds picture of quantum phenomena presents us with the mechanism by which this takes place.

The chief appeal of the Many-Worlds approach is that it appears to resolve some of the most pressing difficulties attending the Copenhagen interpretation of quantum mechanics. For example, Schrödinger's celebrated Cat Paradox, on the Copenhagen interpretation, seems to present us with a view of the quantum wave function in which the cat in question is *both* dead and alive, until one or the other state is observed. The Many-Worlds view would conform to the law of non-contradiction and avoid any "schizophrenic" ontology by maintaining that the world "branches" into distinct space-times where distinct observations are made. Thus, if some process P has a 50:50 probability of culminating in either state X or Y, the culmination of P will yield a universe with observers who observe X and another physically separate universe with observers who observe Y.

It seems to me, however, that there are a number of severe difficulties with the Many-Worlds picture which casts doubt upon the whole project of producing a logically necessary universe model.

The Many-Worlds ontology has a striking analogue in David Lewis' semantical theory for possible worlds known as Counterpart Theory.[14] However, both Alvin Plantinga[15] and Saul Kripke[16] have independently noted some severe logical, semantical and metaphysical difficulties with Counterpart Theory. Kripke argues roughly as follows: Lewis' formal model follows "rather naturally from his philosophical views on counterparts."[17] However, there are formal difficulties with the model; the most serious being a failure of Universal Instantiation for modal properties, e.g., $(\exists y) ((x) \Diamond (x \neq y))$ turns out to be satisfiable, while $(\exists y) \Diamond (y \neq y)$ does not, on the assumption that the standard law $(y) ((x)A(x) \supset A(y))$ obtains, and where $A(x)$ takes on modal operators. Hence, Counterpart Theory allows for intuitively bizarre formal consequences. Kripke quickly adds that, "This view of physics [the Wheeler-Everett interpretation of quantum mechanics] may suffer from the philosophical problems analogous to Lewis' counterpart theory."[18] For his part, Plantinga argues that, along with a number of semantical deficiencies, the Counterpart Theory makes *all* of an individual's properties essential to his or her identity, since it is not the self-same individual, but his or her counterparts which exist in other possible worlds (exactly like the Many-Worlds scenario). This has the bizarre consequence that, say, A. N. Prior in the actual world A could not be A. N. Prior-in-A had just one of the split-ends on one of his hairs been slightly positioned differently. Is such a consequence not outrageous?

I suppose that the Barrow-Tipler response to at least Plantinga might run something like the following: "We grant that the Many-Worlds theory is subjectively counter-intuitive, but what of that? Scientific theories are not required to meet our intuitive expectations so long as those theories can solve theoretical problems and make effective predictions. We thus continue to maintain that the universe does not contain any truly accidental or contingent events or properties in the large."

This conjectured response brings to the fore the underlying commitment to metaphysical determinism which is driving the Many-Worlds ontology. As Barrow and Tipler assert on a number of occasions (*ACP* 106, 193), there is no metaphysical problem of contingency of the actual if the actual is necessary. Of course, the view that the actual is necessary *is* determinism. However, this commitment to determinism entails a commitment to the Strong Principle of Sufficient Reason or PSR (for anything X and its properties P, there is a sufficient reason for the existence of X and its properties P), since the Strong PSR is nothing more than a verbally distinct expression of metaphysical determinism. But it can be argued rather rigorously that the PSR is necessarily false, because it leads to a collapse of modalities in which there is a state of affairs which is neither necessary nor contingent.

Charles Hartshorne contributes to the counter-argument I am about to present in the following way. His Principle of Inclusive Contrast[19] demands that there must be *some* role for contingency in any conceptual scheme which can merit serious consideration, since the concept of necessity cannot be well-defined in pure abstraction from contingency (and *vice versa*); for example, necessity is that which has no *alternative*. Indeed, it is a commonplace of the operator semantics of standard modal logic that the necessity operator can be defined by the use of the contingency operator (coupled with an operator for negation), and likewise, the contingency operator can be defined by the use of the necessity operator (coupled with an operator for negation): (Np iff ~◊~p) and (◊p if ~N~p). Thus, by virtue of the Principle of Inclusive Contrast, determinists must admit at least the logical possibility of a contingency (while denying that the actual world includes any contingency). From this, along with PSR, it can be shown that determinism is conceptually absurd.

The formal argument, indebted to Peter van Inwagen,[20] runs as follows. Since the determinist cannot simply deny the contingent, then there must be at least one state-description or possible world P of which the following could be said: Let X in P stand for the conjunction of any contingent propositions in P into a single proposition (there must be at least one contingent proposition true of P).[21] By virtue of the axiom of modal logic that $(Np \cdot \Diamond q) \equiv \Diamond(Np \cdot \Diamond q)$—in effect, a single contingent conjunct makes a conjunctive proposition contingent—X must be contingent. According to PSR, X must have a sufficient explanation in some state of affairs S. Now, S must be either necessary or contingent, since any true proposition must be either necessary or contingent (or at least I do not know what it would *mean* to deny this[22]). Yet, S cannot be necessary, because if it were necessary, X could not be contingent, since the necessity of an antecedent entails the necessity of its consequent. That is to say, S entails X if S is the sufficient reason for X, and so, $NS \rightarrow NX$. Yet, S also cannot be contingent. For, if S were contingent, then S would be a conjunct of X, and, if S were a conjunct of X, then S would be strictly entailed by X, by virtue of the meaning of conjunction. And, if S is the sufficient reason for X, then S must also strictly entail X, as noted previously. So, if S is contingent, then S both entails and is entailed by X. However, if S both entails and is entailed by X, then, by virtue of the meaning of strict mutual entailment, S *is* X. In the case that S is X, however, a contingent state of affairs is its own sufficient reason, which falsifies PSR. Therefore, if PSR is to be maintained, S can be neither necessary nor contingent, which is conceptually absurd. Thus, the determinist, and by implication Many-Worlds ontologist, is committed to at least one "logically possible" world description which is internally repugnant or impossible.

In light of these logico-philosophical difficulties, I wish to press an argument from Occam's Razor. The Many-Worlds ontology, along with its theoretical cohort—the Feynman "path integral" or "sum-over-histories" approach to quantum mechanics—produces no new testable content which could empirically distinguish it from conventional probabilistic quantum theory with a particle ontology; at least this is the majority opinion.[23] Both interpretations agree with experiment. But, why then should we adopt the Many-Worlds view over the conventional view if the former carries the weight of modal and other sorts of logical perplexity? Now, indeed, particle ontology as well as wave ontology may carry a number of its own philosophical conundrums,[24] but then the proper attitude ought to be one of deep skepticism about our current quantum models, *not* an enthusiastic embrace of Many-Worlds.

The deconstruction of the PSR above might cause some to respond that I have sawed off the limb upon which the natural theologian sits. Doesn't *any* theistic argument require the PSR, since otherwise one could postulate

a basic state of affairs which simply requires no explanation, and by so doing
one could successfully challenge the notion that God must be brought in for
purposes of cosmological explanation? Surely this objection is correct insofar
as it indicates that any natural theological argument needs *a* principle of
explanation, without which such argument cannot get started. However, as
I have argued at some length in my 1987 American Academy of Religion
paper on "Ultimate Explanations,"[25] this principle need not be, indeed
cannot be, the *Strong* PSR, but rather one of the "softer" principles of
explanation, which leaves room for the possibility of the *partial* self-creation
of actual entitles. I prefer the so-called PSR$_5$, a slight revision of William L.
Rowe's PSR$_4$,[26] which reads as follows:

> For every class X whose members are entities (which can be caused
> to exist or which can cause the existence of other entities), there
> must be an explanation of the fact that X has members, and it is not
> the case that members of the class of predicates P which describe
> members of the class X must all have explanations.

PSR$_5$ is perfectly compatible with the wider design argument, since that
argument does not require the absolute explanation of events mandated by
determinism. Rather, it requires that basic or fundamental contingent order
must be explained, and this is compatible with the existence of relative
scopes of chance and/or free agency within parameters set by fundamental
order.

I take these arguments to call into serious question the non-theistic form
of the strong anthropic principle advocated by Barrow and Tipler. Yet, there
is another interesting variation on the anthropic theme discussed by Davies
as an objection to design under the rubric "So what?" Davies states (*GNP*
171):

> . . . the 'so what' proponents reply that, had the universe not been
> arranged in the way it is, we should not be here to marvel at it.
> Indeed, any universe in which intelligent creatures can frame
> philosophical and mathematical questions is, by definition, a
> universe of the sort we observe, however remarkable that universe
> would otherwise have been a priori. In other words, they maintain,
> there is not, after all, anything very extraordinary or mysterious
> about the highly ordered universe we perceive, because we could
> not (obviously) perceive it otherwise.

In a very perceptive review of Barrow and Tipler's work, philosopher
William L. Craig has pointed out that the inference here does not logically
follow.[27] That is to say, it does not strictly follow from the fact that we

occupy an observer compatible universe that, therefore, we ought not to issue surprise at this fact. This is because, when the relevant propositions are quantificationally formalized, the anthropic inference commits the fallacy of contending that sub-implication must hold in first-order quantification. I offer Craig's analysis with some slight alterations in logical notation. (Let S: be a doxastic operator for "being surprised," while F is "a feature of the universe," C is "compatible with our existence," and O is "observed by us.")

(1) We should not be surprised that for all features of the universe we do not observe any which are incompatible with our existence.

~S: (x) [(Fx•~Cx)⊃~Ox] *does not entail the falsity of*

(2) We should be surprised that we do observe features of the universe which are compatible with our existence.

S: (Ex)[(Fx•Cx)•Ox]

For those who prefer a more informal, less rigorous presentation of the logical difficulty here, consider the following analogy provided by John Leslie (as cited by Craig, see note 27). Suppose you were put before a firing squad made up of a hundred marksmen. They aim at your heart and fire, but somehow they all miss the mark and you are still alive. Now, while your response to this situation could indeed be that "you are not surprised that you do not observe that you are dead," it would be equally correct to respond that, "you are surprised that you do observe that you are alive." By analogy, the "so what" proponents are guilty of drawing a subtly illogical inference by issuing an exclusive preference for the first fort of response.

There are, of course, other possibilities for cosmic models which Davies discusses, and which have a bearing on the design thesis. While I cannot exhaust these possibilities here and now, I would like at least to sketch how it is that they seem to me to presuppose, rather than explain, basic order.

Consider the bubble universes and the inflationary scenarios of Alan Guth and others.[28] Davies points out (*GNP* 28) that the question "where does matter come from?" can be answered in terms of new ideas about the expansion of space; that is to say, the exponential expansion of "inflation" of a quantum of space-time can itself "translate" into the production of enormous matter-energy. Further, an arbitrary quantum of space-time could be postulated as appearing acausally *ex nihilo* on the basis of quantum principles of indeterminacy. Thus, the universe might well be, in Guth's celebrated phrase, a "free lunch." The ontological transitions would then be from "nothing"[29] to a quantum of space-time to an expansion of space-time to the energy which constitutes the phenomenal universe. Or, alternatively, what existed primordially might not have been deity, but an elastic plenum of space-time (or quantum vacuum embedded in a space-time substratum, which, again by virtue of quantum indeterminacy, might have begun to warp and eventually separate off into a new bubble of space-time in which inflationary mechanisms would then operate to produce our cosmos.

I should point out at once that inflationary cosmologies have their own technical scientific difficulties. For instance, Hawking rejects the original inflationary model, because it implies variations in the cosmic background radiation which we do not in fact observe (*BHT* 132). The so-called "new" inflationary models of A. Linde have also found little favor among cosmologists because of discrepancies between recent observations and predictions of the models.[30] But our problem is much deeper than this. All such scenarios are making a tacit assumption about laws of physics which govern cosmic behavior. Davies himself points this out in his conclusion to the chapter, "Is the Universe a Free Lunch?" (*GNP* 217): "But what of the laws? They have to be 'there' to start with so that the universe can come into being. Quantum physics has to exist (in some sense) so that a quantum transition can generate the cosmos in the first place." This creates a logico-philosophical difficulty that I find intractable for proponents of Free Lunch cosmology: What sense does it make to say that laws of physics would operate on an absolutely empty domain? In such case, the non-syntactical variables of the mathematical language of physics would fail to have *any* reference whatsoever, and we could not even explain the function of non-syntactical variables in the language. If, on the other hand, we begin with a primordial plenum of space-time, contingencies confront us not merely with respect to laws of quantum physics which govern the emergence of space-time bubbles, but the ontological state of the plenum. Is its volume finite or infinite? If finite, why that particular size? How many dimensions does it have? Three? Seven? Eleven? Why that number? How elastic is it? Is there an upper limit to the speed at which bubbling transitions can occur? Why that limit?

Finally, a brief note on the possibility of plasma models is in order here.[31] The standard big bang model, accepted by a majority of physicists, may yet have some insuperable empirical difficulties. For example, the meaning of the cosmological redshift, the phenomena that big bang theory was originally designed to explain, is still not entirely clear. In addition, the emerging global picture of the observable universe currently reveals a "clumpy" distribution of stars that is not easily accounted for by the idea of uniform expansion from a big bang singularity. Plasma cosmology, based on the behavior of laboratory plasma (nature's "fourth" state of matter) and projections of cosmic behavior predicated on the basic idea that electromagnetism rather than gravity has the significant cosmological effect, dispenses with the need for expansion from a singularity, allegedly has a better explanation for global clumpiness, and in lab simulation models also predicts a microwave background radiation of 2°K (comparing well with the observed 2.78°K). If a plasma model is correct, the natural universe has no beginning in an initial singularity, nor does it oscillate from bang to squeeze to bang to squeeze, but rather evolves different patterns out of a plenum of plasma in infinite space and time.

But here it is to be noticed that the wider design argument (like Aquinas' *secunda via*) is neutral to issues concerning the age or extent of the natural universe. Whether the natural universe (in some form) has existed for an infinite past time or not, it still ought to possess a basic order, or orders, which if contingent require explanation. Thus, in the case of the soundness of plasma cosmology, it is the presumption of the operation of electromagnetism (and other laws) governing the evolution of plasma which requires explanation. As far as I can see, the plasma alternative in no way affects the natural theologian's sense of world contingency, nor does it undermine all evidence for fine-tuning (e.g., the mathematical delicacy of quarks responsible for proton stability).

Conclusion

In conclusion, it appears to me that, for all Davies has shown, his critique of the design argument could be reasonably viewed as wanting, and proponents of design have at least a viable and even strongly plausible hypothesis in light of the new physics. Of course, this is not to say that what I have presented here entitles anyone to make the claim that the theistic design hypothesis has been *shown* or *established*. (For one thing, I have not even touched upon, much less disposed of, at least some of the possible philosophical objections to the wider design argument.) Rather, what I claim is that the above thought experiment shows that a theistic design model of the universe is a more sophisticated and resilient model than some have surmised or proposed. The dialectic of objection and counter-objection between philosophical theologian, philosophical atheologian, and theoretical physicist is thus richer and more robust than might be surmised from a reading of Davies' work. In sum, I am yet convinced that the old issues of natural or philosophical theology are still very much with us. While theoretical physics might someday usurp metaphysics and theology, it is not now clear that it has done so.

NOTES

[1] I wish to acknowledge a number of individuals whose comments on the original version presented at the ILS Conference, or on portions of argument presented elsewhere, have been most helpful: Prof. William J. Wainwright (for comment on the "van Inwagen argument"), Prof. Tom Settle, Prof. William L. Craig, Prof. Dennis Temple, Prof. Donald Viney, and University of Chicago doctoral student Paul Nelson.

[2] Paul Davies, *God and the New Physics* (Simon and Schuster, 1983), hereafter: *GNP*. John Barrow and Frank Tipler, *The Anthropic Cosmological Principle* (Oxford University Press, 1986), hereafter: *ACP*. Stephen W. Hawking, *A Brief History of Time* (Bantam Books, 1988), hereafter: *BHT*. Carl Sagan, *Cosmos* (Ballantine Books, 1980). Robert Jastrow, *God and the Astronomers* (W. W. Norton, 1978).

[3] For philosophers keen on the distinction between logical and physical necessity, my use of the expression "logically necessary" might appear troublesome. However, some of the cosmologists under discussion here intend to say quite sincerely that the existence of the natural universe is a matter of *logical* necessity. In the words of John Wheeler, "Little astonishment should there be, therefore, if the description of nature carries one in the end to logic, the ethereal eyrie at the center of mathematics. If, as one believes, all mathematics reduces to the mathematics of logic, and all physics reduces to mathematics, what alternative is there but for all physics to reduce to the mathematics of logic? Logic is the only branch of mathematics that can 'think about itself'." Cited by Davies at *GNP, p.* 222.

[4] R. G. Swinburne, *The Existence of God* (Oxford University, 1979), Chs. 4 and 7.

[5] It should be pointed out that Davies' stance toward theism in *GNP* is ambiguous. While he presents a running critique of the design argument and theism in general throughout, in some chapters he appears much more sympathetic than in others. This is especially true of Chapter 13 on "Black Holes and Cosmic Chaos." It should also be noticed that *GNP* shows considerable theological naiveté. For instance, queries raised by Davies about the intelligibility of the traditional doctrine of divine timelessness are hardly impressive to theologians who do not hold that God is timeless. In fact, not once does Davies refer to such modern theological movements as process theology or classical free will theism, both of which reject the traditional doctrine of timelessness.

[6]Swinburne, *The Existence of God*, and Charles Hartshorne, *A Natural Theology for Our Time* (Open Court, 1967), hereafter: *NTOT*. Hartshorne develops the argument into one which holds for all genuinely possible worlds. While this *a priori* approach has received criticism, it has never been made clear to my satisfaction what is exactly wrong with Hartshorne's reasoning and intuitions. I will not explicitly argue for the modal form of the argument here, but I will express my sympathy for it.

[7]C. B. Martin has objected that, if natural laws are genuinely fundamental, then they should count as ultimate explanations. Therefore, such laws cannot be contingent and thus subject to causal explanations. But this is to pack too much into our usage of the expression "fundamental." A set of natural laws L can well be "fundamental" for a possible world W in the sense that W has no deeper set of laws for explicating the behavior of its denizens. But it would not follow from this that, therefore, L is fundamental for *all* possible worlds. As long as we are entitled to assume that there are alternative possible worlds and alternative nomological sets definitive of those worlds, Martin's objection appears unwarranted. See C. B. Martin, *Religious Belief* (Cornell University Press, 1959).

[8]C. Hartshorne, *Creative Synthesis and Philosophic Method* (Open Court, 1970), pp. 284-285.

[9]This holds, of course, only on the supposition that there are alternative world orders or nomological sets. If heterotic string theory holds, the sets reduce to four alternatives. If, on the other hand, TOE (The Theory of Everything) obtains—*and* TOE is logically necessary—there is one and only one set. But my argument concerning determinism and Many-Worlds strongly suggests that, at best, TOE will represent the complete physical theory of *this* natural universe, not all possible universes. So, if my arguments are correct, the supposition of alternative world orders is a sound one.

[10]B. Russell and F. C. Copelston, "A Debate on the Existence of God," in *The Existence of God*, ed. by J. Hick (Macmillan, 1964).

[11]G. W. Shields, "Davies, Eternity and the Cosmological Argument," *International Journal for Philosophy of Religion* 21 (1987): 24-26. (The subject of this article is Oxford philosopher Brian Davies, not the physicist Paul Davies.)

[12]This claim will, of course, require supportive argument. (It is at this juncture that the ontological argument supports the design argument.) While I cannot treat this issue here and now, let me simply urge the argument that natural deduction systems of quantification collapse unless we make the assumption of non-emptiness of the Universe Class. If it is not true that there exists at least one object of discourse [as codified, say, in the Whitehead-Russell axiom of PM that $((\exists x)(Fx \lor {\sim}Fx))$], then the rule of Universal Instantiation falters, which seems intuitively bizarre. For further argument see Hartshorne, *Creative Synthesis*, Ch. VIII, and William and Martha Kneale, *The Development of Logic* (Oxford University, 1962), p. 706.

[13]A. Kenny, "Introduction" in his *The Five Ways* (Notre Dame, 1980).

[14]D. Lewis, "Counterpart Theory and Quantified Modal Logic," *Journal of Philosophy* 65 (1968). In conversation during a recent conference (August 1992, Redeemer College, Ontario), Tom Settle has called my attention to the fact that there are disanalogies as well as analogies between Counterpart Theory and Many-Worlds. While this is true, it appears to me that the germane point of similarity is that each theory (in its own way) holds that all possible worlds either are or will become realized. For Lewis, each possible world is real to its own denizens.

[15]A. Plantinga, *The Nature of Necessity* (Oxford University, 1974), Ch. 6.

[16]S. Kripke, *Naming and Necessity* (Harvard University, 1980).

[17]Kripke, *Naming*, p. 45.

[18]Kripke, *Naming*, p. 45.

[19]Hartshorne, *Creative Synthesis*, p. 89. A determinist such as Brand Blanshard might respond that this principle can be accepted without consequence to determinism. Contingency plays the role of "ignorance" or epistemic alternative in the determinist's conceptual scheme—X is "contingent" in that *for all we know* Y might obtain. In effect, one need not accept the notion of contingency in any ontological sense. My reply to Blanshard is that the reduction of the concept of contingency to the concept of *epistemic* contingency will not do for the purposes of logic which at least many, if not most, logicians think are legitimate. While I cannot argue the point adequately here, let me just issue my concurrence with C. S. Peirce's view that "illation" or "entailment" is logically primitive and irreducibly, logically contingent. This will not convince Blanshard, of course, who holds the surely eccentric view that the last advance in philosophical logic was made

with the idealist logics of Bradley and Joachim. For Blanshard's view cf. "Reply to Hartshorne" and "Reply to Rescher" in *The Philosophy of Brand Blanshard* (Open Court, 1980).

[20]P. van Inwagen, *An Essay on Free Will* (Oxford University, 1983), pp. 202-204. Kindred arguments can be found in James F. Ross, *Philosophical Theology* (Bobbs-Merril, 1969), Ch. 7, and Storrs McCall, "Time and the Physical Modalities," *The Monist* 53 (July 1969): 443 (Sec. 6 'A Calculus of Necessary and Sufficient Conditions').

[21]If there were not at least one contingent proposition true in P, then, by our hypothesis, no contingent propositions would be true in *any* possible world. That latter contradicts the assumption of the Principle of Inclusive Contrast.

[22]W. V. O. Quine is celebrated for his critique of the necessity/contingency distinction and the intelligibility of *de re* modality. If Quine is correct, the van Inwagen argument fails. However, in my view, Quine has been answered definitively (or as definitively as is likely to be the case in philosophy) by George L. Goodwin in his *The Ontological Argument of Charles Hartshorne* (Scholars Press, 1978), Ch. 4. Also, see my review of Goodwin in *The Journal of Religion* 60 (April 1980).

[23]John Gribbin, *In Search of the Big Bang: Quantum Physics and Cosmology* (Bantam Books, 1986), p. 243.

[24]Paul Davies has developed an interesting critique of particle ontology in his "Particles Do Not Exist," *Quantum Theory of Gravity: The Bryce DeWitt Festschrift* (Adam Hilger, 1984).

[25]See G. W. Shields, "Ultimate Explanations," *American Academy of Religion Abstracts* (Scholars Press, 1987).

[26]William L. Rowe, *The Cosmological Argument* (Princeton, 1975).

[27]W. L. Craig, "Review Article on Barrow and Tipler's ACP," *International Philosophical Quarterly* 27 (December 1987). I was present at Professor Craig's presentation of this article at the 1987 meeting of the American Academy of Religion in Boston. I benefited greatly from our personal discussions.

[28]A. H. Guth, "Speculations on the Origin of Matter, Energy, and Entropy of the Universe" in *Asymptotic Realms of Physics: Festschrift for Francis Low* (MIT Press, 1983). John A. Wheeler has offered another bubble universe

model with an "oscillating" twist. The universe has gone through an infinite number of cycles with the inception of a new set of laws at each cosmic punctuation. Our "ordered" universe was thus bound to occur given enough cycles. There is therefore nothing "surprising" about our current "ordered" universe and no need to invoke an intelligent designer to explain it. Wheeler has since renounced this "cycle" doctrine on scientific grounds (see his *Frontiers of Time* [North-Holland, 1979]), but Ian Hacking has pointed to deeper logical difficulties: we are not logically entitled to say that the universe's order is a probable occurrence *given enough* cyclic transitions. This is really no different in principle from inferring that a gambler's roll of double six was "probably his one hundredth roll of the evening and in that case not surprising." Contrary to the gambler's and, by analogy, Wheeler's reasoning, the roll has just the unit-probability it has (1/36 given ideal dice), whether it was the gambler's first or one hundredth, or one thousandth try. For Wheeler's earlier view see his contribution to (with C. W. Misner and K. S. Thorne) *Gravitation* (Freeman, 1973), Ch. 44. For Hacking's critique see his "The Inverse Gambler's Fallacy: The Argument from Design. The Anthropic Principle Applied to Wheeler Universes" in *Readings in the Philosophy of Religion: An Analytic Approach*, ed. by Baruch Brody (Prentice-Hall, 1992).

[29]Such transitions are advocated in the "bolder" creation *ex nihilo* scenarios of L. P. Grishchuk and Ya. B. Zeldovich, "Complete Cosmological Theories," in *Quantum Theory of Space and Time*, ed. by M. J. Duff and C. J. Isham (Cambridge University Press, 1982). However, less bold versions employ the concept of a "quantum vacuum" and these have been described as "creation out of nothing" scenarios; but a quantum vacuum is a "state [having] a rich structure which resides in a previously existing substratum of space-time, either Minkowski or de Sitter space-time" (Barrow and Tipler, *ACP*, 441). Thus, it is hardly correct to equate a "quantum vacuum" with "nothing."

[30]For a non-technical discussion of Linde's model, its empirical difficulties, and Linde's rejoinders see John Horgan, "The Universal Wizard: Andrei Linde," *Discover* **13** (1992): 80-93.

[31]For a good discussion of plasma cosmology see Anthony L. Peratt, "Not With a Bang," *The Sciences: New York Academy of Sciences Magazine* (January/February 1990).

FINE-TUNING THE UNIVERSE?

ERNAN MCMULLIN

The question implicit in the title above is, to be sure, an odd-sounding one. A philosopher's question, one might say, or perhaps a theologian's. But, in fact, the metaphor of *fine-tuning* came from scientists; the question of whether or not our universe would have needed some "fine-tuning" to make it capable of sustaining human life was first posed, in that form, by cosmologists in the 1970's. I want to do three things in this paper. I want to say something first of the long and complex history of questions of this sort. Second, I propose to examine the question itself as it is currently posed, and ask what exactly it *means*. And finally, and of necessity rather briefly, I will review the different answers that have been given to the question in the last two decades and assess their merits as the case now stands.

1. The Indifference Principle: Early History

The metaphor of *fine-tuning* may be new, but the issue itself is ancient, as old indeed as speculative philosophy itself.[1]

The first philosophers of the Greek world were concerned with origins, with how things first came to be the way they now are. Out of what materials were they formed, and what sort of agency was responsible for that formation? The Greeks advanced three very different answers to the latter question; we are grappling with a very similar variety of responses today. First of these was that the universe began from an initially formless aggregate; the normal processes of mixing and combination were of themselves sufficient subsequently over the course of time to produce the highly-differentiated world we know. No specification of the initial state, no kind of "directedness," no agency acting towards a *telos* (end or goal), need be postulated. Leucippus, for example, proposed that atoms in random motion came together in the void:

to produce a single whirl, in which, colliding with one another and revolving in all manner of ways, they begin to separate apart like to like. But when their multitude prevents them from rotating any longer in equilibrium, those that are fine go out towards the surrounding void, as if sifted, while the rest abide together, and becoming entangled, unite their motions and make a first spherical structure.[2]

An entirely random original state ("random" relative to the state finally reached), suffices as cosmic starting point: no constraint need be laid upon it in order that the kind of universe in which we now live should ultimately come to be. This we shall call the "Indifference Principle." It is opposed to (and, as we shall see, helps to define) the notion of "fine-tuning" with which we are later going to be concerned. The second part of the atomists' claim is that the order that we see around us can come to be through the operation of mechanical processes alone, so that no sort of teleological explanation of the outcome is required. The two parts of the atomist's assertion (no special initial conditions, and the operation of non-teleological processes only) together amount to what one might call a "General Ateleological Principle," but we shall not be directly concerned with this larger principle in this essay.

Empedocles carried this form of explanation a stage further when he postulated an original epoch when simple organic entities (limbs, organs) joined together randomly to form complexes. Only a few of these complexes would be capable of surviving and these were the ancestors of the diverse kinds of organisms in existence today. The apparent adaptedness manifested by these latter is a necessary outcome of a regime when the non-adapted perished and the survivors propagated according to kind. These early cosmogonies were based on a denial of all forms of teleology; their proponents saw no need of any kind of interposition of mind or purpose or any intrinsic goal-directness in order that the complex should develop from the simple.

Others disagreed, sometimes vehemently. Socrates expressed his disenchantment with the natural philosophy of his Ionian predecessors on the grounds that they had excluded *Nous* (Mind) from its proper role in the world; his response was to turn away from cosmogony altogether. But his pupil, Plato, set out to formulate an alternative cosmogony that would give its due to *Nous*. In the *Timaeus* he describes, in the form of a "likely story," how the *Demiourgos* (Craftsman) imposed geometrical forms that give such reality as they possess to the imperceptibly small constituents of the perceptible world. At every step in the world-making he envisions, the effects of *Nous* are manifest. The underlying principle of Plato's reasoning is a strong teleological one: without the controlling action of mind, a formless matter could never of itself beget order. And so the battle was joined between two diametrically opposite sorts of cosmogony, one based on a strong teleological principle, the other on its denial. (Plato hints elsewhere at a weaker teleological principle involving a World Soul working from within to produce order.)

Aristotle's solution was to challenge the question itself. The natural kinds must be regarded as eternal; there was no natural way in which they could have originated. Thus, there was no Craftsman, no first shaping. Natures act for the good of their own kind and for the preservation (and, if necessary, the restoration) of cosmic order generally. Falling stones return to their natural place when they have been displaced from it, not because of any desire or purpose on their part, but because living and non-living things tend "naturally" to do what is best for them or their kinds. Why? This question, it would seem, is blocked. That is just the way the world is; it didn't come to be that way. The teleological element, though still dominant in Aristotle's system of explanation, is thus of a much weaker kind than Plato's, requiring neither Craftsman nor World Soul for its operation.[3] Over against the views of the atomists, then, there were teleological principles of various degrees of "strength." All of these positions find their analogues in recent cosmological debate.

It is hardly necessary to say that the alternative that found most favor in later Christian ages was the Platonic one, though fundamentally modified, since early Christian thinkers like Augustine insisted that cosmogonic responsibility lay not with a Craftsman, that is, an agent facing a pre-existent material, but with a *Creator*, that is, a Being responsible for the very existence (and not just with the forms or motions) of our world. (This was a solution no Greek thinker would have countenanced; for one thing, it appears to lay responsibility for evil and defect on God's doorstep.) Aquinas combined the Platonic and the Aristotelian modes in an ingenious way within the broader perspective of creation; the fifth of his "five ways" supplements Aristotle in a fundamental way since it asks for the origin of the teleological directedness found in all natural activity, the directedness that Aristotle took for granted. In those ages of faith, the ateleological principle of the atomists got short shrift; it was rejected out of hand by all Christian thinkers.

And now we come to the crucial moment in the early part of our story. In his *Discourse on Method* (1637), Descartes announced in confident fashion that his new mechanics allowed him to defend an Indifference Principle of a highly specific kind. In the treatise *Le Monde* that he had decided to suppress, he had (he says) inquired into:

> what would happen in a new world if God were now to create somewhere, in imaginary space, enough matter to compose it, and

if He agitated the parts of this matter diversely and without order,
so that He made of it a chaos as confused as the poets can imagine,
and if afterwards He did nothing else except lend His ordinary
support to nature, and left it to act according to the laws which He
established.[4]

What would happen? According to all the earlier versions of teleological
explanation, nothing would. The order of our present world could not
possibly have originated from an initial "chaos" (that is, an initial condition
in no way restricted or specified) following merely mechanical law.
Descartes disagreed:

I showed how the greatest part of the matter of this chaos must,
according to these laws, become disposed and arranged in a certain
way which would make it similar to our heavens; how, meanwhile,
some of its parts must compose an earth, some compose planets and
comets, and some others a sun and fixed stars.[5]

He can explain in this way (he asserts) the light that is found traversing
space in an instant, the tides, the formation of the earth's surface. In short:
"there is nothing to be seen in the phenomena of this world which would
not (or at least which could not) appear in the same way in the phenomena
of the world I was describing."
Organisms do present a problem, he concedes:

I did not yet have sufficient knowledge of them to speak of them in
the same style as of the rest—that is, by demonstrating the effects
through the causes and showing from what sources and in what
way nature must produce them.[6]

So for the moment he is willing to suppose that the first animal bodies
came directly from God's hand. But he clearly thinks that a genetic
explanation of the origins of the organic world in mechanical terms ought
eventually to be possible. All that is needed is the operation of mechanical
laws over a lengthy period of time on an originally unspecified distribution
of particles in motion (a "chaos"):

Even if God had given [the world] in the beginning no form other
than chaos, provided that having established the laws of nature He
gave His consent that the world act as it normally does, we can
believe, without slighting the miracle of creation, that through this
alone all purely material things would have been able, with time, to
become such as we now see them. And their nature is much easier

to conceive, when we picture their birth in this way, little by little, than when we consider them merely as completed.[7]

This is what I have called the Indifference Principle, in as clear a formulation as one could wish. There is no need to prescribe any special initial conditions in order to arrive at the complexity of later structure; a random initial distribution of matter and motion suffices. One can see that Descartes, having excluded all forms of teleological explanation from his science, would not even want to admit the hint of teleology that a special setting of the initial conditions would convey. Requiring such a setting is not equivalent to admitting teleology in the strong sense, where one postulates a guiding action urging matter in motion toward a "good" outcome, whether this action be on the part of a Craftsman, World-Soul or just an Aristotelian *telos*. The weaker Indifference Principle has as consequence that a teleological explanation of initial cosmic conditions ("fine-tuning") is unnecessary; if the notion of *principle* be stressed, it would even seem to be excluded. Descartes, of course, defended the much stronger General Ateleological Principle. The unconstrained operation of the laws of mechanics is sufficient (he claims) to bring about order in the world. And indeed these laws themselves cannot be other than they are; he believed he could discover them "without leaning my reasons upon any other principle than the infinite perfections of God."[8] The entire process of cosmic development was thus necessary; the kinds of things that constitute our world are those that *had* to come about. This is surely as blunt a dismissal of teleological modes of explanation as one could imagine.

Right at the origins of natural science in the modern mode, then, Descartes is insisting that no sort of "fine-tuning" is required in order to arrive, in a law-like developmental way, at the world we know. And he is asserting this not just as a methodological principle, but as a categorical assertion. His claim did not, of course, rest on any real achievements on the part of the new science, but on a mechanistic metaphysics with strong theological underpinnings. And it met with fierce opposition in many quarters, especially in England where such an abrupt rejection of traditional teleology seemed to many to border on atheism. No specific role was left for God in Cartesian cosmogony, it seemed, other than as a distant Creator of the initial chaos and a sustainer of an otherwise entirely self-contained system.

2. The Indifference Principle: Later Developments

British natural theology, 1650-1850, may be seen as in large part a response to this challenge.[9] Boyle, Derham, Ray, and other writers noted the presence everywhere in the animal world of behaviors or physiological structures exactly adapted to the good of the organisms in question, and argued that only an intelligent Designer could have originated such a pattern. Newton insisted that the earth had clearly been designed and is constantly maintained as the abode for humankind. The new science, Bentley preached, testifies to God's steadying action at every turn. Without such fine-tuning, the cosmic order on which human life depends would rapidly dissolve. Clarke found everywhere in the universe "order, beauty, and wonderful contrivance, and fitness of all things in the world to their proper ends," testimony to a creative and caring Intelligence.[10]

But it was a rearguard action. Across the Channel in France, an aggressively materialist current was beginning to stir. In his *Pensées philosophiques* (1747), Diderot argued that the only valid mode of reasoning to the existence of a Deity was to be found in the evidences of design in the living world. But in his *Lettre sur les Aveugles* (1749) shortly after, he concluded that the argument from design was inadequate because even the most intricately adapted living structure could have originated during an initial stage when all sorts of random combinations of organs could have occurred, only a few of which would have survived. It was the old argument of Empedocles and Lucretius, now set in the context of a modified Cartesian belief in the dynamic power of a "chaos" to organize itself following the normal laws of mechanics only. Further, this hypothesis would explain (as the other would less easily do) why design so often failed, as in the case of the blind and the deformed. Finally, in *Le rêve de d'Alembert* (written in 1769 but not published until long after his death), Diderot challenged the major exception Descartes had made in favor of teleology, namely the origin and functioning of thinking beings. Even mind, he argued, could have gradually developed through a refining of the powers of sense, provided that matter itself be regarded not as inert, as Descartes and Newton had it, but as active, indeed, as naturally sensitive.

Diderot realized that all of this was promissory (hence his choice of the literary form of a dream for the last and most speculative of these works). His thesis was not just that nothing prevented science from one day showing how all of this could have come about; his conviction, rather, was one of principle, that it would *necessarily* come about. There were clearly two major barriers to be crossed, however, if such a process of explanation were to succeed. The first was to show how the larger structures (stars, planets, the earth's surface) could have formed; the other was to unravel (more plausibly than Diderot had done) the origins of living things. The next century would see both barriers, to all appearances, largely overcome.

The key to the first achievement was Newton's concept of gravity.[11] Newton himself had not been concerned with cosmogonic issues, implicitly assuming that the original ordering of planets and stars had been directly brought about by God. (The more limited problem with which he, unsuccessfully, struggled was how the long-term stability of the system can be assured.) In his *New Theory of the Universe* (1750), Thomas Wright set out to integrate the new mechanics with Biblical theology in an effort to construct a new cosmology. Cosmic collapse could be prevented by supposing that all the stars (including the sun) are in orbital motion around God at the center. The nebulae revealed by the powerful new telescopes are other universes, likewise rotating, and thus maintaining their shapes. Kant read a summary of Wright's book and developed the mechanical ideas in it further, arguing that galaxies, stars and planets might have aggregated in the first place in a rotating whirl of matter, under the influence of gravity alone.

But it was William Herschel who made the most important contribution. Over a twenty-year period (1780-1800), he surveyed the sky systematically in order to construct a taxonomy of nebulae, eventually classifying more than 2500 of these, in an extension of the natural-history approach long familiar to students of the living world. He then used this taxonomy to illustrate the different evolutionary stages that nebulae would go through, supposing them to originate when gravity works on irregularities in the original random distribution of matter. The further development of these hypotheses of galactic and stellar formation through the nineteenth and early twentieth centuries is well-known. No fine-tuning, it gradually became clear, would be needed, either in the setting of the original scene or in guiding the subsequent aggregating of stars, planets, and galaxies under the inexorable pull of gravity.

The living world was, as Boyle and his colleagues had earlier insisted, another matter, but their conviction that only some form of teleological action could account for the adaptedness of the organic realm was effectively challenged by Darwin, whose ingenious account of natural selection operating on individual hereditable variation suggested a plausible alternative. He followed the same genetic mode of explanation already employed by the astronomers, linking later to earlier under a set of laws (though a far more complex and more tentative set of laws than those of mechanics). The adaptation that the earlier natural theologians had seen as incontrovertible evidence of a designing Intelligence could now be explained as the outcome of a perfectly natural and non-teleological process operating over enormous periods of time. One, or at least a small number, of original forms could have been sufficient to have given rise to the immense diversity of living things that would come after. The famous lines with which he closed *The Origin of Species* (1859) come to mind:

> There is grandeur in this view of life, with its several powers, having been originally breathed by the Creator into a few forms or into one; and that, whilst this planet has gone cycling on according to the

fixed law of gravity, from so simple a beginning endless forms most beautiful and most wonderful have been, and are being, evolved.[12]

Darwin was well aware that the mechanisms that he had postulated to explain the transformation of organic species over time would not account for the very first living forms. And he was wary of resorting to an *a priori* principle which would allow him to deduce that even the first forms *had* to have originated in some random process of assembly. So he retained the traditional teleological metaphor of a Creator "breathing" life into matter to initiate the process of evolution, perhaps to indicate that this was a matter about which his science could as yet say absolutely nothing.[13] "It is mere rubbish," he remarked in a letter to Hooker in 1863, "thinking at present of the origin of life; one might as well think of the origin of matter."[14] A few years later, he is a little more sanguine (and remarkably farseeing):

> It is often said that all the conditions for the first production of a living organism are now present, which could ever have been present. But if (and oh! What a big if!) we could conceive in some warm little pond, with all sorts of ammonia and phosphoric salts, light, heat, electricity, etc. present, that a protein compound was chemically formed ready to undergo still more complex changes, at the present day such matter would be instantly devoured or absorbed which would not have been the case before living creatures were formed.[15]

Others were much more confident in their account of how life *must* have begun. Haeckel, for instance, argued that formation of the first cell was analogous to the formation all at once of a crystal. The forces responsible for it must have existed only in the earliest stages of the earth's history, since spontaneous generation of this kind no longer seems to occur.[16] How do we know they ever *did* exist, since there can be no direct evidence for them? Presumably because, in Haeckel's view, they would make a teleological alternative unnecessary. No fine-tuning for him!

The later history of Darwin's theory of evolution is well-known. After a period of severe challenge around the turn of the century, it took on fresh vigor when T. H. Morgan's new science of genetics was able to resolve some of the most pressing of these challenges and open up new and fruitful lines of research. The "new synthesis," as it eventually came to be called, gradually gained authority. It still has its critics, of course, who point to its unfinished agenda and argue (as philosophers like Bergson and Whitehead earlier did) that the neo-Darwinian mechanisms have to be supplemented by a source of directed action; the intricate sorts of order we see everywhere around us cannot in principle be due to these "blind" mechanisms alone.

But the vast majority of biologists disagree, and maintain that there is no in-principle reason why mechanisms of the broadly neo-Darwinian sort might not prove entirely sufficient of themselves to explain the evolutionary process.

As to the origin of the first life-forms, the debate has been much less decisive. Was some kind of "tuning" (fine or otherwise) required? Haeckel was followed by Bernal, Haldane, and others, who clearly saw how crucial this issue was for anyone defending a broadly materialist position. A believer in God could treat the issue as an open question; a materialist could not. Could there be a plausible set of chemical pathways leading towards a first self-replicating complex molecule similar to DNA? The experiments of Stanley Miller and Harold Urey created something of a sensation in 1953 when they produced many organic compounds, including some of the basic amino acids found in protein, simply by mixing the putative constituents of the early terrestrial atmosphere (methane, ammonia, hydrogen, water) under an electric spark for a lengthy period. Headlines in the media announced the synthesis of life in the test-tube. But there was—and still is—a long way to go from organic compounds to a living system. Arthur Kornberg managed in 1956 to synthesize DNA from a "soup" of amino acids but only by using a "primer" of DNA from a living organism. More recent experimental work has not gone much further than this. Theodosius Dobzhansky wrote in 1964:

> The critical step, the appearance of the first self-replicating molecule or a combination of molecules, still seems, however, to be an improbable event. As long as this step is not reproduced experimentally, there will exist a difference of opinion about how it occurred. Some scientists are so headstrong as to believe that the surmise is plausible enough to be accepted as a probable description of what happened in reality. Given eons of time . . . a highly improbable event can take place somewhere, or even in several places, in the universe. . . . On the other hand, some people continue to regard the origin of life not only as an unsolved but also as an unsolvable mystery. They are as firmly convinced as ever that an act of God must have been invoked to contribute that first spark. I strongly feel that this point of view must not be ignored but must be faced honestly . . . .[17]

Dobzhansky makes it clear that he does not himself approve of this latter way of understanding God's action in the world:

> I am convinced that religion in the age of science cannot be sustained by the assumption of miraculous events abrogating the order of Nature. It

should, rather, see acts of God in events the natural causes of which it fully understands.[18]

Fred Hoyle has recently argued that life cannot have originated on earth but must have drifted in on "seeds" borne from outer space. The core of his argument is that the biochemical structures required for even the most rudimentary forms of life involve immensely complicated three-dimensional arrays of amino acid molecules, which could not possibly have come together by random assembly in even the thickest primal "soup" by means of chemical affinities alone.[19]

He considers the structures of enzymes, histones, and t-RNA, all of them essential to living process as we know it, and asserts that the probability of a chance origin for even the simplest version of this process would be of the order of $10^{40,000}$, making it effectively impossible.

Biologists have never been impressed by the logic of this type of argument, similar in kind to that utilized by Lecomte du Nouy in a controversial book forty years ago.[20] Their objections are that the component probabilities are arrived at by conjecture rather than by actual calculation, and further, that there is no question of bringing enzymes, histones, and t-RNA together all at once in a purely random conjunction; there would have to be intermediate simpler chemical forms that would serve as evolutionary bridges to the immensely complicated machinery found in even the simplest cell. The fact that there is as yet no plausible theory of what these might have been does not (they would argue) show that no such bridges could have existed. Hoyle's argument, however logically defective, does serve to remind us, nevertheless, that as our knowledge of the biochemical complexities of DNA-guided replication has deepened, it has not made the problem of origins any easier to solve.

The issue of an original "fine-tuning" has not been resolved in biology, then, even if the majority of biologists would (if asked) express confidence that a way will be found of explaining how a configuration that on the face of it seems so highly improbable might first have come about by purely physio-chemical means. How about physics? Have physicists encountered anything at all similar in their inquiries into origins? In the remainder of this essay we shall see that they recently have, that advances in cosmological theory instead of making the problem of origins simpler have, in the eyes of many at least, made it a good deal more difficult. The reminder we have given of the successes of the Indifference Principle in earlier cosmology should help to explain why this new development came as such a surprise. There was nothing in the history of cosmology from Kant's day down to the middle of our own century that would have suggested that anything other than the original "chaos" postulated by Descartes would prove to be necessary as a cosmic starting-point. No wonder, then, that the inferences associated with the so-called "anthropic principle" were so passionately debated in the 1970's. They appeared to run counter to the entire flow of scientific advance, from Descartes' original bold announcement of the all-sufficiency of ateleological explanation onwards.

3. Anthropic Principles?

We left cosmology in its Newtonian phase, when nothing could be said about the universe as a whole except that it was infinite both in space and in time. Nor could anything be said about the totality of the matter it contained; whether one took it to be finite or infinite in quantity, inconsistencies seemed bound to result. The development of a cosmology proper was the outcome of three major discoveries in less than a century. First was Einstein's creation of a general theory of relativity which made the task of constructing a cosmology, a science of the cosmos as a whole, much more tractable. Non-Euclidean geometry, for one thing, allowed one to represent a universe which was finite but still unbounded. And the new account of gravity implied a much more intimate relation between matter and space-time than the Newtonian relation of container to contained.

The other two developments were observational. First came Hubble's discovery of the redshift in galactic spectra, interpreted as a motion away from us of all other galaxies. Friedman and Lemaitre showed how this motion could be understood in the light of general relativity theory as due to an expansion of space itself from an original "primeval atom," a point-like space containing an unimaginably condensed energy. The "Big Bang" model, as it soon came to be called, at first seemed like nothing more than a speculative extrapolation of relativity theory to an epoch where it never really could be tested. And its implication of an absolute beginning of cosmic time was repugnant to some, on philosophic or broadly religious grounds. Bondi, Gold, and Hoyle formulated an alternative, the steady-state model, which required no such unique beginning. (It *did* involve a multitude of small beginnings, the continuous "creation" of hydrogen atoms throughout space; since this could be represented as obeying a "law," it was thought by its advocates to be less objectionable.)

Then came a second major observational discovery. In 1964, two radio-astronomers, Arno Penzias and Robert Wilson, found an unexpectedly strong microwave radiation at 7.35 cm wavelength that appeared to be constant in every direction. Some fortunate interactions with neighboring cosmologists, P. J. E. Peebles and Robert Dicke, led to the recognition in 1965 that this radiation, which was characteristic of the thermal radiation that would be given off by a "black" (fully radiating) body at 3° K, could well be the "relic" radiation from the Big Bang that Peebles and Dicke had been searching for, and which had, in fact, been predicted by Ralph Alpher and Robert Herman in 1948.[21] It was the first time that a cosmological theory had been made to yield a specific prediction that was borne out subsequently by observation. The result was not only to give spectacular support to Big Bang theory (and to eliminate its Steady State rival), but also to validate early-universe cosmology itself as a respectable branch of science.

Cosmologists were now looking more closely at the earliest stages of cosmic development, making use of the two major physical theories, relativity theory and quantum theory, in order to reconstruct the likely sequence of events during that distant epoch. In particular, they sought out processes that would leave traces (like the microwave radiation) at the present day. Since the initial cosmic conditions were unknown, it would clearly be an advantage were the traces to be independent of any specific initial state. From this it was only a step to the hypothesis that, in general, present traces *would* be independent of initial conditions because of "smoothing" processes, mainly involving intense neutrino fluxes, in the very early universe. The affinity of this hypothesis with what we earlier called the Indifference Principle is obvious, though the new hypothesis had some physics in its support and was not merely a refusal to entertain the possibility that a special initial setting might be necessary in order to arrive at a universe of "our" kind. Charles Misner, the main protagonist of the new approach, gave the name "chaotic cosmology" to it, a reminder of the "chaos" that Descartes envisaged as a sufficient cosmic starting-point.[22] But the proposal did not work out; the viscous processes that were supposed to smooth out any original isotropy proved quite insufficient. Inklings of what came to be called the "horizon problem" (see below) came into view.

Worst of all, when calculations were made as to what sort of initial conditions would, in fact, permit the development of a long-lived isotropic universe of the sort we inhabit, the outcome was exactly the opposite of what chaotic cosmology had envisaged. Collins and Hawking (1973) claimed, on the basis of detailed calculation, that the probability that such a universe would develop from arbitrary initial conditions was vanishingly small.[23] The tendency, they argued, would be for inhomogeneities to increase very rapidly (not to vanish, as chaotic cosmology had postulated), and hence the only way to arrive at a universe as homogeneous as ours after so great a passage of time would be to have an extraordinarily "flat" universe to begin with. Since the antecedent likelihood of such an initial state among all of those consistent with theory was so remote, how is one to explain so blatant a violation of the Indifference Principle?

Their response was a memorable one. Since the existence of galaxies would seem to be a necessary condition for the development of intelligent life, and since galaxies can only develop in a universe which (like ours) is isotropic at large times: "the fact that we have observed the universe to be to develop. Since it *has* developed, the universe *had* to be isotropic. But surely a necessary condition cannot function as an explanation? At this point, Collins and Hawking hit on a further postulate that would, in fact, convert their suggestion into an explanation of sorts. Why not adopt a "philosophy" that had already (they noted) been proposed by Dicke (1961) and Carter (1968), according to which: "there is not one universe but a whole infinite set of universes with all possible initial conditions"?[25] If there are, indeed, many universes actually in existence (merely possible universes will not suffice), then the isotropy of our own universe *is* "explained" by the "because we are here" response. The Indifference Principle is simply shifted up a step to the *ensemble* of universes; it is not violated by the degree of parameter constraint required for a universe of *our* kind, simply because the correlation of human life with the (however rare) flat type of universe is self-explanatory.

The phrase 'anthropic principle' did not make its first appearance until the following year in a paper by Brandon Carter.[26] Physicists had earlier noted the fact that several very large dimensionless numbers (like 10^{40}) seem to occur surprisingly often when the basic constants of physics (such as the velocity of light, the proton mass, and Planck's constant) are combined. The usual reaction on the part of scientists to these coincidences was either to say that there are so many of those constants that almost any large number can be obtained by combining them with sufficient ingenuity, or else to maintain that the coincidences (or at least some of them) were necessary consequences of underlying as-yet undiscovered physical laws. But some more speculative thinkers (Eddington, Dirac, Dicke) associated the apparent coincidences with the presence of observers in the universe (How they did this, each in a different way, we have to leave aside; each of the derivations has come in for heavy—and on the whole deserved—criticism.)[27] Carter revived this linkage between the large-number coincidences and the presence of observers in the universe, adding a further tie to a "Copernican Principle" which, he claimed, had to be rejected or at least strongly qualified, and going on to distinguish between "weak" and "strong" forms of the newly-named anthropic principle. ("What we can expect to observe must be restricted by the conditions necessary for our presence as observers."[28])

There are a lot of threads entangled here; much of the confusion attending later discussions of the anthropic principle can be traced back to the way in which Carter first introduced it. These ambiguities can be dealt with here only in a summary manner. First, the "weak" anthropic principle is relatively trivial and is not really anthropic. It merely states that theories of the universe must take account of the presence in the universe of observers; their presence serves as a constraint on acceptable cosmological models. But so does the presence of beetles or uranium atoms, and the constraints in consequence of these latter would in fact, be much the same as for human observers.[29] *Every* observed feature of a domain serves as an empirical constraint on what will count as an acceptable theory of that domain; the presence of observers is no different in principle than the presence of any other agreed-upon features in that regard. The weak principle clearly is not capable of *explaining* anything; it simply points to the constraint that a particular datum places on theory.[30]

How did *observers* get into the discussion and how did the principle itself come to appear as anything other than a banal consequence of employing empirical method? The same answer can be given both questions. The weak principle was conflated by Carter with a quite different claim, one which is not trivial and which does involve humans (though not primarily as observers). He begins from what he calls the "Copernican principle" to the effect that the cosmic abode of man is in *no* way privileged. (Copernicus would, I suspect, be astonished to have this taken to be an inference from his theory!) By "privileged," he does not mean having an honorific status or advantage attached, rather that the human abode has *no* special features associated with it that would mark it off from any other part of the cosmos. He calls this a "dogma" of earlier cosmologists. On the face of it, it is *obviously* false, since the earth is a planet, has an atmosphere, and has many other features that *do* mark it off from empty space, for example. What he seems to have in mind is the much more limited claim that the earth, the human abode, is not "privileged" (i.e. differentiated in some special way) in its overall spatial or temporal *location*. Let us call this the "Principle of Average Location" (PAL). The reference to the human here (rather than, say, to beetles) comes only from the expectations engendered by religious or philosophical traditions that led people to expect that the human abode *would* be privileged in its cosmic location, privileged in the proper sense of being at the center and not just of being different. Instead of being at the center, we prove to be on an "average" planet, circling an "average" star, in a reasonably "average" galaxy—the sequence is well-known.

Carter (following the lead of Robert Dicke and Martin Rees) points out that PAL (the "Copernican principle" in his terms) has to be qualified in an interesting way in the light of recent cosmological thought. Human beings could exist only when the heavy elements, notably carbon, making them up are already in existence. If the supernova origin for these elements be accepted, human beings (or any other form of carbon-based life) could not exist until two generations of stars would have had time to form and organic evolution would have been in process for a lengthy period, requiring a minimal period of some billions of years. If a universe has human beings in it, it must, according to present theory then, be very old and thus also very large. PAL must therefore be restricted: the location of humans in the cosmos is *not* just "average." It is worth noting that this restriction is not itself a matter of *principle*; it is a consequence of a specific cosmological theory, Big Bang theory.[31] A corollary of the restriction is that any universe that can be directly *observed* by humans has to be very old, and thus of a certain sort (according to current theory) in regard to the type and age distribution of stars, the apparent intensities of visible quasars, and so forth. This is what Carter calls a selection effect. (A selection effect is a feature found in what is observed, due to the circumstances of the observation or to the means used, rather than being intrinsic to the object observed.)

This, then, seems to be where the talk of *observers* in discussions of the anthropic principle comes from; PAL itself is formulated not specifically for humans-as-observers, but more generally for humans-as-humans. The significance of this selection effect is that it qualifies the tentative pre-Big-Bang working principle that the universe *as we observe it* is a fair sample of the universe as a whole. This principle has to be abandoned once one accepts a theory in which the structure of the cosmos changes markedly over time. In an expanding universe, there is nothing particularly surprising about the claim that what human observers see is not typical of what *would* have been seen at a different epoch. It does not, for example, *explain* something we had until then been puzzled by, as some authors have suggested.[32]

One final thread in this tangle around the "weak" principle is Carter's claim that it somehow explains some (or even all) of the so-called large-number coincidences. The suggestion goes back to the speculative work of Dirac and Dicke. But so far as has been shown up to this time, it appears to have no substance. The fact that certain very large dimensionless numbers, like 10^{40}, seem to appear often when we combine the fundamental physical constants in various ways, can in no way be illuminated by pointing to the presence of humans (or beetles) in the universe, or even to a selection effect due to our "non-average" location in time. Such an effect could not pick out relatively precise numerical coincidences. Furthermore, since it is time-dependent, it could not explain numerical relations that are, to the best of our knowledge, time-independent.

Since this is widely-accepted, why is the talk of large-number coincidences retained in standard expositions of the anthropic principle? Perhaps because of a confusion about what is meant by "coincidence" here. What earlier writers, like Dirac, meant was that the same number seems to recur more often than one would have expected on *a priori* grounds. But what Barrow and Tipler, for instance, more often seem to mean is that a restricted range of values of the physical constants was necessary if human life were to develop in the cosmos, and that this looks like a possibly significant coincidence. (This last has, so far as anyone has shown, no relation whatever to the large-number "coincidences" of Dirac *et al.*)

And so we come, finally, to the "strong" form of the anthropic principle (SAP). The strong principle ("strong" in the sense of making a daring claim) was formulated by Carter in a way that easily lent itself to misunderstanding: "The universe (and hence the fundamental parameters on which it depends) must be such as to admit the creation of observers within it at some stage."[33] The problem lies, of course, with the phrase, "must be". If it is conditional, so that the principle merely states that since the universe *does* contain observers (i.e. humans), it evidently "must be" of the sort that would permit the appearance of observers within it, it is not only not strong, it is trivial, and indeed reduces to the weak principle. But if it means that, antecedently, the universe *had* to be of the sort that would make the appearance within it of observers unavoidable, then it is not just strong, it is entirely groundless.[34] Carter makes no attempt himself to argue in its support. The attraction, of course, of this latter reading is that it would make the principle *explanatory*, something Carter clearly wanted. For if the existence of the human can properly be said to be *necessary* (i.e. human beings could not have failed to exist), then this would in some sense explain the apparent coincidences in the physical constants that "just" permit human life to appear.[35] If human life *had* to appear, then the universe *has* to be such as to permit this to happen. But did human life *have* to appear?

Carter had a speculative suggestion to make at this point, similar to the one we have already seen Collins and Hawking to have made in the previous year. If one were to accept some form of many-universe theory (of which more below), then the appearance within this ensemble of co-existent universes of one capable of bearing life might be regarded as (more or less) necessary. In which case SAP (with the addition of a many-universe theory) becomes an *explanation* of the way in which the universe seems precisely adjusted for human life. Why do the physical constants of our universe have the values they do? Because among all the (actual) universes featuring different constants, we (*of course*) will be found in one that permits our existence. Note that this *is* properly anthropic. It is "we" (not beetles) who observe the physical constants and who ask the question. Note also that it is the best example imaginable of a selection effect. But, of course, all this would not make the occurrence of human life necessary *tout court*. Do the many universes *have* to exist? Is their existence a matter of *principle*? Surely not. Does there *have* to be one among them capable of life?

And so, it appears, we have to start over again if we are to extract something worthwhile from this logical tangle. It would be best, perhaps, not to speak of "anthropic principles" at all. WAP is trivial, as we have seen. And SAP, in the formulation often given it, is indefensible as it stands. What remains?

4. An Unlikely Sort of Universe?

Let us return now to the question posed by Collins and Hawking: why is the universe isotropic? The puzzle about the conditions for isotropy came to be called the "flatness problem." The energy density of the universe today is relatively close to the density corresponding to the borderline between an open and a closed universe. The ratio of these densities is usually denoted as Ω, and Ω is, on the basis of present evidence, believed to lie somewhere between the values of 2 and .1. (Since we do not know on which side of unity the energy-density lies, we do not yet know whether the universe is "open," will continue forever to expand, or "closed," will eventually begin to contract.) So the universe in geometrical terms is relatively "flat." The problem is that to achieve this condition today, the value of Ω shortly after the Big Bang would have had to be almost exactly 1; to achieve this, the initial expansion rate would have had to be "tuned" to an accuracy (so one estimate went) of one part in 10^{55}. Since *any* initial value of Ω should have been possible (remember Descartes' "chaos"?), this extraordinarily tight requirement poses a problem. Does it mean that there is something wrong with the model (which left the requirement simply unexplained), or is there some other way to explain it?

A second line of thought also emerged. It was noted that if the values of the fundamental physical constants had been even ever so slightly different, the structure of the universe could have been entirely different. It became a parlor game, indeed, among physicists to ask what would happen if a slightly different set of values were to have been the case. In particular, speculation focussed on the relations between the four fundamental forces. If the strong nuclear force were to have been as little as 2 percent stronger (relatively to the other forces), all hydrogen would have been converted into helium. If it were 5 percent weaker, no helium at all would have formed and there would be nothing but hydrogen. If the weak nuclear force were a little stronger, supernovas could not occur, and heavy elements could not have formed. If it were slightly weaker, only helium might have formed. If the electromagnetic force were slightly stronger, all stars would be red dwarfs, and there would be no planets. If it were a little weaker, all stars would be very hot and short-lived. If the electron charge were ever so slightly different, there would be no chemistry as we know it. Carbon (C_{12}) only *just* managed to form in the primal nucleosynthesis. And so on and so on.[36]

The "coincidence" associated with the flatness problem was very different from those deriving from the relationships between the physical constants. The first had to do with initial conditions; the second concerned the laws of physics themselves. The notion of "improbability" would be very different in the two cases. In the first, one is saying that *within* the rules of the game the initial setting of Ω could (as far as one can see) have been quite different. Countless *possible* initial sets of conditions were permitted (so far as one can tell) by theory. So why is the one actually realized the only one among 10^{55} possible initial states (if this rather speculative numerical estimate be accepted) that would give rise to a long-lived universe of the sort we evidently have? On the other hand, in the second case, one is asking: what if the rules of the game themselves were to be changed slightly? It is difficult to know how to apply the notion of probability in this latter case. Perhaps there are physical reasons why the relations between the constants *have* to be as they are. Further, by what mechanism would they be changed? Would the changes themselves in some second-level sense be lawlike?

5. Anthropic Explanations

What, then, is the puzzle here? *Is* there a puzzle, an explanandum, something to be explained? This is where our brief historical discussion of the Indifference Principle can help. We would not have expected on the basis of earlier science that the overall structures of the world we know would have been so sensitive both to the choice of initial conditions and the "choice" of the laws themselves. (Note: no mention yet of man, or even of carbon-based life.) Focussing for simplicity on just the first of these factors, the initial conditions, it can be concluded that among all the innumerable universes that might have been according to standard Big Bang (SBB) theory, one that is long-lived, permitting planets to develop and evolution to occur, is almost infinitely improbable, in flat contradiction to Descartes' prognosis. What are we to make of this? *Is* there something to be explained?

At this point, the ways diverge. One response is to say: well, that is just the way things are. Any one of the almost infinitely many possible universes, according to the present model, would have been equally "improbable," so why attach any significance to the "improbability" of the one that has actually been realized? Ought it not be taken just as a "given," as the stopping-point in explanation? The other response is to insist that a universe of this kind has a special significance in terms of some system of meaning that would suggest a likely explanation. (Analogy: as we look down from a plane at the boulders scattered over a remote mountainside, we notice one group that spells "help." Is it not more likely that this formation has been deliberately brought about?)[37] If such an explanation exists (so the argument continues), it is to be preferred—at least by those who accept the relevant system of meaning—to leaving the coincidence *merely* a coincidence. Two such broader contexts of meaning appear to exist. Both are properly "anthropic": they hinge on the presence of the human. One is quasi-scientific, the other non-scientific.

The first form of anthropic explanation has already been described. If one adopts a many-universe model, where a multiplicity of *actual* universes co-exist, each realizing a different set of initial conditions and (perhaps) a different relationship between the physical constants, then the fact that we find ourselves in a universe apparently "fine-tuned" for our existence needs no further explanation. All of the other possible universes *have* been realized, and we, of course, are in the one that permits (it need not necessitate) our existence. Provided that the other universes are actual and not just possible, the improbability has been removed. But what kind of plausibility does the many-universe concept itself possess? It is important to underline that there is no independent warrant of any sort for it. Carter cites the Everett "branching worlds" model in quantum theory "to which one is virtually forced by the logic of quantum theory."[38] But one is *not* virtually forced to it; indeed, it has found little support among quantum theorists. But more important, Everett's branching worlds do not provide the range of alternative initial cosmic conditions or alternative physical laws that this version of an anthropic explanation of the initial parameter constraint would require. (We shall use the neutral expression "initial parameter constraint" (IPC) to denote the phenomenon to be explained. The commoner expression "fine-tuning" is more appropriate when a particular *explanation* of that phenomenon, i.e. the conscious operation of a "tuner," is under discussion.)

The second anthropic explanation is of a teleological sort. In the tradition of the "religions of the Book," the universe is the handiwork of a Creator-God as well as being the arena where the story of human sin and human salvation unfolds. The Bible and the Koran present themselves as a record of God's dealings with particular peoples and particular persons. In this framework, it would hardly be far-fetched to suppose that human beings figured in an essential way in the plan of God's creation. A second type of anthropic explanation thus presents itself. If highly specific initial conditions or specific laws of nature were needed in order that human beings would one day appear in the universe, then the Creator could (and would) have ensured that these conditions would be realized. That is part of what, in effect, "Creation" *means* in this tradition.

The explanation here is potentially satisfactory if the theological frame of reference be accepted. It is strongly anthropic; the IPC requirement itself may not distinguish humans from any other sorts of carbon-based life, but the theological *explanation* of IPC does. The explanation would not, as far as we can tell, work for any of the other biological forms requiring similar physical constraints on the work of creation, since we have no reason to suppose them to have been significant in some *special* way for the Creator's designs. It is legitimate in this context to ask about the choice of laws as well as that of initial conditions, since the precise form the laws of Nature should take is also presumably a matter of Divine choice.

If a Creator of the sort described in the Bible is, in fact, responsible for the existence of the universe, then the puzzle of IPC is resolved. But what if the logical order were to be reversed: is the need to explain IPC a sufficient (or at least a fairly persuasive) warrant for belief in a Creator who regards human existence as integral to the work of creation? (The dangers of anthropomorphism in contexts like these have not gone unnoticed by theologians.) Though some Christian apologists have answered this question with an enthusiastic yes, a negative answer seems preferable. There are *far* too many assumptions involved in converting this sort of explanation into a satisfactory existence-proof.

The validity of this form of anthropic explanation as explanation does not depend on whether life could have had a quite different chemical basis, or whether intelligent life requires a planet for its home or could develop in a non-Darwinian way, and so forth. The objections that have been raised on these scores do not affect the validity of an explanation involving a Creator of the sort envisaged in the Bible. Even if intelligent life could originate in a variety of other ways, thus allowing some relaxation of the parameter constraints that originally gave rise to the claim of "fine-tuning," both anthropic explanations (many-universe and theological) of whatever constraints still remain would still hold good *as* explanations. Their cogency as against the third alternative (no explanation needed) would, of course, be weakened, and so one would be less inclined to argue for the superiority of one or the other of them as a way of dealing with the IPC claim. And they could also be considerably weakened as existence-proofs (of the existence of a multiplicity of universes or of a Creator who is concerned about human affairs). But, as already noted, they ought not to be regarded as existence-proofs in the first place.

This separation of explanation from existence-proof may seem odd. In science, the adequacy of a theoretical explanation is often regarded as an adequate testimony to the existence of the entities postulated by the theory. But the debates that swirl around this precise issue among philosophers (the issue of scientific realism, as philosophers call it) ought to warn us of the risks of moving too easily from explanatory adequacy to truth-claim for the theory itself. This sort of inference depends sensitively on the quality of the explanation given, on the viability of alternatives, and on other more complex factors. The anthropic forms of explanation do not function well as existence-proofs, primarily because the explanandum (the IPC claim) is itself highly theory-dependent, and also because the norms for the two proposed types of explanation are far from clear.

In sum, then, there is no such thing as a strong anthropic principle. There is the cosmological puzzle we have dubbed IPC. At least two ways of "explaining" it, of rendering it unpuzzling, have been proposed. Both of these are "anthropic" in that they refer in an essential way to the presence of human beings in the cosmos. There are thus anthropic *explanations* (not principles) of two very different sorts, one cosmological (many-universe) the other theological (choice on the part of a Creator). It would make no sense to call these "strong," so that term can be dropped entirely. The theological anthropic explanation (TAE) challenges the Indifference Principle, which is one reason why scientists have regarded it with suspicion. The other reason is that it does not satisfy the criteria a scientific explanation should. This does not, of course, invalidate it as an explanation, unless one were to hold that only science can explain. One simply would have to look to a different set of criteria, and look (it should be emphasized) just as critically as one would in the scientific case.

6. Postscript: Since 1980

The matter, alas!, cannot be left there. Science has a way of moving on. What appears as a suspicious sort of parameter constraint at one stage of theory may find a perfectly normal sort of explanation at the next. In 1980, Alan Guth proposed a modification of the Big Bang theory which would affect only the first fraction of a second of the cosmic expansion, leaving the remainder of the expansion to be described as in the standard Big Bang theory.[39] Suppose a phase transition were to have occurred, a supercooling that brought about an incredibly rapid cosmic inflation ending around $T = 10^{-30}$ seconds. Even in that brief time the diameter of the universe would have been multiplied by a factor of around 10^{50}. The equations governing such an expansion are very different from those of the "normal" cosmic expansion associated with the Big Bang. No matter what Ω was before the inflation began, the effect of the expansion would be to force its value towards unity, so that an almost "flat" (and thus long-lived) universe is not only not improbable but is a necessary outcome. In this new model, the initial conditions prior to the inflation do not really matter; the expansion is so rapid and so enormous that any peculiarities the initial system possessed are, as it were, "smeared out" and thus lost. There are thus no constraints on the initial conditions; we are back to a "chaos" after Descartes' heart! The flatness problem which first prompted the talk of fine-tuning would thus be eliminated, and the Indifference Principle would reign.

How plausible is the inflationary model? In addition to dissolving the flatness problem, it also eliminates the "horizon" problem. According to the SBB model, as soon as expansion began, the universe broke into an enormous number of tiny regions moving too rapidly apart for them to be in causal connection. How could such a universe give rise to the homogeneities observed today (in the 3° K radiation, for example)? The only way in which these homogeneities could be explained would be to suppose a very tight homogeneity to be imposed as an arbitrary external condition on the initial cosmic state, just the sort of parameter constraint that cosmologists disliked in the context of the flatness problem. The inflationary model, however, could get rid of this obstacle just as it could the flatness problem. Since the region from which the observable universe evolved is so much smaller than the corresponding region in the SBB model, causal connection across it presents no difficulty, and the homogeneity of the observed universe can be causally explained.

But is the postulated phase transition not just a sort of "epicycle" that allows us to eliminate some awkwardness in the SBB model? What other motivation can be offered for a transition of this kind? The Grand Unified Theories (GUTS), now much in vogue in particle physics, do in fact offer a hint. In these theories, three of the four fundamental kinds of forces (electromagnetic, strong nuclear and weak nuclear) are represented as reducible to the same force at energies as high as those of the early universe. These theories, in general, favor phase transitions of the kind the inflationary model requires, though GUTS are still at too tentative a stage to specify this connection as fully as a theoretical account of the inflation would require. One can, however, say that the insertion of the brief but crucial inflationary phase in the first 10^{-30} seconds of the Big Bang gives a more consistent model of how it all may have come about, though at a cost in terms of all-round plausibility.

But the inflationary model faces some difficulties on its own account. The phase transition would give rise to "bubbles," inhomogeneities, that should leave a variety of traces in the observed universe today. These traces are not to be found. And so a further modification was needed. Linde, Lebedev, and Steinhardt suggested that a special sort of phase transition, called a "slow roll-over" transition, would render the inhomogeneities harmless by removing them to great distances from the observable universe. In the new inflationary model, as it is called, different regions of the primordial universe would, through quantum or thermal fluctuations, develop into autonomous domains, each about 10^{-24} cm across. The inflationary expansion would leave the domains more than 10^{26} cm in diameter. Our observable universe would, however, constitute at that point only a tiny region (perhaps 10 cm across) of just one among a vast number of domains. The inhomogeneities are banished to the boundaries of the domains, leaving the domains themselves (and *a fortiori* tiny fragments of the domains like the observable universe) homogeneous.[40] Such a model also offers some hope of explaining the density inhomogeneities that develop into galaxies by invoking quantum fluctuations that occur during the inflationary expansion, though an adequate theory of this process has proved elusive.

Does the new inflationary model make IPC (and, therefore, fine-tuning) unnecessary? This was its principal motivation, and it did succeed in eliminating the sorts of parameter constraint that the SBB model required as additional postulates. Ironically, however, a problem of the familiar kind once again emerged. Guth and Steinhardt note with regret:

> Unfortunately the necessary slow-rollover transition requires the fine tuning of parameters [notably the energy-density, the quantity which occasioned the apparent need for fine-tuning in the original Big Bang model]; calculations yield reasonable predictions only if the parameters are assigned values in a narrow range. Most theorists (including both of us) regard such fine tuning as implausible. The consequences of the scenario are so successful, however, that we are encouraged to go on in the hope that we may discover realistic versions of grand unified theories in which such a slow-rollover transition occurs without fine tuning.[41]

It is curious how the same challenge arises over and over; one level of IPC is explained by the next level of theory, involving a larger-scale universe, but then a new sort of IPC appears. The universe, meanwhile, keeps getting larger and larger. Linde has recently proposed a solution that might (he hopes) eliminate IPC once and for all.[42] He calls it "chaotic inflation" since it begins from an (almost) unspecified initial distribution of scalar fields. This gives rise to a cluster of causally disconnected mini-universes, most of them in a permanent inflationary phase, some (like ours) not, some of them characterizable in terms of classical space-time, some not. There is no initial singularity; the inflations began at different times. There is no need for fine-tuning to bring about the slow roll-over transition needed for "our" kind of universe, since every other possible sort of universe ("with the scalar fields taking all possible values") is out there somewhere.[43] And some of these will embody very different laws of physics, and even a different dimensionality of space-time.

No wonder, then, that we are in a universe whose laws are so neatly correlated to the existence of carbon-based life. Since Linde's "maxi-universe" contains an innumerably large number of mini-universes, exemplifying an enormous variety of physical laws, life will be found in those mini-universes (like ours) where it is capable of developing. The IPC required for life requires no sort of teleological explanation; in such a vast variety of mini-universes, it will surely be found somewhere. Linde's model is thus essentially a many-universe one, with an inflationary twist. Though our mini-universe is governed by Big Bang theory after the initial inflation, this would not (according to him) be true of most of the other mini-universes, so that this is no longer a Big Bang model, strictly speaking.[44]

The price Linde pays for avoiding IPC is very high: the ten-billion-light-year observable universe (which until recently seemed large enough!) has become an almost inconsequentially tiny corner of a mini-universe that has expanded to an almost unimaginable extent[45] from an initial 10^{-33} cm, and this mini-universe itself is only one among an innumerable array of no-longer connected other mini-universes. It illustrates the speculative—some would say extreme—lengths to which cosmologists will go in defence of the Indifference Principle. But it also underlines the danger of relying on a claim of IPC as the basis for an anthropic explanation of the theological sort. Such a claim can always (it seems) be undermined by simply postulating a larger unobservable universe of which the observable region for which parameter constraint is claimed is only a tiny part.

One final remark is directed to those who have been tempted to make "fine-tuning" the basis of a new natural theology, a new and attractively science-based way to persuade waverers that the universe does, indeed, require a Creator in whose designs man played an important role. The course that early-universe cosmology has taken in the twenty years since Carter first introduced the phrase "anthropic principle" ought to warn against this way of reading the signs. IPC is inevitably a challenge to the theorist, an incentive to new efforts of constructive imagination. If a cosmological model requires IPC, one may be sure of one thing; a new stage of theoretical development lies ahead. Apparent fine-tuning can never furnish the warrant for a natural theology of even the most circumspect sort. It may appropriately inspire effort from those who seek to discern a consonance between their religious and their scientific beliefs. The proper response on the part of the religious believer to the vast enlargement of the cosmological imagination in recent decades is not to seek in this enlargement some sort of apologetic argument for theistic belief; rather it is to recognize in it the incentive for a corresponding enlargement in theological horizons.

NOTES

[1]The emphasis given here to the Indifference Principle gives the story a rather different focus than that found in the lengthy historical chapter on Design arguments in John D. Barrow and Frank J. Tipler, *The Anthropic Cosmological Principle* (Oxford University Press, 1986), ch. 2.

[2]Diogenes Laertius summarizing the doctrine of Leucippus. See G. S. Kirk and J. E. Raven, eds. and trans., *The Presocratic Philosophers* (Cambridge University Press, 1960), p. 410.

[3]See McMullin, "Cosmic Order in Plato and Aristotle," in *The Concept of Order*, ed. P. Kuntz (University of Washington Press, 1968), pp. 63-76.

[4]R. Descartes, *Discourse on Method*, ed. and trans. Paul Olscamp (Indianapolis: Bobbs-Merrill, 1965), p. 35.

[5]Ibid., p. 36.

[6]Ibid., p. 37.

[7]Ibid.

[8]Ibid., p. 35.

[9]See, for example, the readings collected in D. C. Goodman, ed., *Science and Religious Belief: A Selection of Primary Sources* (Wright, 1973); see also John H. Brooke, *Science and Religion: Some Historical Perspectives* (Cambridge University Press, 1991), especially chapter 6; Ernan McMullin, "Natural science and belief in a Creator," in *Physics, Philosophy, and Theology*, ed. R. J. Russell et al. (Vatican Observatory, 1988), pp. 49-79, esp. pp. 63-68.

[10]See Michael Buckley, *At the Origins of Modern Atheism* (Yale University Press, 1987), chap. 3.

[11]For a full account of this development, see Michael Hoskin, *Stellar Astronomy: Historical Studies* (Science History Publications, 1982).

[12] Text of the sixth edition of *The Origin of Species* (1872). The phrase "by the Creator" was added in this edition.

[13]Darwin in response to a question from Charles Lyell: "We must assume the creation of one or a few [original] forms in the same manner as philosophers assume a power of attraction without any explanation." Letter from Darwin to Lyell, 11 October 1859, in *The Life and Letters of Charles Darwin*, ed. Francis Darwin (Appleton, 1967), vol. 2, p. 6. There are, of course, some difficulties with this analogy, particularly if one takes seriously the reference to the Creator inserted in the sixth edition.

[14]Darwin to Hooker, 29 March 1863, *Life*, vol. 2, p. 202.

[15]A note written in 1871. *Life*, vol. 2, pp. 202-3.

[16]E. Haeckel, *Natürliche Schopfungsgeschichte*, (Reimer, 1878). See A. I. Oparin, *Origin of Life* (Dover, 1953; reprint of 1938 ed.), chap. 3.

[17]Theodosius Dobzhansky, *Heredity and the Nature of Man* (Harcourt Brace, 1964), pp. 36-7.

[18]Ibid., p. 38.

[19]Fred Hoyle and N.C. Wickramasinghe, *Evolution from Space* (Simon and Schuster, 1981), chap. 2. Hoyle also rejects the Darwinian account of organic evolution, claiming that the absence of intermediate forms in the fossil record and the speed at which major morphological changes appear to have occurred cannot be understood in Darwinian terms. His own proposal is that the gene-pool has been replenished from time to time by genes arriving from space.

[20]Lecomte Pierre du Nouy, *Human Destiny* (Longmans, 1947).

[21]The story is quite a complicated one. Alpher and Herman were co-workers of George Gamow, who was investigating how nucleosynthesis might have happened in the early Big Bang universe. They forecast a microwave radiation with a present temperature of approximately 5° K. Gamow's theory of nucleosynthesis did not work out for elements heavier than helium, and so was more or less abandoned. The prediction was, therefore, forgotten. Peebles himself, unaware of Gamow's work, had predicted a relic radiation with a temperature of around 10° K. Penzias and Wilson had only a single data point (at 7.35 cm); many more were needed in order to establish an actual blackbody spectrum. The characteristic temperature is now given as 2.7° K. Steven Weinberg traces the story of this discovery in some detail in his *The First Three Minutes* (Basic Books, 1977), chaps. 3 and 6.

[22]Charles Misner, "The isotropy of the universe," *Astrophysical Journal*, **151** (1968): 431-457. See also Barrow and Tipler, *Anthropic Cosmological Principle*, pp. 420-426.

[23]C. B. Collins and S. W. Hawking, "Why is the universe isotropic?" *Astrophysical Journal*, **180** (1973): 317-334.

[24]Ibid., p. 319.

[25]Ibid.

[26]Brandon Carter, "Large number coincidences and the anthropic principle in cosmology", in *Confrontation of Cosmological Theory with Astronomical Data*, ed. M.S. Longair (Reidel, 1974), pp. 291-298.

[27]A full, though insufficiently critical, account can be found in Barrow and Tipler, *Anthropic Cosmological Principle*, ch. 4.

[28]Carter, "Large Number Coincidences," p. 291.

[29]See Patrick Wilson, "What is the explanandum of the anthropic principle?" *American Philosophical Quarterly*, **28** (1991): 167-173.

[30]In a lengthy chapter on the weak anthropic principle, Barrow and Tipler discuss the ways in which large physical constants determine the sizes and various other properties of everything from atoms to black holes. But, significantly, there does not appear to be any properly *anthropic* limitation in their exposition. Nor is it clear that there are, in the end, any *coincidences* between the constants (a separate issue) that call for a special form of explanation.

[31]It seems misleading for several reasons to identify this restriction with the weak anthropic principle itself, as Barrow and Tipler do (*Anthropic Cosmological Principle*, p. 16). The non-average location of human beings in time is not a matter of *principle*. It is by identifying WAP with this theoretical result that Barrow and Tipler attempt to defend the principle against the obvious charge that it is trivial. (Though it *is* indeed trivial, it is not strictly speaking tautological, as some have further argued.)

[32]WAP is not *itself* a selection effect, as is sometimes confusingly claimed. The presence of humans (or of beetles) in the universe constrains the sorts of cosmological theories we can plausibly offer. But this kind of constraint is not, except in an exceedingly loose sense, an effect (or, for that matter, a cause) of selection since we are not in this context reviewing the actual effects on observation of some sort of selection bias.

[33]Carter, "Large Number Coincidences," p. 294.

[34]This is the interpretation given to Carter's formulation of SAP by Barrow and Tipler: it "is clearly a more metaphysical and less defensible notion, for it implies that the universe could not have been structured differently—that

perhaps the constants of Nature could not have had numerical values other than what we observe." See *Anthropic Cosmological Principle*, p. 6.

[35]Oddly, Barrow and Tipler discuss these coincidences (in elaborate and helpful detail) under the *weak* principle, not the strong one (chap. 5); one would have anticipated the reverse.

[36]A detailed review is given by John Leslie, *Universes* (Routledge, 1989), chap. 2: "The evidence of fine tuning."

[37]John Leslie has developed and analyzed analogies of this general kind in a series of essays, among them: "Anthropic principle, world ensemble, design," *American Philosophical Quarterly*, **19** (1982): 141-151; "Modern cosmology and the creation of life," in *Evolution and Creation*, ed. E. McMullin (University of Notre Dame Press, 1985), pp. 91-120.

[38]Carter, "Large Number Coincidences," p. 298; see Barrow and Tipler, *Anthropic Cosmological Principle*, pp. 472-489.

[39]Alan Guth, "Inflationary universe: A possible solution to the horizon and flatness of problems," *Physical Review* D, **23** (1981): 347-356; Alan Guth and Paul Steinhardt, "The inflationary universe," *Scientific American*, **215** (1984): 116-128.

[40]See Paul Steinhardt, "The current state of the inflationary universe," *Comments Nuclear Particle Physics*, **12** (1984): 273-286.

[41]Guth and Steinhardt, "The inflationary universe," p. 127.

[42]Andrei Linde, "Particle physics and inflationary cosmology," *Physics Today*, **40** (1987): 61-68.

[43]Ibid., p. 67.

[44]For completeness, it should be added that criticisms of the fundamental assumptions of Big Bang cosmology continue. Among the most vocal critics are H. C. Arp and Eric Lerner. Arp argues against the correlation of red-shift with galactic distance on which the notion of cosmic expansion primarily rests. He claims, for instance, to find objects with quite different red-shifts associated in such a way as to make it highly likely that they are neighbors. Arp makes the red-shift proportional to age rather than to distance, and suggests that the 3° K radiation may be a purely local effect in our own galaxy. See H. C. Arp, *et al.*, "The extragalactic universe: An

alternative view,'' *Nature*, 346 (1990): 807-812. Lerner's provocatively-titled *The Big Bang Never Happened: A Startling Refutation of the Dominant Theory of the Universe* (Random House, 1991) recounts in journalistic style the main challenges facing Big Bang cosmology (notably the difficulties in accounting for galaxy-formation), and suggests as an alternative Hannes Alfren's plasma model which relies on electromagnetic instead of gravitational forces to explain the formation of quasars and galaxies.

[45]Linde mentions an expansion factor of ten to the power of one hundred million!

THE NEW DESIGN ARGUMENT:
WHAT DOES IT PROVE?

DENNIS TEMPLE

The new design argument starts from the claim that the universe was "fine-tuned for life" through delicate balances of physical constants that fell out of the big bang. The argument then goes on to claim (a) that cosmic fine-tuning needs an explanation; (b) that the choice of physical constants by a creator is the best explanation of fine-tuning; and (c) that this in turn confirms the existence of such a creator.

Most discussions of the new design argument concentrate on the scientific evidence of cosmic fine-tuning and give little consideration to the logical requirements of the argument itself. I propose to do the opposite here. I am going to discuss the logic of the argument, what is involved in each of these three claims. I believe that these claims are much more complex, and much more interesting, than has usually been appreciated.

The explanation involved in the new design argument is why-explanation: why the universe was fine-tuned for life. I will begin by sketching out a theory of why-explanation that will be used to clarify the logic of the argument.

1. Why Explanations: A Sketch

A why-explanation may be understood as the answer to a why-question. For example, to explain why Jack was promoted is to answer the question, "Why was Jack promoted?" and to explain why the stock market crashed is to answer the question "Why did the stock market crash?" and so forth. Why-questions consist of the interrogative word "why" followed by a *topic proposition* which expresses the (alleged) fact about which the question asks. For instance, the topic of "Why was Jack promoted?" is "Jack was promoted" and the topic of "Why did the stock market crash?" is "The stock market crashed" and so on. Explanation-seeking why-questions have the form "Why p?", where p is the topic proposition of the question.

What is required for a question of the form "Why p?" to arise? An obvious requirement is that p must be true, since if p is false, there is nothing to explain. For example, there is no explanation why the moon is made of green cheese. Or, what amounts to the same thing, the question "Why is the moon made of green cheese?" does not arise. It is not that we cannot answer the question. We can, and the answer is: it is not made of green cheese. This is a good answer but not an explanation why the topic is true. It is a *corrective answer*: it answers the question by correcting the assumption that the topic proposition is true. An explanation of the topic, by contrast, is a *direct answer* to the question: one which accepts the assumptions of the question and gives a reason why the topic proposition is true. To say that a why-question does not arise, then, is to say that it has no direct answer. If **p** is false, "Why **p**?" has no direct answer and does not arise.

The truth of **p** is necessary for "Why **p**?" to arise but not sufficient. Consider the following example. Suppose one day you happen to run into a friend. Seeing you, the friend asks, apparently for no reason, "Why are you still alive?" That you are still alive is a fact but is it enough to make the question arise? Not at all. It is clear that without further information you would find it impossible to determine what the question is asking for and therefore impossible to decide how to answer it. The natural response would be to ask your friend for more information by saying, "Why shouldn't I still be alive?" or "What do you mean?" Suppose then your friend says, "Oh, I heard you had been run over by a truck." In that case you see that there is some point to the question, and you can answer it by saying, "No, that never happened" or "Yes, I was, but it was a very small truck" or whatever happens to be the case.

According to Bas van Fraassen and some other writers, what is missing in the above case is a suitable *contrast* to the topic proposition: a reason to believe that the topic proposition might not have been true.[1] The question "Why are you still alive?" did not make sense in the first instance because there was no reason to suppose that you would not still be alive. When your friend says that he heard you had been run over by a truck, he supplies such a reason and the question becomes meaningful.

Contrasts can come in a variety of forms. A change in something is one common form. For instance, if your television set suddenly stops working, it makes sense to ask why that change occurred. We see that it is not working, but the fact that the set had been working gives us reason to suppose that it might have continued to work. Contrasts can also come by way of analogy. For example, suppose that Mary and Joan have similar cases of pneumonia; Mary recovers but Joan dies. This is enough to underwrite "Why did Mary recover (when Joan died)?" and conversely. Contrasts can also come from a competing alternative to the topic. Suppose Jack and Jill are both eligible for a single promotion. You believe that Jill is best qualified and most likely to get the promotion. But, as it happens, the promotion goes to Jack. This will be enough to give rise to the question, "Why was Jack promoted (instead of Jill)?"

The epistemic background of "Why p?" must include some reason to believe that **p** is true and a contrast which gives us reason to believe that **p** might not have been true. The contrast locates **p** in the context of a suitable comparison and thereby indicates both that there is something to explain and also what sort of explanation is needed. It is one thing to explain why Bill is still alive on the assumption that he was hit by a truck and another to explain why he is still alive on the assumption that he had a serious heart attack. The truck and the heart attack both give us reason to suppose that Bill might not still be alive, but it is clear that the truck question and the heart attack question will lead us in the direction of quite different answers.

One final point will prove helpful later. A direct answer to "Why p?" accepts the question and attempts to give a reason for **p's** being true in light of its contrast. Corrective answers to "Why p?" come in several forms. One can correct the question by denying that **p** is true, or by accepting **p** and denying that the assumed contrast holds. Finally, one can accept both **p** and the contrast to it, but claim that nevertheless there is no reason for **p** because it happened by chance.

To clarify, let us suppose I win the lottery against odds of one in a million. I might feel moved to ask, "Why did I win and not any of the other contestants?" There might be a direct answer to the question. Perhaps my crooked uncle Bob who works for the lottery board fixed the drawing; that is why I won and not any of the others. But on the other hand if the drawing was honest then there is no reason why I won. All we can say is "It was just chance." To say this is to correct the assumption that there is a reason why **p**, a direct answer to be found. Note, however, that if the question arises, this means that **p** is true and has a genuine contrast, and this is *prima facie* evidence that there is a reason why **p**. So, to accept the answer that **p** happened by chance, there must be independent evidence that a random process gave rise to **p**. It is not enough to say that the process could have been random—we must show that it was.

2. Does Fine-Tuning Need an Explanation?

Does cosmic fine-tuning really need an explanation? Does the question why this universe was fine-tuned for life arise on currently accepted facts of physical cosmology? Let us begin by briefly reviewing these facts.

Cosmic fine-tuning refers to facts such as these.[2] There are stringent requirements for life as we know it to be able to arise in the universe which developed out of the big bang. One is that the universe last long enough. After the big bang, when the universe had cooled enough for the first atoms to form, it is thought that almost all matter existed in the form of hydrogen with a very small admixture of helium. To get enough of the larger atoms (carbon, nitrogen, iron, etc.) necessary for living things, fusion reactions were required in several generations of stars over a period of around 10 billion years. But for this to be possible there must have been a very close balance at the outset between the outward force of the big bang and the inward pull of gravity.

The astronomer P. C. W. Davies explains:

> The universe is . . . the product of a competition of the explosive force of the big bang, and the force of gravity which tries to pull the pieces back together again. In recent years astrophysicists have come to realize just how delicately this competition has been balanced. Had the big bang been weaker, the universe would have soon fallen back on itself in a big crunch. On the other hand, had it been stronger, the cosmic material would have dispersed so rapidly that galaxies would not have formed.[3]

In either case, of course, life as we know it could not have developed. Davies estimates that for the universe to be life-permitting the balance of these forces at the outset (Planck time or 10^{-40} seconds after the big bang) would have to have been on the order of one part in 10^{60}. Davies also points out that if the big bang had featured even very small variations—on the order of one part in 10^{40}—in the strength of the fundamental forces of nature (gravity, the weak and strong nuclear forces, electromagnetism) this would also have led to a universe without life.[4] Here, too, the ability of the universe to permit the development of life depends on a delicate balance.

Behind all this talk of delicate balances is the belief that the big bang could have been stronger or weaker than it was, and similarly for gravity and the other forces of nature which appeared at or after the big bang. As Davies says, even very small differences of this sort would have led to a lifeless universe. This conclusion seems to be accepted by most physicists. For instance, B. J. Carr and M. J. Rees, after an exhaustive review of the evidence of fine-tuning, observe that "The possibility of life as we know it evolving in the Universe depends on the values of a few basic physical constants—and is in some respects remarkably sensitive to their numerical values." They also say that these facts are ". . . remarkable coincidences and they do warrant some explanation."[5] Other physicists concur with this.

But what sort of explanation is needed? What question is supposed to arise from these facts? Carr and Rees do not say, perhaps because the question at issue seems to them obvious in the context. But I think it would be helpful to try to formulate the question that lies behind the claim the facts of cosmic fine-tuning need to be explained. What needs explaining is why this universe was fine-tuned for life. The question at issue in these discussions may be formulated this way: "Why did this universe have just those values of physical constants which would permit the appearance of life in it instead of other values which would have precluded the eventual development of life?" Or, more simply, "Why is this universe life-permitting, not lifeless?"

Does this question arise? Do the facts of fine-tuning need an explanation? Several reasons have been given for saying that they do need explaining. I will briefly review them here.

One reason, which has been advanced by John Leslie, is that fine-tuning needs explaining because we can see how to explain it. He says, "we ought to be guided by the principle that the neatness of an explanation can help show that an explanation is needed."[6] In another place Leslie writes:

> Our universe's elements do not bear labels announcing whether they are in special need of explanation. A chief (or the only?) reason for feeling that something stands in such need, i.e. for reluctance to dismiss it as just how things happen to be, is that one actually glimpses some tidy way in which it might be explained.[7]

This would solve the problem, but unfortunately it is not correct. For example, if I think that you are being stalked by a gang of assassins, I might explain why you are still alive by saying that you are very lucky or very quick witted. But what if there were never any assassins? The fact that I *could* have explained why you are still alive when I thought there were assassins surely does not mean that I still need to explain it when I find there were none. Or take the case of Mary and Joan who both had pneumonia. I might be able to come up with a neat explanation why Mary recovered when Joan dies: perhaps Mary got penicillin and Joan did not. But do I still need to explain this if I discover later that Joan had not died after all? Certainly not. Or suppose there were a terrible thunderstorm that destroyed many electrical appliances in the area. I could explain why my television is still working by pointing out that it has a built in surge protector. But there was no such storm. Do I still need to explain why my television is working? The lesson is clear. For one to see a tidy way in which something might be explained by no means entails that it really needs explaining.

Another reason advanced by Leslie is that the ability of the universe to sustain life needs explaining because "life truly is something to get excited about—something which would *stand out* against any background which lacked it instead of merging like a cherry into a group of equally exciting fruit."[8] In another place Leslie claims that life has a certain intricacy which "ought to be found specially interesting and in need of explanation."[9] It is hard to know what to make of this. That something is exciting or interesting might be taken as an indication that it is unexpected, and this could indicate the presence of a suitable contrast.

An obvious move at this point is to say that a life-permitting universe needs an explanation because it was and is a very improbable outcome of the big bang. Paul Davies, for instance, says:

> If the big bang was just a random event, then the probability seems *overwhelming* . . . that the emerging cosmic material would be in thermodynamic equilibrium at maximum entropy with zero order. As this was clearly not the case, it appears hard to escape the conclusion that the actual state of the universe has been 'chosen' . . . from the huge number of available states, all but an infinitesimal fraction of which are totally disordered.[10]

Davies says we could imagine a creator equipped with a pin choosing a universe from a vast shopping list. If the creator made a random stab with the pin, the likelihood is overwhelming that the choice will go to a disordered and lifeless world. This idea is echoed by other writers. For example, a recent article on the new design argument quotes an estimate that "the odds against the formation of our universe . . . [are] one in $10,000,000,000^{123}$, a number so large that to call it 'astronomical' would engage in a wild understatement."[11] The physicist Roger Penrose similarly calculates that the odds of getting a universe like ours are equally astronomical—one in ten to the 10^{123} power.[12]

One cannot help feeling that these calculations are very speculative at best. As one philosopher put it:

> While the given 'orchestration' of the basic constants does strike the naive consciousness as being 'wildly improbable,' it is very difficult, if not impossible, to quantify the precise degree of improbability. While it may be true that if the force of gravity were only slightly stronger, the whole universe would have collapsed long ago, it seems quite impossible to calculate *a priori* the probability that gravity would have its present value as opposed to some other possible value.[13]

In any case, it is not necessary to show that the universe is improbable. The fact at issue here, that our universe is life-permitting, would still be in need of explanation even if it were not especially unlikely. Suppose, for example, that one could show that any possible universe must be exactly like ours except that the force of gravity can assume either of two equally probable states, one of which would permit the development of life and one of which would not. In this case the appearance of a life-permitting universe would have odds of 50-50. But I submit that the question "Why was this universe life-permitting?" would make perfectly good sense and would arise. And it would do so even if the odds were in favor of life, say 75-25.

According to the theory sketched above, the question "Why was this universe life-permitting?" arises in case its topic is true and there is a suitable contrast to it. The topic is obviously true, so the only issue which remains is whether we have reason to believe that this universe might have been different in a way that would have rendered it lifeless. I pointed out above that most physicists do believe that the universe which emerged from the big bang could have differed from ours in a number of ways that would have precluded the development of life.[14] I conclude then that the question does arise—on what are currently thought to be the facts of physical cosmology.

One final point before leaving this topic. The question "Why a life-permitting universe?" does not and cannot arise simply from the consideration that another sort of universe is and was logically possible. Any contingent state of affairs has logically possible alternatives, but we saw above that many why-questions, even ones with true topic propositions, nevertheless fail to arise. The belief which gives rise to this question must be that lifeless universes are and were physically possible alternatives that might have appeared after the big bang instead of the present universe. Any view which undercuts this belief would also undercut the question.

3. What Could Explain Fine-Tuning?

Supposing that the question "Why a life-permitting universe rather than a lifeless one?" arises, the next issue is how it might be answered. What explains cosmic fine-tuning?

The new design argument, of course, claims that the best explanation of the fine-tuned universe is that the values of physical constants were deliberately chosen by a creator in order to allow for life. The main competition to this creator hypothesis comes from several theories which claim that there are many universes. According to one version of this view, the big bang might have given rise not to just one universe but to a number of isolated "bubble universes," each with different physical characteristics. Some of these bubble universes by chance may well have just those physical characteristics that would allow life to appear. Another theory builds on the many-worlds interpretation of quantum mechanics which holds that all quantum possibilities are realized in different "branch universes" that cannot communicate with each other. All physically possible universes are realized, and we just happen to be in one that allows for life. Yet another version is the oscillating universe theory. According to this view, the universe oscillates endlessly between big bangs and big crunches, with the physical parameters set at random in each big bang. In this particular cycle, they happen to be set just right for life.[15]

Suppose we compare the creator hypothesis to the various many-universe theories. Is there any way to decide which of these explanations is best? According to John Leslie there is. Leslie claims that the creator hypothesis has the advantage of greater *simplicity*. He writes that

> [O]ne would much like to see some detailed and well-evidenced physical theories explaining how many and varied universes came into being. But, alas, the various available theories are rough and tentative. And some of them may offend too drastically against Ockham's razor . . . . But what, then, *is* the excuse for believing in universes in large numbers and with widely varying natures? The answer is that the only thing which speaks at all powerfully in their favor is something that speaks just as powerfully in favor of design. It is that life's evolution appears to have been made possible only by many extraordinarily delicate adjustments of force strengths . . . .[16]

Leslie's point here is that since none of the theories can claim independent confirmation, we have to judge them as alternative explanations of the same facts. In Leslie's view, all of them—the creator hypothesis as well as many-universe theories—would equally explain the facts of fine-tuning. But they differ markedly in one way. The creator hypothesis postulates only a creator, while the many-universe theories are forced to postulate the existence of alternative universes in vast numbers. The creator hypothesis is in this way much simpler than its competitors.[17]

I think that Leslie is right on two of these points. None of these theories has or is likely to get independent confirmation because they are operating beyond ordinary physical knowledge in attempting to explain a characteristic of the physically known. I will suggest below that they should be properly understood as metaphysical theories. Leslie is also right in saying that the creator hypothesis is simpler and that this should count in favor of it. However, I do not agree that all of these theories equally explain the facts of cosmic fine-tuning. There is a significant difference. The creator hypothesis is a direct answer to the question while the many-universe theories are corrective answers. The creator hypothesis says why the universe is life-permitting, while the many-universe theories deny that there is a reason why and say instead that this universe is life-permitting only by chance.

The question "Why is this universe life-permitting?" arises as we have seen from the affirmation that this universe contains life combined with the belief that this universe could have turned out to be different in a way that would have precluded the appearance of life. It is of course open to anyone to challenge the belief that the universe might have turned out differently, and in fact it seems that Stephen Hawking hopes to do so. Hawking recently said that he would like to find additional laws of physics which would show that the universe had to turn out just as it did.[18] If he succeeds, this would certainly undercut the question by denying the assumed contrast. We could not any longer say that things might have come out differently.

The various many-universe theories, however, do not deny that this universe could have turned out differently. They merely postulate that the way it did turn out was due to chance. They try to make this answer seem more reasonable by holding that there were many such chance events—many rolls of the dice, not just one—so that it is not so terribly surprising that one of them—this universe—got everything just right for life.

The point is not that the many-universe theories are not possible answers to the question "Why is the universe life-permitting?" but rather are corrective answers to it. As such they require more in the way of evidential support than a direct answer. To accept that the question arises and to accept that the universe is life-permitting but could have been otherwise, is to affirm that *prima facie* evidence exists for its life-permitting character. Based on the evidence we think the question has a direct answer. Of course, this can be overturned if we have independent evidence that the result in question happened by chance. This was the point made in the earlier example of explaining why I won the lottery. If we can show that the process leading to p was random, then we can say against the *prima facie* evidence there really was no reason why p.

But the sort of evidence required to show the process leading to p was random is lacking in this case. As noted above, the only evidence we have for any of these theories is that each is capable of explaining why this world is life-permitting. But they do not explain equally. The creator hypothesis accepts the question and provides a direct answer to it; the many-universe theories, by contrast, deny the question and provide a corrective answer to it. It takes more evidence to deny a question than to accept it. The creator hypothesis, then, has a decided advantage over the many-universe theories. In fact, it has two advantages: it is simpler and it is a direct answer to the question. My conclusion here is that the creator hypothesis has a good claim to be the best explanation of cosmic fine-tuning proposed so far.

Conclusion

The argument so far upholds the first two claims of the new design argument: that cosmic fine-tuning does need explaining and that the creator hypothesis is the best explanation of those which have been proposed. The next and final issue is to what extent, if any, we should take this as confirming the truth of the creator hypothesis. I want to suggest that the connection between explanation and confirmation is not as obvious as it may seem and in fact needs to be clarified and defended. I will not be able to do that here, but I will briefly indicate the way in which I think it might be done.

To show that there actually is an issue here it suffices to point out that some writers have denied that there is any connection between confirmation and truth. For example, Bas van Fraassen says that the ability of a theory to explain something—to answer a question—gives us no clue to how accurately the theory describes the world: "Nor can there be any question of explanatory success as providing evidence for the truth of a theory that goes beyond any evidence that we have for its providing an adequate description of the phenomena."[19] Not many people would accept van Fraassen's radical empiricism. But if not, the challenge is to say what connection does hold between a theory's ability to explain something and our decision to accept that theory.

I think that the key point in understanding this connection here is to see that the creator hypothesis and the many-universe theories are *metaphysical theories*. To say that they are metaphysical is just to point out the obvious fact that all of these theories are in fact "world hypotheses"—attempts to give an ultimate explanation of the way the world is. As such they project an hypothesis beyond all that is known in order to explain something about all that is known. The purpose of a metaphysical theory is to explain something at the boundary of knowledge.

To be sure, there are those who claim to have no interest in metaphysics and who do not like a discipline that seems so speculative and so insecure. And there are others who argue that come what may we all do care about metaphysics and cannot avoid taking some positions on the ultimate nature of things. But whatever may be the case here I think it is obvious that, first, if we are going to have a metaphysic at all we are usually going to be forced to choose between competing theories of the universe and, second, that when we do so our main, if not sole, criterion must be to choose the metaphysical theory that does the best job of explaining whatever we are trying to explain. This means, among other things, favoring theories that are clear, simple, and give direct answers over their opposites.

The creator hypothesis and the many-universe theories are not scientific theories even though they resemble scientific theories in postulating an explanation of something. They are not scientific because they are postulating something well beyond the boundaries of what is scientifically known or knowable at this time. That is why it is not appropriate to judge them as J. L. Mackie would by asking whether they provide detailed predictions of phenomena.[20] It is not the purpose of a metaphysical theory to describe the phenomena. Its purpose is to give an explanation which goes somewhat beyond the boundary of scientific knowledge. But here I do want to enter a *caveat*. Metaphysical theories sometimes cross that boundary and become physical theories. For Demokritus and Lucretius the atomic theory was metaphysical, but it is so no longer. Now it is understood as a description of phenomena and is the source of many detailed predictions.

It is also important on the other side to realize that the creator hypothesis is not a theology. To be sure, the "creator" of the creator hypothesis bears only a passing resemblance to Yahweh or Allah, but to make this creator into Yahweh or Allah would be to introduce features which have nothing at all to do with the purpose of the hypothesis: the explanation of cosmic fine-tuning. For this purpose it would be useless to insist that the creator hypothesis be supplemented with the claim that this creator was also the God of Abraham or the one who spoke to Mohammed through the angel Gabriel. But this does not mean that theologians should ignore the design argument. Theologies are not metaphysical theories but they do have metaphysical implications. Theologians should not be uninterested in how well the metaphysical implications of their theologies bear up against opposing interpretations of the universe.

In sum, I think that if we understand that the creator hypothesis is a metaphysical theory, and are clear about what that means, the fact that it is arguably the best explanation of cosmic fine-tuning does speak strongly in its favor. So, the new design argument does prove something after all.

NOTES

[1]The requirement that **p** be true was articulated by Carl Hempel in *Aspects of Scientific Explanation* (The Free Press, 1965), p. 335. The contrast theory is found in Bas van Fraassen, *The Scientific Image* (Clarendon Press, 1980), Chapter 5, and Alan Garfinkel, *Forms of Explanation* (Yale University Press, 1981). I discuss van Fraassen and Garfinkel and compare their views to Hempel in "Discussion: The Contrast Theory of Why-Questions," *Philosophy of Science*, 55 (1988). The view sketched here is a further development of some of the ideas presented in that article.

[2]Cosmic fine-tuning has been the subject of a number of recent works. Some of the more prominent are: Steven Weinberg, *The First Three Minutes*, updated edition (Basic Books, 1988); P. C. W. Davies, *The Accidental Universe* (Cambridge University Press, 1982) and *God and the New Physics* (Simon and Schuster, 1983); B. J. Carr and M. J. Rees, "The Anthropic Principle and the Structure of the Physical World," *Nature*, **278** (1979): 605-612.

[3]Davies, *God and the New Physics*, p. 179.

[4]Ibid., pp. 186-188.

[5]Carr and Rees, "The Anthropic Principle," p. 612.

[6]John Leslie, "Modern Cosmology and the Creation of Life," in *Evolution and Creation*, ed. Ernan McMullin (University of Notre Dame Press, 1985), p. 100.

[7]John Leslie, "How to Draw Conclusions From a Fine-Tuned Cosmos," in Robert John Russell, William R. Stoeger, and George V. Coyne, eds., *Physics, Philosophy, and Theology* (Vatican Observatory, 1988), p. 302.

[8]John Leslie, "Anthropic Principle, World Ensemble, Design," *American Philosophical Quarterly*, **19** (1982): 150.

[9]Leslie, "Modern Cosmology," p. 101.

[10]Davies, *God and the New Physics*, p. 168.

[11]L. Stafford Betty and Bruce Cordell, "God and Modern Science: New Life for the Teleological Argument," *International Philosophical Quarterly*, **27** (1987): 416.

[12]Roger Penrose, *The Emperor's New Mind* (Oxford University Press, 1989), p. 344.

[13]John Jefferson Davis, "The Design Argument, Cosmic 'Fine-Tuning,' and the Anthropic Principle," *International Journal for Philosophy of Religion*, **21** (1987): 145.

[14]This seems to be the consensus view, but there is some dissent. Alan Guth has proposed what he calls an "inflationary model" of the very early universe which would explain some of the balances cited as examples of fine-tuning. See Alan Guth and Paul Steinhardt, "The Inflationary Universe,"

in *The New Physics*, ed. P. C. W. Davies (Cambridge University Press, 1989). Stephen Hawking has suggested that time, like space, might be considered "finite but unbounded"; in this case there would not be a beginning of the universe at a big bang singularity. See his "The Edge of Spacetime" in Davies, *The New Physics*, pp. 68-69.

[15]Many-universe theories are discussed in Ian Barbour, *Religion in an Age of Science* (Harper and Row, 1990), pp. 135-140 and in many of the sources cited earlier: Davies, *God and the New Physics*, pp. 171-174; Leslie, "Anthropic Principle," pp. 145-147 and elsewhere; Betty and Cordell, "God and Modern Science," pp. 417-419; Davis, "The Design Argument," pp. 143-144. Other explanations have been suggested, including the idea that the structure of the universe is due to the presence of observers. However, many-universe theories are still regarded as the only serious competition to the creator hypothesis.

[16]Leslie, "Modern Cosmology," pp. 111-112.

[17]Ibid., pp. 113-114.

[18]Hawking, "The Edge of Spacetime," pp. 68-69.

[19]Van Fraassen, *Scientific Image*, p. 156.

[20]J. L. Mackie, *The Miracle of Theism* (Clarendon Press, 1982), pp. 138-139.

PART III

STUDIES IN THE
HISTORY OF SCIENCE—RELIGION
INTERACTION

WILLIAM MCDOUGALL AND THE REACTION AGAINST VICTORIAN SCIENTIFIC NATURALISM

MARK SHALE

During the Jubilee-year celebration of Queen Victoria's reign, Thomas Henry Huxley, the leading spokeman and defender of scientific naturalism, proudly announced that Francis Bacon's ideal of science "coming to the aid of man's estate," had become reality. Huxley claimed there now existed a "new Nature created by science" which formed

> the foundation of our wealth and the condition of our safety . . . ;
> it is the bond which unites into a solid political whole, regions larger
> than any empire of antiquity; it secures us from the recurrence of
> pestilences and famines of former times; it is the source of endless
> comforts and conveniences, which are not mere luxuries, but
> conduce to physical and moral well-being.[1]

The influence of science had become so pervasive that it had "fully transformed" the life of the average Victorian and brought about an "almost complete reorientation in the thought and expectations of men and society."[2] George Henry Lewes, positivist, historian, psychologist, and a member of Huxley's camp, added his own praise of the advancement of science, saying, "in the struggle for life with the facts of existence, Science is a bringer of aid; in the struggle of the soul with the mystery of existence, Science is a bringer of light."[3]

The optimism of Huxley and Lewes was shared by their compatriots, a loosely allied group that historian Frank Miller Tuner has called the Victorian scientific naturalists. They included such notables as the social philosopher and social Darwinist Herbert Spencer; Charles Darwin's cousin, the founder of the eugenics movement and modern statistics, Francis Galton; the physicist John Tyndall; the outspoken mathematician at University College, London, W. K. Clifford; and the anthropologists Edward Tylor and John Lubbock. Although these individuals differed on the particulars, they agreed on the general character of Huxley's New Nature and the methods to be used in understanding it.

The Victorian scientific naturalists viewed the knowable universe as mechanical and materialistic. It conformed to the metaphor of the Newtonian world-machine, a conception of nature in which only physical phenomena existed, phenomena which were ultimately reducible to particles of matter that moved according to the laws of mechanics. The knowledge and understanding of this mechanical universe could not come from revelation, which the scientific naturalists believed was tantamount to superstition; nor could it come from metaphysics, which the physician and physiological psychologist Henry Maudsley said was "nothing more than supernaturalism writ fine." Knowledge could only come from an empirical approach tempered with the method of experimental science. Science so conducted would lead to "truth," "the description of the phenomena of the external world . . . and [the] description of the law of [the] succession and coexistences of those phenomena."[4] The only truths accessible to humanity—and those on which a new, better world would be built—were defined by the naturalists' own conception of the methods used in the physical sciences: empiricism, experimentalism, and reductionism.[5] Concepts that defied reduction to mechanistic/materialistic explanation, such as the human spirit or soul, an efficacious consciousness, or a mind capable of free will, were not merely beyond the purview of science, so defined, but illusions. Indeed, for the psychology of the Victorian naturalists the "mind" was little more than a passive agent in experience: it received sense impressions of the material world which arranged themselves according to the mechanical laws of association.

Scientific naturalists saw the great achievements of nineteenth-century science—Dalton's atomic hypothesis, the conservation of energy concept, and Darwin's theory of evolution—as achievements that came without the help of, or in spite of, Christianity, and they thought it imperative that humanity take itself out of the hands of traditional priests and ministers and instead place its destiny in the hands of a priesthood of scientists. In the world-view of the Victorian scientific naturalists there was no room for traditional Christianity with its emphasis on human sin, the saving power of God's grace, or divine revelation as an avenue to truth. Yet, as historian of science A. Hunter Dupree has convincingly demonstrated,[6] they recognized the *power* that relgious beliefs, rituals, and institutions had over society, even if the basis for them was no more than superstitious carry-overs from a more primitive age. Accordingly, Huxley, the self-appointed high priest of the movement, repeatedly borrowed Christian symbols in his effort to bring others into what he called the "church scientific." He wished for nothing less than to be a leader of what he called a "new Reformation" in which the divinely revealed "truths" of Christianity would be supplanted by the empirically demonstrated truths of science. In a letter to Charles Kingsley, an Anglican clergyman sympathic to the aims of science, Huxley preached,

If that great and powerful instrument for good or evil, the Church of England, is to be saved from being shivered into fragments by the advancing tide of science . . . it must be by the efforts of men who, like yourself, see your way to the combination of the practice of the Church with the spirit of science. Understand that all the younger men of science whom I know intimately are *essentially* of my way of thinking . . . . Understand that *this new school of prophets is the only one that can work miracles*, that it is right and you will comprehend that it is of no use to try to barricade us with shovel hats and aprons, or to talk about our *doctrines* being "shocking" [my emphasis].[7]

The Anglican church was to be reformed and would become a nineteenth-century version of Bacon's Salomon's House, where ignorance of science was sin and salvation lay in accepting the power of the scientific method as defined by Huxley's Holy Office of scientific naturalists.

Not all philosophers and scientists near the end of the nineteenth century wished to follow Darwin's apostle into the "church scientific," at least, that is, they did not want to join an institution that had as its dogma the philosophy of scientific naturalism. For them, scientific dogma was just as damaging to the advancement of scientific knowledge as theological dogma. Among those who rejected the creed of scientific naturalism was the psychologist William McDougall. McDougall was the junior member of a small but influential group of prominent scientists and English men of letters who chose to battle the Philistines of scientific mechanism, and to argue no less zealously for a philosophy of science that was not bound by mechanistic materialism. The group included such notables as biologist Alfred Russel Wallace, animal behaviorist George John Romanes, writer Samuel Butler, psychical researcher Frederic W. H. Meyers, philosopher Henry Sidgwick, and psychologists James Ward and G. F. Stout.

McDougall was a full generation younger than the others but he vigorously carried their banner against scientific naturalism out of the nineteenth and three decades into the twentieth century. He was eminently well-qualified to do so. Possessing a medical degree from Cambridge University, which included a four-year neurophysiology residency under Charles Sherrington at St. Thomas Hospital in London, McDougall had engaged in anthropological field work in the Torres Straits and spent a year in the physiological psychology laboratory of G. E. Müller in Göttingen. He held academic positions first at University College, London, then Cambridge and Oxford, where he carried on a vigorous research program in experimental psychology. In 1920 he immigrated to the United States to accept the William James Chair of Philosophy and Psychology at Harvard, and in 1927 became Chairman of the Duke University Department of Psychology. At

Duke he and his graduate students J. B. and Louisa Rhine established the world's first laboratory devoted exclusively to research into parapsychology.[8] Over a career that spanned nearly forty years, McDougall wrote twenty-two books, including the groundbreaking *An Introduction to Social Psychology* (1908), which went through thirty-three editions. He also published 150 research articles and reviews. Superbly trained, possessed of a penetrating intellect, acerbic, and contentious, McDougall was recognized by his peers as among the most articulate and formidable opponents of scientific naturalism.

McDougall opposed scientific naturalism not just because he thought it inadequate to explain the phenomena of life and mind, but because he thought it morally imperative to do so. Religion was the bedrock on which the moral and ethical values of culture rested. The major religions of the world, past and present, had at their center belief in a being or beings that were spiritual, not mechanical, in character, and such religions appealed to a spiritual essence in man that caused him to transcend the animal aspect of his nature. Take away the spiritual aspect of life and only a shell of a man or of civilization remained. McDougall said, "There is no good reason to think that in the absence of such beliefs, any high moral tradition could have been evolved by any branch of the human race. Are we then justified in assuming that, if the foundations are sapped away, the superstructure of moral tradition will continue to stand unshaken and unimpaired, powerful to govern conduct through the long ages to come? I gravely doubt it."[9]

Huxley's religion of science, McDougall believed, could not provide adequate guidance for individuals to live meaningful lives because its mechanistic philosophy was inadequate to address fundamental issues of human existence: For what purpose am I here? Why should I act morally? Is there life after death? If so, what will it be like? Equally reprehensible was the dogmatic claim of Huxley, Tyndall, Clifford, and their compatriots that the methodology of scientific naturalism was the sole means to truth. Their methodology required the reduction of phenomena to discrete units of matter, precluding even the possibility of a spiritual, or non-material, existence. That people of all cultures the world over subscribed to some kind of belief in a deity or deities, to an afterlife, and made claims of witnessing miracles or ghostly apparitions of one kind or another, were phenomena that could not be rightfully dismissed from scientific investigation simply because they defied explanation according to a "billiard-ball" model of mechanism. McDougall, and those like him, believed the quest for the spiritual an essential undertaking for individuals in order to lead purposeful, meaningful lives and to strive for improvement in the human condition. He said,

> If materialism is true, human life, fundamentally and generally speaking, is not worth living; and men and women who believe

materialism is true will not in the long run think themselves justified in creating, in calling to life, new individuals to meet the inevitable pains and sorrows and labours of life and the risks of many things far worse than death. Human life as we know it is a tragic and pathetic affair, which can only be redeemed by some belief, or at least some hope, in a larger significance than is compatible with the creed of materialism, no matter how nobly stoic a form it may be held.[10]

Like his older counterparts, McDougall was not a traditional Christian and never intended that his efforts to combat a materialist philosophy of science be interpreted as a defense of orthodox Christianity, whether it be Protestantism in general, Anglicanism in particular, or Catholicism.[11] Neither he nor they believed in original sin, the incarnation, redemption, the second coming of Christ, the power of prayer, or the Bible as divinely inspired. Thus their intent was not to defend a "Biblical scientism," as had the authors of the Bridgewater Treatises or as had William Paley with his "watchmaker" analogy, nor to prove or find evidence for the existence of God. In fact, they abhorred the efforts of clergymen to reconcile Scripture with Nature. But they believed themselves religious men in the sense that they engaged in a search for what Ward referred to as "a supreme spiritual unity" and Meyers called the "essential spirituality of the universe."[12]

In their search for this "spritual unity," McDougall and his compatriots insisted upon using an empirical method and experimental investigation. That involved not only carefully controlled techniques of introspection to analyze conscious experience, it also requried the control—as far as it was possible—of conditions under which occurred alleged supra-normal phenomena: trance mediums, automatic writing, telepathy, apparitions, and so forth. All were engaged in what was called psychical research, and some, such as Wallace and Meyers, became avowed believers in spiritualism, that is, that the souls of the dead continued to exist and communicate with the living. Like doubting Thomas of the gospels, they were not content merely to believe on faith in a world beyond mechanism, they needed evidence that forces beyond those known to physics and chemistry existed.

For the scientific naturalists that was a paradoxical position, one which raised the old interactionist issue of Descartes: how is it possible for that which is not matter to influence matter? If belief in a world on the other side of this one rested on the necessity of experiencing it directly, then that world must also be physical for the senses reacted only to the physical.[13] McDougall's intent was to show that a paradox, in fact, did not exist because the paradox itself was due to the false premise of materialism that lay behind Victorian scientific naturalism. Using his early experiments on consciousness and the psychology of perception, McDougall developed a view of nature and of mind contrary to the world view of the scientific naturalists.

In their account of the mind, Huxley, Spencer, and the scientific naturalists claimed that "consciousness" was merely a byproduct of the neural activities in the brain. It had no causal efficacy at all in behavior. It was, as Huxley claimed, an epiphenomenon as powerless to alter the course of neural processes and behavior as was the whistling of a locomotive to change the motion of its wheels.[14] McDougall responded that based upon the theory of evolution, which the scientific naturalists themselves ardently championed, such an answer did not make sense. If consciousness was useless, then why in the evolution of life had neural processes which had consciousness as a correlate come to play an increasingly large role relative to the unconscious processes of reflex action? To McDougall, the theory of evolution dictated a growth in consciousness because it was a useful, purposive agent: it gave the organism a selective advantage in the struggle for life. McDougall said,

> We have learnt to believe from innumerable instances, among which there is no established exception, that any phenomenon constantly appearing in every group of animals has, or has had, a useful part to play in the developemnt of the individual of the species, and the more constant and widely distributed the phenomenon, the more certain is this inference. This special case of teleology has acquired a strong and reasonable basis in the theory of natural selection.[15]

To explain, in part, what was occuring in the mind, McDougall turned to the newly formulated energy concept. The physicist James Prescott Joule, along with Huxley, Tyndall, and Spencer, interpreted the energy concept according to their own philosophy of science: energy was the result of atoms and molecules in motion. But physicists Ernst Mach and Wilhelm Ostwald, and the physiologist William Benjamin Carpenter, rejected the "billiard-balls-in-motion" model of nature and interpreted energy as an abstraction. Ostwald and Mach, physicists of enormous prestige, warned scientists against interpreting physical processes as solely caused by matter in motion.[16] McDougall quoted Ostwald as writing that matter was "nothing but a group of various forms of energy coordinated in space, and all that we may try to say of matter is really said of those energies." Mach had a somewhat different perspective but agreed that "when we treat of matter mechanically we are regarding it from only one of many posssible aspects."[17] Carpenter, emphasizing that interconvertibility of forms of energy depended on appropriate physical conditions, claimed that unique energy transformations occurred in living organisms. If one stimulated a nerve with an electric current, the *electrical* energy became *nerve* energy; when a nerve excited an electrical organ (as in an electric eel), a reverse transformation occurred. These interpretations of Mach, Ostwald, and Carpenter helped inform McDougall's own theory of the mind and its operation.[18]

McDougall developed what he called a "psycho-physical" model of the mind. On the physical side was the nervous system, which provided the physical conduits for transmission of nerve energy, which he also called "neurin," "neurokyme," or "psychic energy." He thought it legitimate to form the hypothesis that neurin was a fluid, for "just as the fluid theory of heat, the two-fluid theory of electricity and the corpuscular theory of light furnished probably the most useful working conceptions for the sciences of heat, electricity, and light at certain stages of their development," so would neurin serve as a basis for understanding psycho-physical processes.[19] Although it was tempting, he said, to regard it as a known form of energy, such as electricity or magnetism, neurin was different. Consciousness, the "psychical" side of the model, so far as anyone knew, was *only* associated with energy transformations *within* the body and it was *purposive*, it operated to direct the organism toward a goal. Therefore, he said, "the forms of energy concerned must be of a highly special and peculiar nature" that obeyed laws as yet undiscovered by science.[20] Neurin propagated through the nervous system by traversing the synaptic gaps among neurons. Transmission of sufficient neurin across a numerically sufficient number of synaptic gaps resulted in the phenomenon of consciousness. But because the individual experienced consciousness as a "unitary" phenomenon, McDougall believed it necessary to hypothesize an agent—the soul—to bring about that unification. It thus served the purpose analogous to that of the concept of ether in physics. Just as physicists, who desired more than mathematical equations for describing the effects of radiant energy, light, electricity, and magetism, postulated an ether to serve as the medium for the propagation of those energies, so did McDougall postulate a soul as the medium of propagation and unification for the energy released at the synapses. Thus consciousness was not a "thing," not a substance, but a disturbance in the soul much like a magnetic field was a disturbance in the ether. Searching for an analogy to represent his interpretation of consciousness, he turned to the phenomena manifest by wires when an electric current passed through them. Consciousness produced by the neurons in the brain was the analog of the magnetic field produced around the wires. Consciousness was as real as the magnetic field. Both were inferred from their ability to affect the behavior of physical objects: a compass needle in the case of magnetism, the neuro-muscular system in the case of consciousness.

With this model McDougall was able to provide an explanation for how consciousness, a non-material entity, could affect neural processes. The principle he invoked was the inductive influence that electric currents and magnetic fields have on each other. His explanation ran as follows. Imagine two wires, A and B. Passing a current through A results in a magnetic field around it; sending a different current through B creates a magnetic field about it different from the one surrounding wire A. However, if the two wires are side-by-side, McDougall noted, the currents and magnetic fields of each are changed due to a reciprocal electromagnetic influence. If other wires are added and currents passed through each of them, the addition of each one would modify in some way the magnetic fields of the others and, hence, the flow of current in them. In a similar way consciousness affected neural processes. Using that example to sum up his psycho-physical model of the mind, McDougall wrote,

> In this crude simile the wires stand for nervous arcs, the electric current for the flow of nervous energy [i.e., neurin] through each arc, the magnetic field generated by the current in each wire flowing separately for a psychical element, and the total magnetic field, when several or many wires are in action, for the state of consciousness. . . . Are the wires the only existents presupposed by, and necessary to, the production of these effects? Is all else fleeting process? No, we are compelled to postulate, as a necessary condition of the development of the magnetic field, a medium or substance which we call ether. Just so we are compelled to postulate an existent, an immaterial being, in which the separate neural processes produce the elementary affections which we have called psychical elements, and this we call the soul. The soul then is the ground of unity of psychical process, of individual consciousness.[21]

The early experiments McDougall performed in a search for evidence to support his hypothesis of efficacious concsciousness were on spatial reorientation and binocular rivalry. The first phenomenon revealed itself when observing a "reversible cube" like the one to the right. In the experiments he conducted McDougall discovered that as one stares at the cube a spatial reordering occurs, with the bottom of the cube suddenly be-

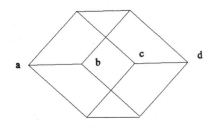

Reversible Cube

coming its side. The "meaning" of the cube changed: it may be seen as a cube with edge "a b" nearest the eye, or as one with edge "c d" nearest, or it may simply appear as a flat drawing. This shift in meaning could occur without any apparent expenditure of "psychical energy." He noted, however, that it was possible "to will" a change in the spatial configuration, to alter the meaning of the drawing. He hypothesized that the psychical phenomenon of "willing" affected brain processes and produced a neural reordering. He said the mind "may influence the processes whose phenomena we conceive as brain-processes in a way which would appear to us a spatial redistribution of energy or transference of energy from one part of the brain to another . . . and without alteration of the quantity of energy." In other words, the "meaning" we give to objects was the initial product of psychical energy affecting the soul and was not directly caused by physical processes in the brain.[22]

McDougall's claim directly contradicted the sensori-motor explanation of volition that predominated in psychology at the turn of the century. Alexander Bain, Wilhelm Wundt, Hermann von Helmholtz, and Ernst Mach all defended the position that volition required a "feeling of innervation" in the muscles prior to the willful act. That is, in addition to the memory of past muscular sensations that stemmed from the commission of a similar act, the individual had a kinaesthetic sense of which muscles of the body would be used before he used them. Without such a sense, they claimed, volition was impossible.[23] Thus association psychologists would explain the change in the reorientation of the cube as due to the sensori-motor fluctuations of the eye muscles and not the result of transferrence of psychical energy.

McDougall prepared an experiment to exclude the possibility that the change in reorientation of the cube was due to sensori-motor fluctuations. William James had supplied helpful clues for its design. In *The Principles of Psychology* James had pointed out that clinical evidence revealed anaesthetic patients could perform acts without any feelings whatsoever in their limbs. McDougall performed experiments in binocular rivalry in which he paralyzed the muscles of his visually strongest eye with atropine and verified that through an effort of will he could significantly change the rate of fluctuation between two different fields presented before each eye.[24]

McDougall believed his vision experiments gave results of tremendous significance. The Victorian scientific naturalists previously had the advantage over anyone who attempted to explain consciousness and volition in any terms other than sensori-motor psychology. To claim that consciousness and volition were due to a mysterious power or faculty of the mind was, for naturalists, to earn the appellation of "vitalist" and, hence, "unscientific." McDougall thought his discoveries invalidated those charges. The "will" was not simply a feeling of innervation that resulted from neurochemical brain processes leading to an action; it represented the conscious transference of patterns of neural energy from one area of the brain to another. He thought the evidence of the power of volition, of conscious purpose, acting independently of the motor system vindicated the position he shared with James, Ward, Sidgwick, and Stout that mechanistic material-ism was inadequate to explain the phenomena of both life and mind.[25] One can detect the cautious triumph and relief he felt when writing the conclusion to his paper on the attention process:

> I suggest then that, while all attention involves concentration or convergence of free nervous energy from all or many parts of the brain into some one neural system, voluntary effort results in a further degree of this concentration of energy. . . . It is here, if anywhere, that the interactionist must seek in the insufficiency of physical causes *evidence of psychical efficiency*; here possibly we have a residual effect which . . . may be *evidence of psychical guidance of physical process*. If such power of guidance be granted to the interactionist, he has all that is needed for his purposes. *The world is then not purely mechanical*, and biological evolution may be regarded as increasingly teleological, as swayed in an ever-increasing degree by final causes, and we may hopefully look forward to the time when man will control by voluntary effort the further evolution of his species.[26]

McDougall's conclusions were met with the greatest interest by individuals pursuing psychical research. The idea that consciousness was similar to a magnetic field effect which could influence neural processes gave psychical researchers a powerful theoretical boost. Telepathy, in particular, which seemed inexplicable by the tenets of scientific naturalism, seemed a more plausible possibility after McDougall's work, because it was a reasonable hypothesis that a "conscious field" produced by one mind could influence another.[27] As a member of the BSPR, president of the American Society for Psychical Research, and a founder of the Boston Society for Psychical Research, McDougall never tired of championing psychical research as a field of science which he believed was the foremost hope of combating the "destroying tide of materialism against which revealed religion and metaphysical philosophy [were] equally helpless."[28]

One can see that McDougall fought against the Victorian scientific naturalists with weapons from a common arsenal: principles of physics, evolutionary biology, empiricism, and experiment. They also shared a belief that the sea of faith which had once surrounded their world was now, to borrow a phrase from Matthew Arnold, "retreating to the breath of the night wind, down the vast edges drear and naked shingles of the world." McDougall and the naturalists believed that, in the future, science was to be the final arbiter of truth. The scientific naturalists wished to transform a religion of faith into a rational religion of science. So, in effect, did McDougall. The principal difference was that McDougall desired to preserve what he thought was the essence of religion—the quest for the spiritual—within the body of science itself.

NOTES

[1]Thomas Henry Huxley, *Collected Essays* (D. Appleton, 1894), vol. 1, p. 51; Frank Miller Turner, *Between Science and Religion: The Reaction to Scientific Naturalism in Late Victorian England* (Yale University Press, 1974), p. 8. Miller's book provides an excellent, succinct summary of the position of the Victorian scientific naturalists.

[2]Quoted in Turner, *Between Science and Religion*, p. 8.

[3]George Henry Lewes, "On the Dread and Dislike of Science," *Fortnightly Review* **29** (1878): 805.

[4]Henry Maudsley, *Natural Causes and Supernatural Seemings* (Kegan Paul, Trench and Company, 1886), p. 104; Turner, *Between Science and Religion*, p. 18.

[5]See Thomas Henry Huxley, "On Improving Natural Knowledge," in *Collected Essays*, vol. 1, p. 41.

[6]A. Hunter Dupree, "Christianity and the Scientific Community," in *God and Nature: Historical Essays on the Encounter Between Christianity and Science*, ed. David C. Lindberg and Ronald L. Numbers (University of California Press, 1986), pp. 351-368. See especially pp. 362-365.

[7]Leonard Huxley, *Life and Letters of Thomas Henry Huxley*, 2 vols. (D. Appleton, 1901), vol 1., p. 238.

[8]Many of the important details regarding the high points of McDougall's life are recalled in his short autobiography in Carl Murchison, ed. *A History of Psychology in Autobiography*, 6 vols. (Clark University Press, 1930), vol. 1, pp. 191-223.

[9]William McDougall, "The Need for Psychical Research," in *Religion and the Sciences of Life* (Duke University Press, 1934), p. 57. This article was originally an address delivered in Boston on May 25, 1922 to the American Society for Psychical Research.

[10]Ibid., p. 58.

[11]McDougall, "Autobiography," in Murchison, pp. 196-197.

[12]James Ward, *The Realm of Ends or Pluralism and Theism* (Cambridge University Press, 1911), p. 185; Frederic W. H. Meyers, *Science and a Future Life with Other Essays* (Macmillan, 1893), p. 131.

[13]The German psychologist Wilhelm Wundt said, "I see in spiritualism . . . a sign of the materialism and barbarism of our time. From early times . . . materialism has had two forms; the one denies the spiritual, the other transforms it into matter." From "Letter to Prof. Hermann Ulric," *Popular Science Monthly* 15 (September 1879): 593. Also see Robert Laurence Moore, *In Search of White Crows: Spiritualism, Parapsychology, and American Culture* (Oxford University Press, 1977), pp. 23-24.

[14]Thomas Henry Huxley, "On the Hypothesis that Animals are Automata and Its History [1874]," in *Collected Essays*, 9 vols. (Georg Olms Verlag Hildescheim, 1970), pp. 199-250.

[15]William McDougall, "A Contribution Towards an Improvement in Psychological Method," *Mind*, New Series, 7 (1898): 27.

[16]Thomas Kuhn, "Energy Conservation as an Example of Simultaneous Discovery," in *Critical Problems in the History of Science*, ed. Marshall Clagett (University of Wisconsin Press, 1959), pp. 321-356.

[17]McDougall, "Towards an Improvement in Psychological Method," pp. 25-26, quotations of Ostwald and Mach appear on p. 385.

[18]William Benjamin Carpenter, "On the Mutual Relations of the Vital and Psychical Forces," *Philosophical Transactions of the Royal Society of London*, part 2, 140 (1850): 727-757; Thomas S. Hall, *History of General Physiology*, 2 vols. (University of Chicago Press, 1969), vol.2, pp. 272-274. It is interesting to note that Ostwald also had a theory of consciousness as the product of energy transformations in the nervous system very similar to McDougall's theory. See his *Vorlesungen über Naturphilosophie* (Leipzig, 1902). McDougall, "Towards an Improvement in Psychological Method," pp. 385-386; McDougall, "On the Seat of the Psycho-Physical Process," *Brain* 24 (1901): 614.

[19]McDougall, "On the Seat of the Psycho-Physical Processes," p. 614.

[20]Ibid., p. 615.

[21]McDougall, *Physiological Psychology* (J. M. Dent, 1905), pp. 167-169.

[22]McDougall, *Body and Mind: A History and Defense of Animism* (Methuen, 1911), pp. 215, 308-311; Harold G. McCurdy, "William McDougall," in *Historical Roots of Contemporary Psychology*, ed. Benjamin B. Wolman (Harper and Row, 1968), pp. 116-117.

[23]James provides an excellent summary account of the theory of innervation in *The Principles of Psychology*, 2 vols. (Henry Holt, 1890), vol. 2, ch. 24, "Will," pp. 486-591.

[24]McDougall, *Body and Mind*, pp. 215, 308-311; McCurdy, "William McDougall," pp. 116-117.

[25]McDougall, "Physiological Factors of the Attention Process (IV)," *Mind*, New Series **15** (1906): 359.

[26]Ibid.

[27]A modified version of McDougall's idea emerged in the 1920s among psychical researchers, who referred to telepathy as "mental radio," and numerous experiments to uncover telepathic ability were performed in France, the United States and Great Britain. The French chemical engineer Rene Warcollier, for example, in explaining the theoretical basis for a series of experiments he conducted to discover telepathic abilities, extended McDougall's hypothesis: "like wireless, telepathy requires some sort of harmony, or tuning, between stations . . . . But the analogy cannot be pressed too far, since telepathy uses no code, does not seem to operate at a determinable speed, and apparently does not obey the inverse square law. . . . In any case, keeping the lessons of modern physics in mind allows us to understand . . . how the vibrations . . . can influence by induction other nervous systems in other brains." See Rene Warcollier, *La Telepathie; recherches experimentales* (Alcan, 1921), p. 337. The term "mental radio" owed its popularity to Upton Sinclair's book *Mental Radio* (Monrovia, California: privately published, 1930), which was Sinclair's report of "his wife's apparently laregely successful attempts to reproduce telepathically" drawings that he had made.

[28]McDougall, "The Need for Psychical Research," in *Religion and the Sciences of Life*, p. 59. For an excellent discussion of the directions psychical research took in the twentieth century and the role played by McDougall and his

graduate student J. B. Rhine, see Seymour H. Mauskopf and Michael R. McVaugh, *The Elusive Science: Origins of Experimental Psychical Research* (Johns Hopkins University Press, 1980).

A CLASH OF WILLS:
VOLUNTARISM IN THE THOUGHT OF ROBERT BOYLE

RON LEVY

1. The Traditional Voluntarist Thesis and its Limitations

When he referred to law, Robert Boyle (1627-1691) made some astounding comments. These are his words: "I look upon law as a moral, not a physical cause, as being indeed but a notional thing, according to which, an intelligent and free agent is bound to regulate its actions."[1] With this thought, Boyle addresses the conception of laws of nature, the physical laws of universal order so fundamental to modern assumptions. In the later seventeenth-century such assumptions were just in the making; as these words suggest, Boyle could not simply accept physical laws of nature, at least not without qualification. Confessing his confusion, he acknowledges something enigmatic about their very conception.

Robert Boyle's legacy takes root in his genius for observation and analysis. As a founding member of London's Royal Society, his fame as a brilliant virtuoso was only eclipsed by his younger contemporary, Isaac Newton. He was perhaps the first great experimental scientist working in a distinctly modern vein.[2] If the conceptions of laws of nature confused him, it was not for lack of wit. Boyle's concerns were both frank and simple, the practical concerns of a man of common sense. He asks questions which might perplex anyone who thinks seriously of what laws of nature imply. "It is plain," he says, "that nothing but an intellectual Being can be properly capable of receiving and acting by a law. For if it does not understand, it cannot know what the will of the legislator is."[3] "Inanimate bodies," he elsewhere concludes, "are utterly incapable of understanding what a law is, or what it enjoins, or when they act conformably to it."[4] In other words, Boyle suggests that one cannot properly say that any purely corporeal, non-thinking entity behaves in accordance with "law."

The simplistic candor of Boyle's perplexity makes his comments all the more astounding. For one thing, the conception of laws of nature had already become central to the new science when Boyle worked in the later seventeenth-century. Boyle's work overlapped with Newton's, and when Newton devised his brilliant laws of cosmic order he was only perfecting what such men as Kepler and Descartes had attempted generations before. No doubt, Boyle knew well of Newton's use of law, as he also did of

Descartes', a knowledge to which Boyle's own statements give testimony.[5] It thus seems odd that the very conception of nature's laws should pose such problems to Boyle, for it was essential to the new language of science.

But these statements are surprising in yet a further sense: they sound so unlike the Boyle whom scholars have recently portrayed. Generations of students have encountered Boyle only through the law bearing his name, and while the significance of "Boyle's Law" itself has receded from the fore of recent scholarship,[6] the commentary has nonetheless reiterated Boyle's respect for laws of nature. I refer explicitly to the portrayal cast by an important and influential group of commentators who interpret Boyle's appeal to law in terms of his fundamental theological convictions.[7] They cast Boyle within the broad context of the theological voluntarism of the Reformation, and particularly of seventeenth-century England. Theirs is a tremendously provocative portrayal, and warrants some consideration.

The voluntarist thesis, or the "traditional" voluntarist thesis, as I shall call it, defines a prominent historiographical posture. It serves to relate theology and epistemology in such fashion as to explain the manner of seventeenth-century natural philosophy. The thesis finds base in formulations according the will of God a preeminence over and above all other of the divine attributes—formulations of theological voluntarism. While conceptions of a willing God exist in all periods of Christian thought, historians have been drawn to a particular flourish of theological voluntarism attributed to the Protestant Reformation.

Both Luther and Calvin explain this Protestant orientation. They appeal to a God of unbound omnipotence whose power is but divine will made manifest. "God . . . foresees, purposes and does all things according to His immutable, eternal and infallible will,"[8] Luther had declared, for "God is God . . . whose will . . . is itself the measure."[9] Such statements, of course, permeate the Catholic, and even the Hebraic commentary; but they take on special meaning in the Reformation. Recall that the Reformation flared over issues of the efficacy of works over faith, and the relation of each to grace and salvation. Luther and Calvin were unequivocally clear: grace is a unilateral gesture of God, it cannot be solicited, as it is a pure act of God's unprovoked will. Divine will thus becomes central to Protestant thought, and particularly so, commentators have claimed, within the Puritan setting of seventeenth-century England.

As Perry Miller, the undisputed dean of Puritan scholarship, explained, "the Puritans . . . emphasized certain conceptions of [God] at the expense of others, and even came close to identifying these conceptions with His essence."[10] In consequence, absolute sovereignty became the essential defining attribute of God. Miller continued:

the Puritan's intense belief in unremitting supervision by a supernatural power, coupled with his equally intense awareness that the power was beyond human comprehension, made it difficult for him to speculate about the reasons for God's actions or to discover clearly wherein they were always good. Meanwhile, what befell him in life . . . 'this Will of God, is the First Cause of all things,' and we cannot understand it or trace its logic.'[11]

By virtue of this emphasis on divine will, Puritan's propound a voluntarist theology. And this informs the cast of mind in seventeenth-century England.[12]

I do not seek to defend this portrayal, but rather to note its consistency and its implications. Theological voluntarism, as Miller's description reveals, speaks directly of the creative prowess of God. In so doing it informs natural philosophy. If the Creator, in relation to man, is first and foremost a willing God, then the natural order, as man understands it, exists first and foremost as the consequence of divine will.

This premise generates a nexus of thought. In accepting nature as the consequence of an omnipotently willing God, man inevitably acknowledges the ineptitude of his own faculties of intellection. A deity whose creative prowess stems from his omnipotent will shows no respect for human understanding; in short, divine will far transcends human reason, and the voluntarist can in no way apprehend the essential design of the created order. The rationalist's project, as found in such thinkers as Descartes or Leibniz, dissolves outright.

Trusting the integrity of human reason and allying it directly with the realm of divine ideas, Descartes had sought to uncover the truths of creation by properly engaging human thought. Cartesians thinkers insisted that the human mind, when rightly directed, could apprehend the divine ideas compelling the design of creation. The rationalist thus allies the order of nature and the order of knowledge; his certainty is rooted in a direct appeal to divine reason. But the ascendence of divine will severs this alliance and bars this appeal: the theological voluntarist has no choice but to seek a different route to apprehend the natural order.

Rather than presuming to emulate divine reason to discern the truths of nature, in the manner of the rationalist, the voluntarist respects the bounds of man's intellect. In consequence, he appeals directly to the observed facts of creation, querying only what the divine has actually and in fact willed into being. From here he may slowly and carefully piece together the truths of the created order. As Francis Bacon, the great philosopher of empiricism, had insisted,

the universe to the eye of the human understanding is framed like
a labyrinth . . . . No excellence of wit . . . can overcome such
difficulties as these. Our steps must be guided by a clue, and the
whole way from the very first perception of the senses must be laid
out upon a sure plan.[13]

For Bacon, experimentation provided this clue.[14] With collective effort, the
order of nature and the order of knowledge will fall into alliance over time,
but this alliance is always tentative, never absolute. This describes the
epistemology of the nominalist and the empiricist, the precise epistemological orientation of the new experimental science of seventeenth-century
England.

A host of important scholars have unveiled early modern science in this
light, carefully and convincingly arguing this relation between religion and
epistemology, and depicting its manifestation in natural philosophy.[15] The
richness of the traditional voluntarist thesis lies in its far ranging scope and
integrative synthesis. Its fundamental heuristic takes root in the nature of
the man-God relation, and from this spins a provocative nexus of ideas
embracing issues of cosmology, ontology, and epistemology. Its founding
principle, and the reason that English Puritanism serves so well to illustrate
the thesis, relies on post-lapsarian man and his severed link with God.
God's will attains primacy at the cost of human integrity and potential. Man
emerges as both inconsequential and inept in the face of his magnificent
Creator. Recognizing this immense disparity between himself and the forces
of creation, man relies upon the modest epistemology of the empiricist to
assert cautious, carefully induced truths of the created order. Founded on
the severed relation of man and God, the traditional voluntarist thesis is
constructed upon what I label as a *disjunctive* voluntarism.

This thesis has been used, and rightly, I think, to account for Boyle's
epistemology. Man's understanding is a function of his relation to an
omnipotently willing God. Boyle says this precisely: "The distance betwixt
the infinite creator and the creatures, which are but the limited and arbitrary
productions of his power and will is so vast, that all the divine attributes or
perfections do by unmeasurable intervals transcend those faint resemblances
of them, that he has been pleased to impress, either upon other creatures,
or upon us men."[16] Denying man's apprehension of the essential truths
of the Creator, Boyle concedes his apprehension of the essential truths of the
created order only to a slightly greater extent. This is his explanation:

For, whatever our self-love may incline us to imagine, we are really
but created and finite beings . . . and we come into the world but
such, as it pleased the almighty and most free author of our nature
to make us. And from this dependency and limitedness of our

natures, It follows . . . that the means or measures, which are furnished us to employ in the searching or judging of truth, are but such as are proportionable to God's designs in creating us, and therefore may probably be supposed not to be capable of reaching to all kinds . . . of truths . . . has given us light enough to perceive, that we cannot attain to a clear and full knowledge of them.[17]

Boyle casts man at great distance from a willful God. By divine intent, man must struggle for those few certain truths he can ascertain. And he does this, as Boyle says, by "convers[ing] with things themselves."[18] Such is the manner of experimentation.

This is how theological voluntarism generates Boyle's epistemology, accounting for his empirical mode of thought. I endorse this explanation. But the same voluntarism has been evoked to explain Boyle's use and understanding of laws of nature, and this I am less willing to accept. Listen to the way Margaret Osler recently expressed it:

Central to Boyle's theology, metaphysics, and natural philosophy was his solidly voluntarist conception of God's relationship to the creation. Accordingly, the laws of nature are what they are because God created them so; it is not the case that he created them because they are true; and he can alter them at will. Miracles are evidence of his acting freely, since nothing, not even the laws of nature, can obstruct God from exercising his will freely.[19]

Some years back J. E. McGuire expressed the same idea, but with greater breadth of perspective. He described Boyle's conception of physical laws of nature as "a natural grammar imposed on nature by God's will,"[20] and then he proceeded to characterize Boyle's achievement in terms of the broad sweep of history. "Boyle was affecting a shift from laws conceived as part of the fabric of things," he explains,

to laws conceived as edicts imposed upon nature by a mandate of the Sovereign Will. With this shift from *logos* to *nomos*, Boyle also rejected the conception of God as immanent in nature; if laws are imposed on it then God is to be conceived as a transcendental sovereign *over* nature.[21]

McGuire and Osler epitomize the historiography of the traditional voluntarist thesis. In Boyle's thought, these scholars suggest, laws of nature stand as the imposed mandates of an omnipotently willing God. But we have cause to reconsider this long accepted interpretation of Boyle's position if we now return to our point of departure.

Those of Boyle's statements sounded at the outset challenge the conception of law as a pervasive force of will. When Boyle insists that law is a "moral, not a physical cause," he frankly tempers what Osler and McGuire have just affirmed. By describing law as a "notional thing," something to which only an "intelligent and free agent" may respond, Boyle reveals law as an expression of reason, not of will. For Boyle, law seems preeminently rational in its source; and in its object, only an active principle of reason secures its efficacy. This view need not impugn the will of God, but may rather subordinate it to, temper it with, or define it in terms of, other of the divine attributes.

And this view leads to a dismissal of the traditional voluntarist thesis as an explanation of Boyle's conception of law. In its stead, I propose that a tradition of "natural law" thought informs Boyle's treatment of physical laws of nature. The conception of *logos* has not been abandoned, as McGuire insists, but is in fact underscored by Boyle's appeal to laws of nature. Understanding this, we can see further that voluntarism does intersect with Boyle's general notion of law, but a different sort of voluntarism from that I have described. A *conjunctive* voluntarism, one linking rather than severing man and God, pushes Boyle's ideas. Largely anthropological rather than theological, this voluntarism determines an ethic of behavior rather than an epistemological orientation; at once it both complements and contradicts the traditional voluntarist thesis. Casting Boyle's laws of nature in their proper frame leads to an appreciation of the role and mechanics of this revised conception of voluntarism.

2. The Dual Spheres of Boyle's Thought

Commentators such as McGuire and Osler have not respected Boyle's guarded appeal to and appreciation of law. The fact is that as working conceptions, laws of nature are not integral to Boyle's most careful scientific work, for Boyle brackets the notion of laws of nature, relegating it to a certain sphere of his discussion, but not that of his most rigorous observation and analysis, i.e., of his science proper. This division of thought hinges on Boyle's distinction between "particular" and "universal" natures, a distinction mandated by Boyle's own rigid criteria of explanation in natural philosophy.

"[T]o explicate a phaenomenon," Boyle had insisted, "it is not enough to ascribe it to one general efficient, but we must intelligibly shew the particular manner, how that general cause produces the proposed effect.[22] Emphasizing "the particular manner," or the "how" of a phenomenon's cause, Boyle sought to abolish the all too pervasive reliance on occult explanation, a device of interpretation central not only to those influenced by scholastic schools of thought, but to many who had themselves condemned and abandoned Aristotle.[23] Rejecting the language of substantial forms, plastic natures, the soul of the world, and the like—a language which seemed to shroud rather than to unveil truths—Boyle enthusiastically embraced the new mechanical explanation.

Mechanism, or corpuscularism, offers clear and comprehensible explanation. Its appeal takes root in the ordinary events of human experience: our world confirms that as things push against and bump into one another, they move, turn, stop, cause further collisions, and the like. Mechanism provides explanation in precisely these terms, attributing all of the world's phenomena to interactions of the smallest particles of matter, corpuscles whose variance in size, shape, and configuration mandate their behavior. The mechanical outlook renders occult explanation unnecessary.

Boyle's commitment to mechanism leads him to set forth a curious alternative: "[W]e shall perhaps find the more catholick and primary causes of things," he observes,

> to be *either* certain, primitive, general, and fixt laws of nature (or rules of action and passion among the parcels of the universal matter), *or else* the shape, size, motion, and other primary affections of the smallest parts of matter, and of their first coalitions or clusters . . . .[24]

Here Boyle virtually equates laws of nature with laws of motion, a point worthy of note. But Boyle then proposes the viability of such laws, along with another explanatory construct, the "primary affections" of matter, suggesting an appeal to one, but not both, as the fundamental heuristic of his science. The fact is that in his most careful discussion, at the very core of his natural philosophy, Boyle strives to account for phenomena in terms of the latter conception. Appealing to the "shape, size, motion, and other primary affections of the smallest parts of matter," Boyle exploits his corpuscularism, not laws of nature, to account for the vast array of observations marking his experimental endeavors.

This appeal to the language of corpuscularism at the cost of language of law relates to what Boyle treats as the two grand spheres of the natural order, those of "universal" and of "particular" natures. This is an epistemological, not an ontological distinction. Boyle confines his careful explanatory science to the province of the particular.

The particular nature of things concerns, as he says, "individual mechanism."[25] With this reference, Boyle points towards the mechanical interactions of corpuscular reality. "[T]he particular nature of an individual body," he notes,

. . . consists in a convention of the mechanical affections (such as bigness, figure, order, situation, contexture, and local motion) of its parts . . . as the concourse of all these is considered as the principle of motion, rest, and changes in that body.[26]

Cast in these terms, particular natures afford explanation wholly compatible with the experimental criteria of mechanism. Note that in this realm of query the individual structure of matter founds and explains the interrelations and interactions of different particles of matter. Motion is essential at this level of Boyle's thought, but laws of motion—that to which laws of nature inevitably reduce—are not.

To explore the particular nature of things, Boyle must accept motion as fact: he simply assumes the motion of matter as a "mechanical affection," as he describes it, along with the size and shape of individual corpuscles.[27] Boyle's science can then proceed uninhibited by the disturbing questions— and indeed, these are perennial questions—concerning the provenance of motion itself. With motion thus assumed, the naturalist directs his focus to the mechanical interactions of moving particles. Left behind are the questions surrounding motion's law. The consequence of these laws is accepted without perplexing over the laws themselves.

Boyle offers a pointed illustration of his turn to particular natures. The milling of corn offers an analogy. "[I]f corn be reduced to mean," he explains,

the materials and shape of the milstones, and their peculiar motion and adaptation, will be much of the same kind . . . whether the corn be ground by a water-mill or a wind-mill, or a horse mill, or a hand mill; that is, by a mill, whose stones are turned by inanimate, by brute, or by rational agents.[28]

In this instance, explanation of the materials, shape, motion, and interaction of the milstones may be propounded clearly and without doubt. This explanation, cast in the new language of mechanism, remains confined to the realm of particular natures. But the more fundamental questions of agency—here addressed in terms of the inanimate, brute, or rational—are withdrawn from the domain of this realm.

Laws of nature inevitably raise these more fundamental questions. So, while the consequences of such laws are assumed in Boyle's science, the laws themselves are not addressed, for they transcend mechanical explanation. Had Boyle incorporated mathematics into his science with the rigor of either Descartes and Newton, for example, perhaps he would have concerned himself with the content or description of laws of nature, as had they. But significantly, he did not. And so while local motion is fundamental to his science, laws of motion are not.

As case in point, consider Boyle's extensive writings on the "spring" of the air, the source of the famed "Boyle's Law." Recounting an extensive series of experiments with his new air-pump, Boyle sought to describe the air in terms of his new mechanistic conceptions. In pages upon pages of prolix description Boyle strives to persuade his readers that particles of air work mechanically, very much in the manner of a spring. His image is simple: we must conceive of "the air near the earth," he says,

> to be such a heap of little bodies, lying one upon another, as may be resembled to a fleece of wool . . . of many slender and flexible hairs; each of which may indeed, like a little spring, be easily bent or rolled up; but . . . also, like a spring . . . endeavour to stretch itself out again.[29]

Nowhere does Boyle cast his observations in terms of law. A statistical table whose figures directly suggest the inverse relationship between the volume and the pressure of gasses illustrates what we know as "Boyle's Law," but this is our language, not his. Boyle sought only to offer a mechanical accounting of the goings-on within his air-pump.

Excised from the sphere of his most careful exposition and explanation, considerations of law are thus relegated to the realm of "universal" natures. As its name suggests, this realm is far broader than that of the particular. Boyle describes universal natures in terms of the connections and conveyances between the component parts of creation, the "cosmical mechanism" by which the order of creation adheres as a whole.[30] Here the interrelation of and external connections between particulars takes priority over the internal structure and configuration of an individual thing. "Universal nature," he says, comprises "the aggregate of the bodies, that make up the world, framed as it is." It is "contrived in the present structure and constitution of the world, whereby all the bodies, that compose it, are enabled to act upon, and fitted to suffer from one another."[31] Concerns of both the breadth and the unity of creation are now drawn within the ken of consideration.

Boyle's concentration on particular natures, the central thrust of his experimental program, focuses purely on corporeal reality. An appeal beyond this violates the principles of mechanism, inviting the speculations of occult explanation. Nonetheless, his discussion of universal natures unabashedly extends beyond the material sphere. The "aggregate of bodies," when taken as a whole, stands as more than an assembly of particulars. What demands attention, Boyle insists, is

> the great variety, and consequently number, of [particular bodies];
> of their symmetry, as they are parts of the world; and of the
> connexion and dependence they have in relation to one another.[32]

The turn from internal structure to external relations, calling attention to
such things as the "variety," "symmetry," and "connexion and dependence" of particulars, invites reflection upon the order inherent to the
aggregate as a whole. Query of the interconnection of particulars yields
acknowledgment of the design of their relations. Boyle's discussion
inevitably passes from the design to the designer of creation. He thereby
addresses a new dimension of concern, reaching far beyond the realm of
particular natures. "I plead only for such a philosophy," Boyle had
exclaimed, "as teaches but to things purely corporeal, and distinguish[es]
between the first original of things, and the subsequent course of nature."[33]
The sphere of the particular, at the crux of Boyle's natural philosophy,
probes this "subsequent course," mandating a focus on corporeal reality.
But as he withdraws from the particular and turns towards the universal,
Boyle unabashedly addresses "the first original of things." And then his
narrow criteria of discussion dissolves. "[I]n physics we should indeed
ground all things upon as solid reasons as may be had," he says,

> but I see no necessity, that those reasons should be always precisely
> physical; especially if we be treating, not of any particular phaenom-
> enon . . . but of the first and general causes of the world itself.[34]

This is no slight concession. Here Boyle seems to abandon his rigorous
manner of explication, in violation of his own stern admonitions. But
viewed more properly, Boyle has stepped from one to the other of his two
grand categories of understanding. Placing things of creation in their
universal frame, "the first original of things" and "the first and general
causes of the world itself" inevitably come to the fore. Metaphysics, so
carefully removed from the sphere of particular natures, invariably bleeds
into the realm of physics.

"To discern particular truths is one thing," Boyle admits, but "to be able
to discover the intercourse and harmony between all truths, is another thing,
and a far more difficult one."[35] The turn from the particular to the universal, while the more demanding, is also the far more noble challenge.
"[T]hings merely corporeal" are worthy of study, he notes, but when
compared with the truths of the grand harmony "the greatest discoveries we
can make of them are but trifles."[36] Having been omitted from his more
narrow sphere of discussion, laws of nature, in this more wide sweeping
realm of inquiry, are evoked as principles of this "grand harmony."

I am not suggesting that under the rubric of the "universal" Boyle unveils the explicit manner and content of physical laws of nature, as he refused to do elsewhere. But I do contend that Boyle's references to law, as they stand within the context of universal order and design, are relegated to and informed by this more comprehensive sphere of his discussion.

This is why laws of nature, while revealing God's will, serve fundamentally to express something far broader, giving indication of the reasoned order of the universe and the teleology of the cosmos. In turning from the particular to the universal nature of things the natural philosopher confronts a cosmic unity, a "grand harmony." And as Boyle discusses the "shape, size, motion, and other primary affections of the smallest parts of matter," i.e., the particular nature of things, in terms of a specified language of the particular—a quasi-technical language of Boyle's own design which need not be considered here[37]—the grand truths implied by universal natures demand a far broader language of their own. Boyle evokes such truths in the terms by which he addresses the Creator himself: he relies upon his consistent and pervasive language of divine attribution.

Repeatedly, throughout Boyle's work reference is made to the goodness, wisdom, and power of God. Boyle co-opts this triad of divine attributes from a long tradition of theological discourse; but his own formulations are telling. While the omnipotence of God is but a manifestation of divine will, divine will maintains no obvious ascendence over other of the divine attributes, in the manner of theological voluntarism.

For Boyle, the coherence and order expressed by the interrelations of nature clearly suggest a divine will prompted by divine wisdom. The grand design of the mechanistic world, Boyle says,

> suppose[s] no other efficient of the universe, but God himself, whose almighty power, still accompanied with his infinite wisdom, did at first frame the corporeal world, according to the divine ideas, which he had.[38]

Admitting the creative force of God as a willing force, Boyle nonetheless honors the priority of reason. Wisdom "accompanies" the creative force of will; "divine ideas" precede it. Surely, Boyle here concedes a principle of intellection, alluding to the grand context of his "notional" laws. The "attribute of God that shines forth in his creatures, is his wisdom," Boyle elsewhere insists,

> which to an intelligent considerer appears very manifestly expressed in the world, whether you contemplate it as an aggregate or system of all natural bodies, or consider the creatures it is made up of, both

in their particular and distinct nature, and in relation to each other, and the universe, which they constitute.[39]

Embracing the particular natures of things within his universal vision, here Boyle notes the symmetry and harmony of their interaction. Considered in the context of the universal, particular natures warrant respect as a testament of divine wisdom. God's wisdom is manifest in the design of creation.

"[I]t cannot be rationally pretended," Boyle explains,

> that at the first framing of the world, there was a sufficiency in the stupid materials of it, without any particular guidance of a most wise Superintendent, to frame bodies so excellently contrived and fitted to their respective ends.[40]

For Boyle this "first framing," by which matter was set into motion, established the laws of nature as reasoned principles of divine order. Boyle's "most wise Superintendent" is no doubt a most wise lawgiver.

From this perspective, the voluntarist conception of law as imposed will recedes in the face of assumptions of law as an immanent and pervasive principle of cosmic order. When Boyle insists on law "as being indeed but a notional thing,"[41] he evokes its status as a rational entity. Through law, divine reason pervades the cosmos; divine will expresses the content of divine reason. And despite Boyle's great care in explicating physical phenomena in physical terms, moral dicta embrace the entire realm of creation.

3. Natural Law and Conjunctive Voluntarism

This imposition of the moral upon the physical evokes a well defined tradition of natural law. Originating in antiquity and first refined by Stoic philosophers, notions of natural law eventually became central to Christian thought.[42] The natural law finds its most articulate Christian proponent in Thomas Aquinas, but in post-Reformation England we can note Richard Hooker, certainly the greatest Anglican voice during Elizabeth's reign, as its most representative champion. Natural law thinkers conceive of a vast legalistic hierarchy pervading the cosmos. A single, divine law—one virtually equated with God's reason—blankets all of creation. The physical laws of the universe form but one species of law.[43] Of equal profundity is the natural law itself, a mandate of divine reason accessible to men and guiding human action. This type of scheme shapes Boyle's fundamental convictions.

A full account of this orientation of Boyle's thought and its provenance extends beyond the scope of this study; but the validity and value of this portrayal may be secured by complementing Boyle's epistemology with his ethics, or moral philosophy.

It is not odd that a goodly portion, perhaps as much as one-half of Boyle's writings, are reflective pieces on religion and ethics. Having insisting that he "had much rather have men not philosophers than not Christians,"[44] Boyle sought to prove that the new endeavors of natural philosophy reinforce rather than threaten traditional Christian belief. Boyle's outlook as a Christian moralist thus emerges in a wealth of religious and ethical works, providing a rich and important complement to his scientific writings. Without consideration of these texts Robert Boyle cannot be fully understood.

Here, Boyle's ethics conform to Renaissance rather than to Reformation ideals. The portrayal of Boyle as a theological voluntarist now invariably dissolves. Denying the Reformers' disjunction of man and God, Boyle asserts a more auspicious vision placing man and God in accordance. In Boyle's ethical writings, man's reason readily discerns the natural law, and this guides man's behavior. In consequence, the conjunctive, anthropological voluntarism to which I have alluded now appears, as the will of man is in fact exalted for its kinship with divine will.

This conception permeates Boyle's moral philosophy. I draw from Boyle's most comprehensive ethical statement, a piece entitled the *Aretology*, after the Greek *arete*.[45] As its title suggests, its main concern is with the nature of virtue; Boyle here focuses particularly on moral rather than intellectual virtue, turning to the sphere of human action rather than that of human thought. Within this work Boyle explicitly evokes natural law—truly a divine law—by which man can distinguish between proper and improper behavior. "The Law of Nature," he explains, "is that natural light of knowledge or that inborn law of God, that he lights in every man's heart, showing us the difference between good and evil."[46] This conception, he insists, both parallels and replicates the essential mandate of Scripture. "The rudiments of the law of nature are in our hearts," Boyle explains, "but the lineaments are in the Ten Commandments."[47] This fusion of the natural and the written law has a rich lineage rooted in Scripture itself, perhaps most notably in Paul's admonition to the Romans.[48]

In Boyle, as in Paul, a pure and simple mandate emerges from the equation of natural and Scriptural law. Boyle offers this insight: "For the light of nature and mere human reason tells [sic] every man that there is a God, whom . . . we are bound, both to Love and Adore; as also that we ought to love our neighbors as ourselves." And he confirms, "these two are the summary of the Decalogue, as Christ himself teaches."[49] To the extent that such statements epitomize Boyle's ethical vision, and I believe that they do, the oppressive onus of the Reformers' creed is lifted. Boyle does not bemoan the ineptitude of post-lapsarian man, an ineptitude so prevalent in the discourse of the Reformers. He rather exalts the moral aspirations and the moral capacities of man.

Perhaps nothing illustrates this as neatly as Boyle's distinction between theological and civic virtue.[50] The former, as Boyle explains it, embraces the Reformers' plight in full, for this is a virtue wholly reliant on the grace of God. The theologically virtuous will attain salvation, but tellingly, Boyle gives this scant attention when he addresses human ethical concerns. Civic virtue, on the other hand—also called simply moral virtue—is a secularized conception, a thing unto itself which man can obtain on his own accord. Man needs this virtue in his dealings with other men. As it is gained or lost by man's own efforts, it is Boyle's concern.

Rather than derogating both the will and reason of man in the face of divine greatness, as implied both by theological voluntarism and by theological virtue, Boyle's notion of civic virtue honors the godly nature of both. This is an essential tenet of natural law thought: the natural law, a principle of divine reason, is accessible to man when he appeals to his own reason. It may be realized by initiatives of his own will.

Boyle thus invalidates the oft cast image of the Godly English Puritan, dutifully scurrying to and from the pew and the workplace, selfishly marking his divine status all the while.[51] Boyle's is an ethic which, while demanding perhaps no less toil, reassures man of his own worth. Integrity is granted the man as man, not merely the man as Puritan.

This betrays Boyle's conjunctive voluntarism. The potentials of man's will are exalted, and they are seen in kinship with the will of the divine, for man wills in a manner emulating God himself. In practical terms, this faith in man's willing capacities—something found amongst Renaissance, but not Reformation thinkers—is of the greatest consequence.[52] It informs a nascent utilitarian ethic both prodding and justifying the activities of the seventeenth-century English virtuosi.

Historians refrain from placing "utilitarianism," as a doctrine of thought, prior to Jeremy Bentham and the later eighteenth century.[53] Only at this late date is a criterion of utility espoused as part of a full-blown social philosophy, a rationalized theory of statecraft overtly severed from Christian ties. But the fundamental impulse of this later utilitarianism, that the beneficence of human actions determines their intrinsic worth, blossoms with real force—and as a secularized ethic—in the setting of Boyle's England.

We see this as a humanist ideal in the parallel visions of the two great English utopians, Thomas More and Francis Bacon. Separated by more than a century, both sketch societies founded on the willful cooperation of men. Theirs are rationalized societies: when they openly embrace Christianity, the imposing edifice of the Church is nowhere to be found—nor is the notion of sinful man. Christianity is adopted for its tenets of natural religion, and the achievements of both Utopia and Bensalem are the produce of the beneficent, willful actions of their citizens. A current of natural law runs through both fantastic social visions.

When Francis Bacon emerged as something of the 'patron-saint' of the Royal Society his explicit empirical program assumed the efficacy of man's will. In Bacon's vision, man is not hamstrung by his own nature, patiently awaiting for some essential change wrought by the grace of God. Rather, man is a Prometheus of hope and potential whose mastery of the natural order replicates God's own wise and good governance of his creation. I argue that this spirit compels a generation of English virtuosi; the willfulness of man bursts the limiting vision of theological voluntarism.

This is Boyle's ethical bent. But is it possible that a theological *and* an anthropological voluntarism can coexist in Boyle's thought, the one compelling his epistemology, the other his ethical outlook? Along with his century, Boyle stands at the confluence of the intellectual and theological currents of both the Renaissance and the Reformation. In consequence, he may very well grapple with complementary and competing visions. Perhaps Boyle sees himself alternately as both a Renaissance and a Protestant Christian, alternately in conjunction with the humanists' and disjoined from the Reformers' God. If this suggests an inconsistency of thought, it nonetheless creates an enormously productive dynamic. It yields a new body of learning and the promise of its use. And this marks a great watershed, forever quickening the pace of Western, and then of global history.

NOTES

[1]Robert Boyle, *The Works of the Honourable Robert Boyle*, 6 vols. (T. Birch, 1772; facsm. reprint ed.), vol. 5: *The Christian Virtuoso*, p. 521.

[2]In their seminal treatment of Boyle in *Leviathan and the Air Pump: Hobbes, Boyle, and the Experimental Life* (Princeton University Press, 1985), Steven Shapin and Simon Schaffer focus on Boyle to examine the manner of later seventeenth-century experimental science. For these scholars, Boyle's scientific writings offer the clearest model of the new manner of research and report. In a very real sense, Boyle pioneers that which ultimately evolves into the modern laboratory report and the modern scientific paper.

[3]Robert Boyle, *A Free Inquiry into the Vulgarly Received Notion of Nature*, in *Works*, vol. 5, p. 170.

[4]Boyle, *The Christian Virtuoso*, p. 521.

[5]Boyle refers to Descartes frequently, and with great respect. He refers explicitly to Descartes' notion of laws of nature, e.g., in his *Of the High Veneration Man's Intellect Owes to God*, in *Works* vol. 5, p. 140 and his *Disquisition about the Final Causes of Natural Things*, in *Works*, vol. 5, pp. 396-397, 400. On the other hand, Boyle does not explicitly refer to Newton, but Newton's correspondence with Boyle would indicate that Boyle was nonetheless familiar with Newton's work. Some of Newton's extant letters to Boyle are reprinted in Birch.

[6]Marie Boas' rendering of Boyle in *Robert Boyle and Seventeenth-Century Chemistry* (Cambridge University Press, 1968) typifies the treatment and interests of the "internalists." Boas sought to explain Boyle's achievements in terms of modern chemistry. "Boyle's Law," treating of the inverse relationship between the pressure and volume of gasses, thus falls under her purview. The historiography of the "externalists," concerned more with appreciating early modern science in its own terms, has subsequently sought to understand Boyle's natural philosophy as he himself understood it.

[7]The following represent the most important, and the most recent contributions to this literature: Francis Oakley, "Christian Theology and the Newtonian Science: The Rise of the Concept of the Laws of Nature," *Church History* 30 (1961): 433-457; J. E. McGuire, "Boyle's Conception of Nature," *Journal of the History of Ideas* 33 (1972): 523-542; Eugene Klaaren, *Religious Origins of Modern Science: Belief in Creation in 17th Century Thought* (William B. Erdmans, 1977); Edward Davis, "Creation, Contingency, and Early Modern Science: The Impact of Voluntaristic Theology on 17th Century Natural Philosophy" (Ph.D. dissertation, Indiana University, 1984); Margaret J. Osler, "The Intellectual Origins of Robert Boyle's Philosophy of Nature: Gassendi's Voluntarism and Boyle's Physico-Theological Project," in *Philosophy, Science, and Religion, 1640-1700*, ed. R. Ashcraft, R. Kroll, and P. Zagorin (Cambridge University Press, 1991), pp. 178-198; Jan Wojcik, "Robert Boyle and the Limits of Reason: A Study in the Relationship Between Science and Religion in Seventeenth-Century England" (Ph.D. dissertation, University of Kentucky, 1992).

[8]Erasmus and Luther, *Discourse on Free Will*, trans. and ed. Ernst F. Winter (Frederick Ungar Publishing Co., 1982), p. 106.

[9]Ibid., p. 130.

[10]Perry Miller, *The New England Mind: The Seventeenth-Century* (Harvard University Press, 1982), p. 14.

[11]Ibid., p. 16.

[12]Many of the concerns addressed in this essay intersect with the discussion surrounding the notion of Puritan science. This discussion follows in the wake of Robert Merton's *Science, Technology and Society in 17th Century England*, originally published as a book-length article in *Osiris* **4** (1938): 360-632. An overview of this historiography and its significance can be found in I. Bernard Cohen, ed., *Puritanism and the Rise of Modern Science: The Merton Thesis* (Rutgers University Press, 1990).

[13]Francis Bacon, *The Great Instauration*, ed. Jerry Weinberger (Harlan Davidson, Inc., 1989), p. 13.

[14]Bacon describes this in terms of the natural history. As history is experiential, experiment is associated with the history of nature. But nature often conceals her secrets. Bacon thus pleads for natural histories artificially induced—the history created by manipulating nature in the laboratory.

[15]The works cited in note no. 7 assume this relation and develop its varied aspects.

[16]Boyle, *Veneration*, pp. 148-149.

[17]Boyle, *A Discourse of Things Above Reason*, in *Works*, vol. 4, p. 410.

[18]Boyle, *A Proemial Essay. . . Touching Experimental Essays in General*, in *Works*, vol. 1, p. 299.

[19]Osler, "Intellectual Origins," p. 185.

[20]McGuire, "Boyle's Conception of Nature," p. 537.

[21]Ibid., p. 538.

[22]Boyle, *Free Inquiry*, p. 245.

[23]While arguing against such men as Henry More and Franciscus Linus, who appealed to occult explanation even as they rejected the manner of the scholastics, Boyle also took a stance against those "Epicureans" who founded all reality on the chance interactions of Democritus' atoms. For

Boyle, this appeal to chance in fact offered no explanation at all. See, e.g., his *Some Considerations Touching the Usefulness of Experimental Natural Philosophy*, in *Works*, vol. 2, pp. 42ff.

[24]Boyle, *Usefulness*, p. 37 (my italics).

[25]Boyle, *Free Inquiry*, p. 178.

[26]Ibid., p. 177.

[27]Boyle refers to motion as a mechanical affection elsewhere as well. See, e.g., *The Sceptical Chymist*, in *Works*, vol. 3, p. 557 and *The Origin of Forms and Qualities according to the Corpuscular Philosophy*, in *Works*, vol. 3, p. 13.

[28]Boyle, *About the Excellency and Grounds of the Corpuscular or Mechanical Philosophy*, in *Works*, vol. 4, p. 73.

[29]Boyle, *New Experiments Physico-Mechanical, Touching the Spring of the Air, and its Effects*, in *Works*, vol. 1, p. 1.

[30]Boyle, *Free Inquiry*, p. 178.

[31]Ibid., p. 177.

[32]Boyle, *Veneration*, p. 136.

[33]Boyle, *Excellency . . . of the Mechanical Philosophy*, p. 68.

[34]Boyle, *Disquisition*, p. 399.

[35]Boyle, *Advices in Judging of Things Said to Transcend Reason*, in *Works*, vol. 4, p. 466.

[36]Boyle, *Veneration*, p. 151.

[37]In his *Origin of Forms*, e.g., Boyle defines such terms as "situation," "posture," and "order" to explain the configuration of individual corpuscles in relation to one another. See *Origin of Forms*, pp. 16ff.

[38]Boyle, *Free Inquiry*, p. 179.

[39]Boyle, *Usefulness*, p. 21.

[40]Boyle, *Disquisition*, p. 444.

[41]Boyle, *The Christian Virtuoso*, p. 521.

[42]A definitive study on the natural law tradition is yet to be written. The best treatments of natural law are found in discussions of the idea in particular thinkers (for example Hugo Grotius, or John Locke, in the seventeenth century) or in a particular group of thinkers (such as the early Stoics). The works of Alessandro d'Entreves, Richard Tuck, and Heinrich Rommen serve as much as any as general and comprehensive overviews of the tradition of natural law thought.

[43]Richard Hooker offers a particularly explicit discussion of the relationship between the varied types of law in Book I of his *Laws of Ecclesiastical Polity*. Here, he acknowledges the "law of natural agents," the "law of angels," and the "law of men" as all descending from the "first eternal law" of God. "Natural law," in opposition to "law of natural agents," falls under the rubric of "the law of men."

[44]Boyle, *Usefulness*, p. 15.

[45]In *Robert Boyle and the English Revolution* (Franklin Press, 1977), J. R. Jacob was the first to call close attention to the significance of Boyle's *Aretology*. The work itself exists among the Boyle Papers in the Royal Society, but its recent publication, in *Early Essays and Ethics of Robert Boyle*, ed. John T. Harwood (Southern Illinois University Press, 1991), the edition cited here, now makes this important work accessible. Coincidentally, a microfilm of the manuscript of the *Aretology* is also included in the newly available microfilm series, *Papers and Letters of Robert Boyle* (University Publications of America, 1991), but Harwood's careful annotations and insightful commentary make his edition invaluable.

[46]Boyle, *Aretology*, p. 46.

[47]Ibid.

[48]Romans, 2:15.

[49]Boyle, *Aretology*, pp. 54-55.

[50]Boyle's explicit discussion of this distinction is found in *Aretology*, p. 49 ff. But his statements go far in explaining why his extensive theological reflections so rarely address issues of salvation and election.

[51]This image of the English Puritan is cast by Max Weber, who profoundly influenced the thought and work of Robert Merton. See note no. 12.

[52]While the debate between proponents and detractors of free will is extensive and complex in the sixteenth and seventeenth centuries, it cannot be denied that the earliest Reformers denied free will to man. The famous exchange between Erasmus and Luther serves as case in point. Vehemently denying man's free will, Luther notes, quite significantly, that this issue is "the real thing, i.e., the essential point" at the core of his theology. See Winter, *Erasmus and Luther*, p. 137.

[53]Anthony Quinton, for example, in his *Utilitarian Ethics* (St. Martin's Press, 1973) is willing to tie the roots of Bentham's thought to Hume in the mid-eighteenth-century, but he attributes very little to seventeenth-century thinkers. See Quinton, pp. 15-23.

GALILEO AND THE CHURCH

EDWARD L. SCHOEN

Although he wrote hundreds of years before the time of Copernicus or Galileo, Aquinas provided the fundamental model for integrating Aristotelian theology with distinctively Christian themes. Aristotle's was the fundamental position against which so many early modern scientists struggled. According to Aquinas, the understanding of the nature of theological science Aristotle had was now complicated by the introduction of revelation. So, while he agreed with the Aristotelian view that theology was a science and that sciences were hierarchically structured, Aquinas departed from that tradition by adding:

> sciences are of two kinds: some work from premises recognized in the innate light of intelligence, for instance arithmetic, geometry, and sciences of the same sort; while others work from premises recognized in the light of a higher science. . . . In this second manner is Christian theology a science, for it flows from founts recognized in the light of a higher science, namely God's very own which he shares with the blessed . . . . Christian theology takes on faith its principles revealed by God.[1]

Furthermore, because this latter form of science was based upon the revealed word of God, Aquinas argued that Scriptural teaching took precedence over all other scientific insights:

> Holy teaching assumes its principles from no human science, but from divine science, by which as by supreme wisdom all our knowledge is governed . . . whatsoever is encountered in the other sciences which is incompatible with its truth should be completely condemned as false . . . .[2]

The ticklish problem, of course, was to determine precisely what was taught by Scripture. Aquinas readily admitted that God's revelation might be presented metaphorically or symbolically. Indeed, the words of Scripture

177

could bear a multitude of senses beyond the merely literal, including spiritual and historical ones.[3]

Nevertheless, whatever these other senses of Scripture might be, Aquinas believed they were all built upon and presupposed the literal sense. This literal sense was both fundamental and incontrovertibly true because it was "that which the author intends, and the author of holy Scripture is God who comprehends everything all at once in his understanding . . . ."[4] Aquinas warned, however, that the literal sense of Scripture was not always what the casual reader might expect it to be. Sometimes, for example, it lurked behind the apparent meaning of the text. When Scripture speaks of the arm of God, the literal sense is not that he has a physical limb, but that he has what it signifies, namely the power of doing and making. This example brings out how nothing false can underlie the literal sense of Scripture.[5]

Since nothing could be true that contradicted the literal sense of Scripture, once that sense was properly extracted from the text, Aquinas found it necessary to reshape much of Aristotle's understanding of the Unmoved Mover. Particularly problematic was Aristotle's view regarding the Unmoved Mover's relation to the world. Since it was self-absorbed in thinking upon thinking, the Unmoved Mover's action could only be traced in terms of the desire to emulate its changeless self-sufficiency. Heavenly bodies struggled after the eternal by spinning in unceasing, perfect circular motions, while humans felt this same lure toward eternality in the intimacy of their desire to reproduce. According to Aquinas' reading of Scripture, however, the Christian God's attention was turned much more directly toward his creation. Instead of being completely self-absorbed, God "knows all things that are in any way whatever."[6] For Aquinas, this meant that God knows fully actual things, he also knows of potentially existent things that they are potentially existent.[7] Furthermore, God's focus upon his creatures was not entirely intellectual. "God loves all existing things"[8] and acts both mercifully and justly toward his creation.

These deviations from Aristotle should not be overemphasized, however. In his essential nature, the God of Aquinas shared much with the Unmoved Mover. He was eternally changeless and without parts. Bodiless and purely actual, he was perfectly good, limitless, self-sufficient and necessarily existent.[9] As such, this God remained a far cry from anything like the Olympians of Homer and Hesiod. Utterly different from human beings, his manifestations of love, mercy or justice did not conform to human patterns. Nevertheless, though God's attributes were unlike those of human beings, for the observant who knew where to look, manifestations of God could be found nearly everywhere. With respect to God's love, for example, Aquinas explained that since the very existence of each single thing is good, and . . . God's will is the cause of things . . . . God therefore wills some good to each existing thing, and since loving is no other than willing good to someone, it is clear that God loves everything.[10]

Similarly, God's mercy could be found in the way he drove away misery. According to Aquinas, misery means the presence of defect and defect is eliminated by goodness. God, as the first source of goodness, mercifully eliminates defects in the very production of a good Creation.[11] The manifestation of the justice of God was more straightforward, appearing in the fact that *"he grants what is proper to all existing things according to their worth . . . ."*[12]

In his discussion of the five ways, Aquinas outlined an intricate account of God's causal interaction with Creation. Going beyond Aristotle's Unmoved Mover, the God of Aquinas operated both as "first and final cause of the entire universe . . . ."[13] As might be expected, God's final causal attraction produced the same motions in the heavenly bodies as were enticed by the Unmoved Mover. Like Aristotle's heavenly spheres, the celestial bodies of Aquinas could change only in place and never in substance.[14] Moved by their desire for God, their circular, single, uniform motion bore silent witness to the changeless and utterly simple divine object of their desire.[15] On the terrestrial plane, God provided proper direction for those creatures that were unaware of their goals. With respect to human beings, however, Aquinas shifted emphasis away from Aristotle's focus upon the drive to reproduce. Ultimate human happiness lay in the knowledge of God.[16]

Turning to first-causal roles, Aquinas conceived God as the original changeless source of change, the fixed initiator who originated those chains of cause and effect that have coursed incessantly through the history of Creation. As first cause, God provided the necessitating ground for all contingent being. He was the ultimately perfect source of all that is less than perfect.

At this point, it is obvious that Aquinas, armed with his literal sense of Scripture and some help from Aristotle, had transformed the coldly distant god of Xenophanes into a divine presence nearly as ubiquitous as the pantheon of the ancient Greeks. Being so different from Zeus or Athena, of course, this God showed up in rather different places. Nevertheless, when properly understood using the theological method initially fashioned by Aristotle, he fit tightly and systematically into the overall scheme of things. God's eternal changelessness was as evident to Aquinas in the constant circling of the stars as the wrath of Zeus had been to the Greeks in the thundering flash of lightning. Unfortunately, just as Xenophanes had come along to challenge the ancient Greek places for the Olympians, so Galileo came along to question those new places where Aquinas thought his Christian God had been revealed.

In his *Letter to the Grand Duchess Christina*, Galileo complained of what he regarded as petty and unfair treatment by the Church. He accused Church leaders of refusing to face honestly either his own arguments or those of Copernicus in their response to his claim that the sun was "situated motionless in the center of the revolution of the celestial orbs while the earth rotates on its axis and revolves about the sun."[17] Instead, these officials had hidden behind the authority of misinterpreted Scripture. As Galileo saw it, the situation was clear and simple. His opponents

> would have us altogether abandon reason and the evidence of our senses in favor of some biblical passage, though under the surface meaning of its words this passage may contain a different sense.[18]

In this particular statement of his complaint, Galileo implied a straightforward incompatibility between his own approach to Scripture and that of the Church. Strangely, though, his position regarding Scripture seems surprisingly close to that of Aquinas. Like Aquinas, Galileo did not question the truth of Scripture rightly understood. Also like Aquinas, he believed that Scripture "may say things which are quite different from what its bare words signify."[19] In fact, to illustrate how the signification of the bare words might contrast with the deeper Scriptural sense, Galileo chose precisely the same example as Aquinas. Aquinas had used Scriptural references to God's bodily parts to demonstrate that the literal sense of Scripture was not that God really had such parts, but rather that he had the capacities signified by such parts. Similarly, Galileo argued that when the bare sense of a Scriptural passage taught that God had bodily parts, this teaching must be abandoned in favor of a deeper sense.[20]

If anything approaching the position of Aquinas were taken as normative regarding the interpretation of Scripture, it would seem that the views of Galileo could be reconciled quite easily with those of the Church. This dispute amounted to little more than a tussle over terminology. Neither side was prepared to accept what Galileo termed the bare sense of Scripture. Instead, both embraced something more fundamental, what Galileo called the deeper sense and Aquinas had called the literal sense.

Why, then, was the disagreement so bitter? Galileo's characterization leaves the matter baffling. Were Church leaders of his time utterly unfamiliar with the teachings of Aquinas? Were they so completely naive regarding the problem of Scriptural exegesis that they could not even make the elementary distinction between an apparent, superficial sense of Scripture and the deeper truths that lay beneath this surface?

To avoid such grotesque interpretations of the situation, Galileo's description of the conflict must not be taken as the final word on the subject. Galileo was well-known for his masterly polemics. Unfortunately, his caricature of his enemies, though it may have given him the argumentative advantage of oversimplification, also trivialized the seriousness of his conflict with the Church.

In order to appreciate more clearly the genuine depth of this conflict, Galileo's depiction of the situation to the Grand Duchess must be compared with the details of his actual assault upon the religious teachings of his day. In his letter to the Grand Duchess, Galileo described his task as one of discovering physical truths by deriving them from sense experience and necessary demonstrations. The task of Scripture, on the other hand, was to communicate divine mysteries of religious importance. These two enterprises were cleanly separable. As Galileo put it,

> since the Holy Ghost did not intend to teach us whether heaven moves or stands still, whether its shape is spherical or like a discus or extended in a plane, nor whether the earth is located at its center or off to one side, then so much the less was it intended to settle for us any other conclusion of the same kind . . . . I would say here something that was heard from an ecclesiastic of the most eminent degree: 'That the intention of the Holy Ghost is to teach us how one goes to heaven, not how heaven goes.'[21]

Occasionally, in the course of communicating spiritual truths, Scripture may seem to teach something regarding the physical world. But Galileo believed such teachings should be taken casually as mere accommodations to the needs of unsophisticated, common minds.[22] Since "the holy Bible and the phenomena of nature proceed alike from the divine Word,"[23] genuine truths gleaned from each sphere can be expected to harmonize. When apparent conflicts arose, however, Galileo was inclined to use truths gleaned from nature to correct the human understanding of Scripture rather than the other way around. In his assessment,

> nothing physical which sense-experience sets before our eyes, or which necessary demonstrations prove to us, ought to be called in question (much less condemned) upon the testimony of biblical passages . . . , having arrived at any certainties in physics, we ought to utilize these as the most appropriate aids in the true exposition of the Bible and in the investigation of those meanings which are necessarily contained therein, for these must be concordant with demonstrated truths.[24]

While Aquinas would have been uneasy with Galileo's decided preference for physical truth, he would have to agree with Galileo's ultimate conclusions. Like Galileo, Aquinas believed that God was the source of all truth. As a result, any truths revealed in nature must harmonize with a proper understanding of Scriptural teachings. Furthermore, if what Galileo meant by sense-experience and necessary demonstrations were interpreted along properly Aristotelian lines, then Aquinas would have to agree that properly derived physical truths must necessarily be true. Thus, by necessity, such truths could never conflict with the genuine teachings of Scripture. In principle, then, Aquinas would seem committed to Galileo's conclusion that truths properly extracted from nature could be used to correct various misinterpretations of Scripture. In fact, he himself had used this very strategy to correct naive misunderstandings of Scriptural references to God's bodily parts. Since Aristotelian methods had established God's necessary incorporeality independently of Scriptural teachings, the literal sense of Biblical references to God's bodily parts could not be taken to imply that God has a body.[25]

The insuperable barrier to this easy reconciliation, of course, was Galileo's refusal to embrace properly Aristotelian methods. His investigations of natural phenomena bore little resemblance to the approach taken by Aristotle. Consider, for example, his study of sunspots. Galileo began by collecting relevant sense experiences. Unlike Aristotle, however, Galileo never systematized any of these experiences of sunspots to stabilize universals in his soul. Nor did he try to use his intuitive reason to extract any necessarily true or universal first principles. Instead, he simply recorded an extraordinarily wide diversity of very detailed and apparently random observations of the sun.

Quite unlike Aristotle, Galileo did not even limit himself to what might be considered direct observations. Though he certainly took direct observations, these were supplemented with additional data collected by peering through his newly constructed telescope. Even more perversely, Galileo devised exotically indirect ways of using his telescope to gather data. For example, by properly positioning a piece of paper behind his telescope and darkening his room, he found that he could trace out precise diagrams of the sunspots he observed by outlining the images cast upon his pieces of paper.[26]

Galileo was well aware of the controversial status of his telescopes. Not only was their use utterly unorthodox from an Aristotelian point of view, by Galileo's own standards, telescopic data were not always reliable. Near the beginning of *The Starry Messenger*, he warned, ''it is necessary to prepare a quite perfect telescope, which will show all objects bright, distinct, and free from any haziness . . . .''[27] He accompanied this warning with suggestions of tests that could be performed to check the adequacy of the data that could be obtained from particular instruments.

From an Aristotelian point of view, Galileo's defense of the quality of data from particular telescopes was not very convincing. Instead of constructing syllogisms from necessary first principles, he used analogies. Galileo pointed his telescopes at terrestrial objects, comparing the telescopic images with those obtained with the naked eye. For instance, the magnification of a particular telescope could be checked by tracing

> the contour of two circles or two squares of which one is four hundred times as large as the other . . . . Then, with both these figures attached to the same wall, observe them simultaneously from a distance, looking at the smaller one through the telescope and at the larger one with the other eye unaided. . . . the two figures will appear to be of the same size if the instrument magnifies objects in the desired proportion.[28]

When turned to the heavens, Galileo assumed his telescope would perform similarly. If it produced images of a particular magnification and quality on earth, he believed his instrument would produce analogously magnified images of similar quality when pointed toward the moon, the sun or other celestial spheres.

After collecting his data and defending their integrity in such unorthodox ways, Galileo went on to employ them in an equally unsatisfactory manner. His procedure clearly ran counter to the Aristotelian tradition. Despite avowals to the contrary, Galileo did not use his observations as a basis for constructing necessary demonstrations. Instead, he explicitly argued by analogy. Consider one of his hypotheses about the nature of sunspots. Galileo said,

> if, proceeding on a basis of analogy with materials known and familiar to us, one may suggest something that they may be from their appearance, my view would be exactly opposite to that of Apelles. To me it seems that none of the essentials belonging to stars are in any way adapted to the spots, while on the other hand I find in them nothing at all which does not resemble our own clouds.[29]

Galileo was extremely confident that his use of analogies could provide genuine insight into the reality of sunspots. While he was willing to confess a certain degree of ignorance regarding their precise nature, admitting that the "substance of the spots might even be any of a thousand things unknown and unimaginable to us,[30] Galileo concluded forcefully, "I have no doubt whatever that they are real objects and not mere appearances or illusions of the eye or of the lenses of the telescope."[31]

Furthermore, though it was easier to say what sunspots were not than what they were, Galileo believed that at least some things could be said positively about their nature by using careful observations coupled with specially selected analogies. For instance,

> we need not assume the material of the sunspots to be very dense and opaque, as we may reasonably suppose with regard to the material of the moon and the planets. A density and opacity similar to that of a cloud is enough, if interposed between us and the sun, to produce the required obscurity and blackness.[32]

Such positive descriptions, though initially vague, could be refined almost indefinitely. One of Galileo's chief methods of increasing the precision of his descriptions was to use initially crude analogies as a basis for making predictions. The outcome of such predictions could be used to modify his descriptions appropriately. For example, the similarity of sunspots and clouds with regard to thickness and opacity determined nothing regarding their relative permanence. Assuming that sunspots were permanent, however, one would expect that after passing across the visible hemisphere of the sun in a period of fifteen days, they would return again to sight about fifteen days later. Since this does not happen, Galileo concluded that sunspots must not be permanent. Their impermanence was further confirmed by the fact that even while crossing the visible hemisphere of the sun, sunspots sometimes rather suddenly disappear.[33]

While this particular conclusion regarding the relative impermanence of sunspots helped to tighten the analogy with clouds,[34] the outcome of other predictions moved the description of sunspots in new directions of analogy. For instance, if sunspots, like clouds, were in the atmosphere relatively close to the surface of our earth, one would expect to find some perceptible parallax when observing them. But the

> lack of any perceptible parallax shows that we must conclude them to be not in the atmosphere; that is, not near the earth within the space commonly assigned to the element of air.[35]

Galileo's conclusion that sunspots were constantly appearing and disappearing as well as changing in size and shape was based directly upon observational data, much of which was collected by using telescopes. His conclusions that these spots were real and located either on or near the surface of the sun were derived by combining his observations with a series of arguments employing analogies. Guided by his analogies, Galileo increasingly refined his understanding of sunspots on the basis of the outcome of predictions.[36]

Obviously, Galileo's affirmation of the existence of changeable spots on or near the surface of the sun directly contradicted the claim of both Aristotle and Aquinas that the heavens must, of necessity, be incorruptible. Galileo was not only aware of this clash, he emphasized it, claiming that his own conclusions should be preferred to those of the tradition:

> [I]t is better Aristotelian philosophy to say, "Heaven is alterable because my senses tell me so," than to say, "Heaven is inalterable because Aristotle was so persuaded by reasoning." . . . Now we, thanks to the telescope, have brought the heavens thirty or forty times closer to us than they were to Aristotle, so that we can discern many things in them that he could not see; among other things these sunspots. . . . Therefore we can treat of the heavens and the sun more confidently than Aristotle could.[37]

Here, at last, something of the true gulf between Galileo and the Church is revealed. Not only did he collect much of his data by the questionable use of telescopes, Galileo failed to use his observations in a properly Aristotelian way to stabilize universals in his soul. Instead of trying to establish first principles from which necessary conclusions could be derived syllogistically, he employed a series of analogies refined by the skillful use of predictions to draw his conclusions. As if all of this were not scandalous enough, Galileo made no attempt to minimize the impact of his claims by using the time-honored contention that he was only "saving appearances." To the contrary, he remained trenchantly realistic regarding the nature and location of sunspots. Ultimately, when his highly unorthodox methods led to conclusions that conflicted with those derived by more traditional techniques, Galileo cheerfully repudiated the findings of orthodoxy and embraced his own instead.

Galileo recognized that his repudiation of the incorruptibility of the heavens threw into question one of the most fundamental manifestations of God to be found in the natural world. If the heavens were corruptible, they obviously could not provide indications of divine changelessness. Instead of shrinking from this implication, however, Galileo challenged the basis from which divine changelessness traditionally had been derived, the Greek assumption, enshrined by Aristotle and his contemporaries as a necessary truth, that the incorruptible is superior to the corruptible. In his assault on this ancient belief, Galileo once again argued by appealing to a series of analogies.

> For my part I consider the earth very noble and admirable precisely because of the diverse alterations, changes, generations, etc. that occur in it incessantly. If, not being subject to any changes, it were a vast desert of sand or a mountain of jasper, or if at the time of the flood the waters which covered it had frozen, and it had remained an enormous globe of ice where nothing was ever born or ever altered or changed, I should deem it a useless lump in the universe, devoid of activity and, in a word, superfluous and essentially nonexistent. This is exactly the difference between a living animal and a dead one; and I say the same of the moon, of Jupiter, and of all other world globes.[38]

As his analogies make clear, Galileo saw no reason to think that incorruptibility was better than corruptibility. He felt no compulsion whatever to "keep the heavens free from even the tiniest alteration of material."[39] To the contrary, he valued change and complexity over static simplicity. From Galileo's point of view, a universe filled with unimaginable diversity seemed more naturally to fit with the richness of nature and the omnipotence of the Creator and Ruler."[40] Put somewhat differently, Galileo still found a place for the manifestation of God in the heavens. But it was their changeability rather than their static incorruptibility that allowed the heavenly bodies to provide an appropriate indication of the divine.

At this point, Galileo fell into a stance remarkably similar to that of Xenophanes. Xenophanes had threatened the traditional religion of the Homeric age by suggesting a new conception of the divine coupled with a distinctively different methodology. Rather than embracing imperfect gods conceived anthropomorphically, he proposed a distant, unchanging god understood in conformity with the quite novel standards of moral excellence and fittingness. In the same fashion, Galileo challenged the traditional methods and beliefs of his age. Instead of demonstrating necessary truths from certain first principles, he argued by analogy. As a result of his arguments, he not only repudiated the immutability of the heavens, but also rejected the traditional belief that the infinitely wise and all-powerful Creator must, of necessity, remain utterly changeless.

Few theologians of his day were ready to brave the conceptual frontier so hazily mapped by Galileo. Their hesitancy did not stem from any unwillingness to use analogies for characterizing the divine. Centuries before, Aquinas had argued painstakingly for the importance of analogical predication as a compromise between the excesses of univocity and the uninformativeness of equivocation.[41] The problem lay with Galileo's arrogant confidence in the productivity of coupling observations, analogies and predictions. He claimed not only that his investigative techniques could be used to discover the true nature of reality, but also that they could be used as a basis for challenging supposedly necessary First Principles as well as the consequences derived syllogistically from those Principles. From the orthodox point of view, Galileo's bold conclusions not only were improperly derived, they contradicted the eternal truths of theological and natural science. Contrary to his protestations in his *Letter to the Grand Duchess Christina*, Galileo was not merely quibbling over the finer points of Biblical hermeneutics, he was challenging the most fundamental methods as well as the most secure findings of the sciences of his day.

NOTES

[1]Thomas Aquinas, *Summa Theologiae*, ed. Thomas Gilby (Image Books, 1969), vol. 1, pt. 1, q. 1-13, p. 44.

[2]Ibid., p. 51.

[3]Ibid., pp. 56 and 59.

[4]Ibid., p. 60.

[5]Ibid., p. 61.

[6]Thomas Aquinas, *Summa Theologiae*, ed. Thomas Gilby (Image Books, 1969), vol. 2, pt. 1, q. 14-26 , p. 34.

[7]Ibid., p. 35.

[8]Ibid., p. 133. For a discussion of God's mercy and justice, see pp. 144-148.

[9]Aquinas, *Summa Theologiae*, vol. 1, pt. 1, q. 1-13, pp. 71-165.

[10]Ibid., p. 133.

[11]Ibid., p. 145.

[12]Ibid., p. 141. Emphasis in original.

[13]Aquinas, *Summa Theologiae*, vol. 1, pt. 1, q. 1-13, p. 50.

[14]Ibid., pp. 141 and 153.

[15]See Thomas Aquinas, *Summa Contra Gentiles, Book Two: Creation*, trans. James F. Anderson (University of Notre Dame Press, 1975), p. 211, and Thomas Aquinas, *Summa Contra Gentiles, Book Three: Providence, Part I*, trans. Vernon J. Bourke (University of Notre Dame Press, 1975), pp. 92-93.

[16]See Aquinas, *Summa Theologiae*, vol. 1, pt. 1, pp. 67-71 and 167-168, as well as vol. 2, pt. 2: p. 208.

[17]Stillman Drake, trans., *Discoveries and Opinions of Galileo*, (Doubleday Anchor Books, 1957), p. 177.

[18]Ibid., p. 179.

[19]Ibid., p. 181.

[20]Ibid., p. 181 for Galileo's discussion of this example. For Aquinas' treatment, see *Summa Theologiae*, vol. 1, pt. 1, p. 61.

[21]Ibid., pp. 185-186.

[22]Ibid., p. 182.

[23]Ibid., p. 182.

[24]Ibid., pp. 182-183.

[25]See Aquinas, *Summa Theologiae*, vol. 1, pt. 1, p. 73 for the demonstration that God has no body and p. 61 for the way in which Aquinas uses this to extract the literal sense from Scriptural references to God's arm.

[26]For an example of data collected with his telescope, see Drake, *Discoveries*, pp. 106ff. For the details of his method for tracing sunspots, see pp. 115ff.

[27]Ibid., p. 30.

[28]Ibid., p. 30.

[29]Ibid., p. 98.

[30]Ibid., p. 98.

[31]Ibid., pp. 90-91.

[32]Ibid., p. 93. For his comments regarding the relative ease of negative, as opposed to positive, characterizations, see p. 90.

[33]Ibid., p. 95.

[34]Ibid., pp. 98-99.

[35]Ibid., p. 92.

[36]Ibid., pp. 90ff.

[37]Stillman Drake, trans., *Galileo: Dialogue Concerning the Two Chief World Systems*, 2nd rev. ed. (University of California Press, 1967), p. 56.

[38]Ibid., pp. 58-59.

[39]See Drake, *Discoveries*, p. 142.

[40]Drake, *Dialogue*, p. 101.

[41]See Aquinas, *Summa Theologiae*, vol. 1, pt. 1, q. 13.

PART IV

DESCRIPTIONS OF CONFERENCE PAPERS

DESCRIPTIONS OF CONFERENCE PAPERS 1990

(PRESENTED IN ALPHABETICAL ORDER
BY AUTHOR'S LAST NAME)

FRANK ANGOTTI
Liberal Studies, Gannon University

JOSEPH A. LEU
Department of Physics, Gannon University

TECHNOLOGY, RELIGIOUS VALUES AND MORAL RESPONSIBILITY

Because of the computer charged, microchip symbolized *weltanschauung* of the new scientific/technological community, one more and more approached, measured and understood in terms of "matter," and the "fingertip" ability to successfully manipulate quantity, there is less and less room for religious idealism, questions of normative human values, ideals, and goals. In the new conceptual context, the discourse becomes self-serving; technology judges itself, it is no longer constrained by metaphysical considerations. In the telling observation of Jacques Ellul, "technology exists beyond good and evil."

Our proposal is to expand upon and share the above reflections, and we hope to contribute some insights and perhaps hazard a suggestion or two about what we can do to preserve the operative ideal of human moral responsibility *vis à vis* science and technology.

D. BRIAN AUSTIN
Department of Philosophy, Cumberland College

RANDOMNESS, CHAOS, AND OMNISCIENCE

Contemporary physical science, with its discoveries that magnify the role of random events, may give the theist reason to revise her view of God's omniscience. Both quantum mechanics and "chaos" research give us reason to believe that random events play a critical role in the natural universe. If omniscience is defined as knowledge of all that is knowable, then the

193

presence of random events would seem to reduce the contents of the category of the knowable, thus attenuating the scope of omniscience. From this point of view, God may still be said to possess omniscience so defined, but lack the ability to know future random events, since they would be by definition unknowable. These conclusions have significant impact on the foreknowledge/freedom debate and on theodicy.

MICHAEL BARNHART
Department of Philosophy, Temple University

WHICH SCIENCE? WHOSE RELIGION? TECHNOLOGIZATION FROM A ZEN PERSPECTIVE

In this paper I undertake to examine the possible conflict and its resolution between science and religion from the standpoint of the "Kyoto School" of philosophy in Japan. This conflict is investigated in terms of certain typical ways of thematizing the human condition within Buddhism. I then turn to the question of the significance for Buddhism of mediating the perceived tensions between religion and science.

JAMES BARRY
Department of Philosophy, Indiana University Southeast

THE QUESTION OF TECHNOLOGY IN THEOLOGICAL GROUND OF BACONIAN SCIENCE

In this paper I argue that the strongest tie between the Baconian and Cartesian views of science (and the way in which Bacon is therefore most "modern") may be said to involve the impact of their respective theological/philosophical commitments on their visions of science. In my view, Bacon announces "modern science" because he sets the stage for it *theologically*. Further, I seek to show that Bacon's theological view (through its coalescence with the mathematical commitments of Descartes) provides an indispensible ground for Newtonian physics—what I would call the first accomplishment of modern science.

GREG BEABOUT
Department of Philosophy, St. Louis University

CAN ENGINEERS LEARN TO BE ETHICAL?

This paper is an examination of the possibility that engineers can benefit in the area of moral development from college ethics courses. Engineers are a unique group since: 1) their curriculum leaves little room for humanities courses, 2) personality studies indicate that engineering students often have relative indifference to human relations and public affairs, and 3) empirical evidence of the engineering faculty, who are likely role models for engineering students, shows that they tend to be more authoritarian and prejudiced than faculty members from other disciplines. After a tentative affirmative conclusion, I call for an empirical study of the moral development of engineering students modeled after Kohlberg's studies of moral development.

JOANNE CHO
Department of History, The University of Chicago

TROELTSCH'S RESPONSE TO TOENNIES:
The Healthy Interaction Between History of Science and Religion

Contra Toennies, Ernest Troeltsch argued for the healthy interaction between religion and science. He did not consider the natural sciences a serious threat to Christianity, and therefore did not defend Christianity against them. For Troeltsch, the threat to Christianity came from the historical sciences rather than from the natural sciences. However, he was willing to "correct" traditional Christianity according to the new discoveries of both the natural and historical sciences.

KATHY J. COOKE
Fishbein Center, The University of Chicago

PROGRESS ACCORDING TO THE ETHICS OF SCIENCE:
Edwin Grant Conklin's Call to Christian Morality and Social Evolution

Edwin Grant Conklin was a leading embryologist at Princeton University who spent the latter half of his career, spanning the first half of the twentieth century, writing about the social implications of biology. He claimed that further evolutionary advance among humankind could only occur in the realm of the social. Science provided a rational basis for social cooperation among human beings, in contrast to traditional religious foundations, and biology provided a particular model upon which human beings could base their behavior.

RICHARD A. DEITRICH
Religious Studies Program
Science, Technology, and Society Program
Penn State University

PAUL TILLICH AND TECHNOLOGY:
His Importance for Science, Technology and
Society (STS) Studies

Paul Tillich has developed both a concept (the Multi-dimensional Unity of Life) and a method (Correlation) which are invaluable for science education. His work provides an important approach for integrating the various knowledge specialities. This integration occurs because Tillich correlates modern science and technology with traditional faith and religion, thereby exposing the ethical and transcendant aspects of each—individually and interactively. By including these aspects within interdisciplinary instruction, a more robust Science, Technology, and Society (STS) education results.

GREGG DE YOUNG
Whitney Young College, Kentucky State University

THE ISLAMIZATION OF NATURAL SCIENCES TODAY

Calls for Islamization of the natural sciences in the Islamic World imply the necessity to restructure the existing scientific community along Islamic lines so that it will be governed by norms of activity and directed toward ends of the envisioned Islamic world-power. These calls for the re-formation of an Islamic scientific community are often based on a newly resurgent form of Pan-Islamism that is replacing the traditional Palestinian question with broader political and intellectual goals.

DANNY L. FRANKE
Department of Philosophy, University of Tennessee

TECHNOLOGY AND RELIGION:
The Hospital as Battleground

Both technology and religion play important roles in the health of individuals. The nature of technology and religion is such, however, that they approach this differently, often leading to conflict.

In this paper I will explore four aspects of health and the human condition that technology does not address: (1) Technology does not ask questions; (2) Technology does not have feelings; (3) Technology does not know when to quit; (4) Technology does not look at the overall view.

DANIEL C. FOUKE
Department of Philosophy, University of Dayton

METAPHYSICS, APOLOGETICS AND THE EUCHARIST IN THE EARLY LIEBNIZ

In Leibniz's early work, Transubstantiation was a central concern. In attempting to demonstrate the possibility of substantial change in the Host, Leibniz introduced a central metaphysical role for minds as the basis for substantiality, which stimulated the development of his later dynamical system. However, when in his later metaphysics he introduced mind-like entities with active principles into all bodies, Leibniz undermined his earlier ability to give a metaphysical basis for Transubstantiation.

JAMES W. FLANAGAN
Paul J. Jallinan Professor of Religion
Case Western Reserve University

HOLOGRAMS AND HOLOGRAPHY: New Constructs for Understanding the Biblical Past

This paper examines holograms and holography as metaphors and models for the biblical past and its examination. Images of composite holograms are suggested as analogous to "mesoforms," i.e., intermediate and unstable realms between integrative levels of nature. Analogies are drawn between mesoforms and the intermediate zone between archaelogy and literary studies as used by biblical historians. It suggests that space and time categories and referential grids are no longer completely useful for discovering meanings in ancient religions.

ROBERT S. GALL
Department of Humanities, Sinclair College

THE PIETY OF THOUGHT: Heidegger, Religion & the Question of Technology

This essay explores the ways in which Heidegger suggests that science, technology, and religion concern one another in the contemporary world.

What results is a recognition of the futility of trying to overcome our scientific-technological thinking with simple assertions of faith. Instead, we are led to recognize the tragic possibilities of religious thinking and the fragility of faith in the "postmodern" world, where the promise of salvation lies in questioning—the piety of thought.

WILLIAM V. GRIMES
Department of Philosophy
State University of New York at Albany

WAVEFIELD REALITY AND MENTAL ACTIVITY

The move in physics from Newtonian to wavefield concepts supports an analogous move in concepts of mind from episodic-dispositional models to process models in which consciousness-states are conceived to occur both as overt sensations and as subliminal feelings—about and ideations. Such states are not epiphenomena, but are bound up with physical states (neural and behavioral) as interdependent *dual emergent aspects* of an organizational unity.

PETER M. HESS
Department of Philosophy, University of San Francisco

"NATURE" AND THE KNOWLEDGE OF GOD:
The Depth of Scientific Understanding
in Seventeenth-Century Natural Theology

How successful were seventeenth-century theologians in accommodating the traditional concepts of Christian philosophical discourse to the radically new world perspectives emerging from the Scientific Revolution? This paper investigates the cosmological presuppositions underlying the teleological argument for the existence of God during the period of transition from a pre-Copernican to a Newtonian world view, with the object of determining the relative awareness on the part of the theological community of contemporary scientific developments.

JOHN HILL
Kent School of Law,
Illinois Institute of Technology

BEYOND BIOLOGY:
Toward An Intentional View of Parenting

Collaborative reproduction, including artificial insemination, *in vitro* fertilization and surrogate parenting, often create parent-child ties where no biological relationship exists. This paper rejects "biological theories" of parental rights, which limit the permissible use of collaborative reproduction, and proposes an "intentional theory" of parenthood, which focuses on the intentions of the parties prior to conception of the child. The theory is then applied to the conflict in surrogate arrangements between surrogate mothers and intentional parents.

TOM M. HUGHES
Department of Computer Science
Kentucky State University

HOW IS UNIFICATION OF SCIENTIFIC AND
THEOLOGICAL DISCOURSE POSSIBLE?

Throughout the history of ideas attempts to reconcile science and theology by separating their referents into mutually exclusive domains have failed. Also unsuccessful have been attempts to integrate them by fusing their referents into a common domain. How their unification can be achieved, in the Kantian framework, is by recognizing that each are part of normative discourse about what sensory and action states of affairs ought to be fact, by virtue of synthetic *a priori* normatives.

WILLARD JOHNSON
Department of Religious Studies
San Diego State University

RELIGION-SCIENCE INTERATIONS IN
PRIMAL AND MODERN SOCIETIES

This essay examines the paradigmatic and actual relations of scientific ideas (facts) and religious ideas (myths) in primal and modern societies. Though in the wake of modernity the actual relation of science and religion has been adversarial, they are in fact complementary, both paradigmatically and in primal times. By sorting out their separate appropriate epistemologies, their true complementarity emerges in post-modern hermeneutics which transcends the narrow limitations of scientism and reductionism.

W. B. JONES
Department of Philosophy and Religious Studies
Old Dominion University

TOWARD UNDERSTANDING SCIENCE, TECHNOLOGY, AND RELIGION

To facilitate fruitful discussions of the science-technology-and-religion triad, a series of suggestions for approaching this complex topic is offered. First, it is suggested that the temporal and historical character of each of the three always be kept in mind. It is also suggested that in such discussions only rational-sciences (in the sense of Margenau) be considered, and that the content of science and technology be distinguished from their historical and sociological aspects.

CHARLES D. KAY
Department of Philosophy, Wofford College

IS CREATION A PSEUDO-PROBLEM?

In a recent article that has already been included in a textbook anthology, Adolf Grünbaum insists that there is nothing in the theories of modern cosmology that can in any way support a notion of divine creation *ex nihilo*. Indeed, creation is only a pseudoproblem in physical cosmology.

I argue that to define such a question as a pseudoproblem would be to beg the question against a theory unless the term "pseudoproblem" were itself construed only in a neutral sense indicating that the question does not arise within the context of a competing theory. A theory that *included* some theory of modern cosmology and posed additional questions regarding the nature of the initial event and even its *creation* cannot *therefore* be ruled illegitimate.

RICK KENNEDY
Department of History, Indiana University Southeast

THE APPLICATION OF MATHEMATICS
TO CHRISTIAN APOLOGETICS:
The Use of Geometry and Infinity by Arnauld and Pascal

In the midst of a Cartesian era of new mathematical influence, Blaise Pascal and Antoine Arnauld were among the first and probably most influential thinkers to apply mathematics to Christian apologetics. In the *Pensees* and *The Port-Royal Logic*, they integrated geometrical demonstration into arguments against skepticism and appropriated the increasingly influential concept of infinity into discussions of proportional relationships between humans and God and the existence of the inconceivable. Finally, they mixed probability theory with the concepts of proportion and infinity in order to demonstrate the wisdom of being a Christian.

DANIEL C. KOLB
Department of Philosophy, Radford University

A TALE OF TWO TELEOLOGIES:
Life and Purpose in England and Germany
in the First Half of the 19th Century

This essay explores 19th-Century ideas of teleology. The dominant British conception, rooted in the Design Argument, has little to offer the working biologist and provides no coherent defense against Darwinian reductionism. The dominant German conception, *Naturphilosophie*, forms the basis of a rich biological tradition and provides a number of alternatives to Darwinian reductionism. The immediate and complete "triumph" of Darwinism is puzzling.

NORMAN LILLEGARD
Department of Philosophy and Religion
University of Tennessee-Martin

RELIGIOUS OBJECTIONS TO SOME TECHNOLOGICAL
PICTURES OF THE SELF
[or "No Good News for Data"]

I attempt to show that (1) Turing maching functionalism is in one sense dualistic, and thus incompatible with JudeoChristian anthropology and (2) that functionalism ignores the "parochiality" inherent in many psychological concepts. The parochiality of "feels pain" is rooted in those bodily and biological limits to human life which are emphasized in the nondualistic Judeo/Christian anthropology. Functionalism and popular "androidology" violate both religious sensibility and plain sense.

THOMAS S. MARTIN
Department of Humanities, Sinclair Community College

DEEP ECOLOGY AS A RELIGIOUS WORLD VIEW

Deep ecology represents the first comprehensive effort to synthesize ecological science and human spirituality. Its urgency sets it apart from other philosophies: it proposes that if we do not adopt its precepts soon, all life is doomed. Deep ecology is a religion: it offers a path to self-realization via intuition of the interconnectedness of nature. But it also transcends ordinary definitions of religion, and may be a first step toward a post-western worldview.

JOHN L. MEEKS
Maryknoll School of Theology

NATURE AND HUMAN REORGANIZATION:
A Theo-Critical Response to C. R. Badcock

I argue that, at least from the perspective of a Freudian sociobiology (à la Badcock), we cannot discuss social institutions in terms of what ultimately becomes genetic manifestation; rather, the notion of the biological realm as ground of human social instincts must be reinterpreted for an animal that in many ways has created its own (second or social) nature. It is in this light that I introduce the concept of a sociobiological history of repression of the body which suggests the messianic "resurrection of the body."

RICHARD J. MCGOWAN
Department of Philosophy, Saint Joseph's College

ARISTOTELIAN BIOLOGY AND THE TRANSMISSION OF
ORIGINAL SIN IN ST. THOMAS AQUINAS

Aristotelian biology permeates the corpus of St. Thomas Aquinas. Scholars unaware of Thomas' commitment to the "one-semen" theory of reproduction often misinterpret and misconstrue his positions. For instance, McLaughlin does not understand the grounds upon which Thomas asserts that (1) Eve's sin was graver than Adam's, but (2) her sin did not corrupt human nature. Thomas' doctrine of original sin can only be understood through awareness of his biological commitments.

G. STEVEN NEELEY
Department of Philosophy, Xavier University

THE TERMINATION OF LIFE-SUPPORT:
Invasive Medical Technology, Religious Interdiction
and the Proscription of Self-Directed Death

Decisions to disemploy life-support are often swept under broad legal proscriptions of suicide. Legal scholars have accordingly proposed recognition of a constitutional right to elective death. A historical analysis of the legal proscription of self-destruction reveals that the origins of this taboo are rooted in theological dogma and that the rationale behind the common law prohibition of self-willed death will not survive modern-day constitutional scrutiny.

PAUL A. NELSON
Department of Philosophy, University of Chicago

THE ROLE OF THEOLOGICAL ARGUMENTS
IN CURRENT EVOLUTIONARY THEORY

It is widely held that evolutionary theory—as a rational science—is grounded on a metaphysics according to which any reference to "God" or "the creator" in explanation or theory justification is methodologically illicit (Beck, 1982; Riddiford and Penny, 1984; Hoffman, 1989). Yet the arguments from imperfection (Gould, 1980) and homology (Ridley, 1985) are formulated in theological terms, which is plainly inconsistent with the methodological naturalism on which evolutionary theory is grounded.

In my paper, I address this problem and I examine the imperfection and homology arguments for descent, while considering some difficulties with commonly held views.

HERBERT T. NEVE
Department of Religion, Wright State University

MARVIN B. SEIGER
Department of Biological Sciences, Wright State University

GENETICS AND ETHICS:
Colloquy for Interdisciplinary Course
on Evolution, Religion, and Ethics

Drawing upon a colloquy conducted at Wright State University in 1989, we examine the application of genetic engineering and the dialogue it is evoking between geneticists and ethicists. This study summarizes the presentations of Professors Elof Carlson and Thomas McElhinney. The issues raised by genetic engineering, the Human Genome Project and the *Novo Report* are featured. The paper closes with observations and conclusions about the ongoing genetics/ethics dialogue.

ROBERT O'CONNER
Department of Philosophy, Wheaton College

THEOLOGICAL REALISM, REFERENCE AND TRUTH

This paper looks at the recent work of Janet Martin Soskice, who in *Metaphor and Religious Language* argues for what she calls a "critical realist" interpretation of those terms employed by religious explanations to account for certain experiences of the world. I argue that Soskice fails to provide sufficient reason to endorse a realist perspective on scientific, much less religious, explanations. Furthermore, I argue that the problems which arise for the support of theological realism, though not necessarily insurmountable, are largely ignored in Soskice's account.

From this I conclude that, though surely valuable for the insight it provides on the general methodological approach to the justification of belief in God, Soskice's account ultimately fails to provide convincing reason for thinking that the theoretical terms of a theological explanation are, as she argues, "reality depicting."

PHILLIP W. OTT
Department of Philosophy and Religion
University of Evansville

JOHN WESLEY STUDIES THE PHYSICIANS:
Formative Influences on a Concept of
Health as Wholeness

This paper explores the formative influences of medical science on Wesley's concept of health. Three themes—the idea of the well-working of the body as a whole, the view of "sympathy" throughout one's whole being, and belief in the natural means of promoting health—are interconnected. Because of the symbiotic relationship between body and spirit, a well-working body is fundamental to Wesley's wholistic view of health. Furthermore, sensible regimen is the key to a life of health as wholeness.

TERRY PENCE
Department of Philosophy,
Northern Kentucky University

IN DEFENSE OF THE STEWARDSHIP ETHIC:
Christianity, Deep Ecology, and Animal Rights

The burden of this paper will be to argue that Christianity in its more orthodox forms is incompatible with the philosophical expressions of both the Animal Rights/Liberation and Deep Ecology movements. Nevertheless, a sympathetic exploration of the stewardship ethic should incline Christians to endorse much of the practical agendas of these movements and at the same time avoid many of their philosophical and practical shortcomings.

ALAN R. PERREIAH
Department of Philosophy, University of Kentucky

THEOLOGY: SCIENCE OR RHETORIC?
Medieval and Renaissance Views

In this paper I examine two pre-Reformation models of the nature of theology. The Scholastic professors in the universities of the Middle Ages believed that religion should be modelled after science. The Humanistic scholars of the Renaissance claimed that religion should not be patterned after science but rather after poetry and rhetoric. It is hoped that study of these models will help us clarify some relationships between science and religion.

DONALD B. PRIBOR
Department of Biology, The University of Toledo

TRANSCENDING THE OPPOSITION BETWEEN SCIENCE AND RELIGION

One approach to transcending the opposition between science and religion is to acknowledge that science has two aspects: (1) objective knowledge of how things interact and (2) explanatory stories of nature using analogies and metaphors. This second aspect allows science to be integrated with not-literal myths of religion-philosophy. As an example, I show how an ideal heat machine first described by Carnot can also be understood to represent the Taoist ideas of Yin-Yang and of *wu wei*.

RICHARD O. RANDOLPH
Ethics Program, Graduate Theological Union

HUMAN NATURE AND TECHNOLOGY

Although we have recently experienced very dramatic technological break-throughs, there are some serious problems associated with these advances. This essay suggests that there is an indissoluble link between technology and human nature. One's assessment of the future prospects for resolving the problems associated with technology depend upon one's assessment of human nature. Using the theological analysis of Reinhold Niebuhr, the essay concludes that we can be cautiously optimistic about the future.

ALBERT B. RANDALL
Department of History/Philosophy
Austin Peay State University

NINETEENTH-CENTURY APES, ANGELS, AND EMERGENTISM: Science Opens a Door for Natural Theology

Before the nineteenth century, evolutionary views were more metaphysical than scientific. The 1859 publication of Darwin's *The Origin of the Species* changed this. At the center of the evolutionary whirlwind were Lyell, Darwin, Wallace, and Huxley. Each, for different reasons, opened a door in the edifice of science for a new natural theology. Through that door marched the emergent evolution of Morgan and Alexander. This paper explores the door opened by those scientists and examines emergent evolution as a response which intervened between science and religion.

EDWARD L. SCHOEN
Department of Philosophy and Religion
Western Kentucky University

THE ROLES OF PREDICTIONS IN SCIENCE AND RELIGION

The evidential role of predictions in the sciences has long been recognized. Less often noticed is the variety of nonevidential roles played by scientific predictions. In this discussion, a diversity of both evidential and nonevidential roles for scientific predictions is delineated. Once these roles are clearly understood, it is possible to find certain parallels with religious predictions. Such parallels indicate that religious and scientific perspectives share, at least partially, a common epistemic structure.

DOUGLAS K. STUART
Department of Humanities
Illinois Institute of Technology

THE *SINE QUA NON* FOR A POST-MODERN COALESCENCE OF SCIENCE AND RELIGION

This paper discusses how the incipient holistic paradigms emerging within and cross-fertilizing the sciences may function as a living mythology in Joseph Campbell's sense, an umbrella for the sciences, philosophy, and theology under which the West may heal the age-old split of body/mind and begin to accept its share of the universal responsibility for cooperation and community essential for the survival of humanity in the 21st century.

DENNIS TEMPLE
Department of Philosophy, Roosevelt University

HUME AND MODERN COSMOLOGY

This paper is concerned with Hume's claim that the uniqueness of the universe is, in itself, a bar to any scientific account of the origin of the universe. This is offered by Hume a an objection to the argument from design. I argue that the uniqueness objection made sense when applied to a Newtonian steady state universe, but not when applied to the expanding universe of modern physics. The expanding universe allows both modern cosmology and modern design arguments to escape the uniqueness objection.

DAVID A. VALONE
Fishbein Center for the
History of Science and Medicine
The University of Chicago

SCIENCE, THEOLOGY, AND THE HUMAN SCIENCES:
Cambridge and the Rejection of Utilitarian
Moral Philosophy 1815-1833

Sciences which study moral and social relations face questions similar to those traditionally discussed in religious contexts. In 19th-century England several such sciences were in direct competition. The utilitarians called upon a system of expedience as their ultimate authority. In opposition to this movement, a group formed at Cambridge led by William Whewell which drew instead on the ideas of German romanticism to formulate a science based on historical and religious principles.

DONALD WAYNE VINEY
Philosophy Program, Pittsburg State University

THE WARFARE BETWEEN
SCIENCE AND THEOLOGY REVISITED:
Reflections on the Creation/Evolution Controversy

The Creation/Evolution controversy is fueled by the assumptions that science and theology are in the business of explaining certain natural phenomena and that the success of one explanation entails the failure of the other. These assumptions also inform the so-called warfare of science with theology. Evidence for these assumptions is paltry. Moreover, the characteristics that make God weak as a postulate of science make God strong as a postulate of the life of faith.

DARYL J. WENNEMANN
Department of Philosophy, St. Louis University

DESACRALIZATION AND THE DISENCHANTMENT
OF THE WORLD:
An Introduction to
Jacques Ellul's Sociology of Religion

In this paper, I explore Jacques Ellul's sociology of religion in terms of Weber's disenchantment thesis. In contrast to Mircea Eliade's depiction of modern persons as nonreligious, owing to scientific and technological development, Ellul argues that traditional religions have merely been replaced by new ones. This has occurred, according to Ellul, because the desacralization of one realm of experience results in the resacralization of another realm of experience.

DAN WETMORE
Department of Philosophy
Bowling Green State University

RELIGION AND TECHNOLOGY:
Parallel Pursuits

The thesis of this paper is that strong parallels may be drawn between the religious and technological facets of Western society. Their display of continued vitality and on-going development throughout Western history have marked them as driving forces in the shaping of the Western tradition. I believe that examination of the two in a comparative framework offers new insights that will further our understanding of each.

PAUL S. WHITE
Fishbein Center for the
History of Science and Medicine
The University of Chicago

SCIENCE AND THE RELIGIOUS OTHER:
Victorian Psychology and the
Politics of Social Control

In Victorian psychology, a hierarchical relationship in the mind, where reason was both purveyor of knowledge and director of action, and emotion a blind motive force, furnished foundations for a hierarchical society. The relationship between reason and emotion grounded the relationship between science and religion, and the relationship between scientific elite and the working classes. Religion, defined solely in terms of "emotion," could ally its motive power with reason by impelling and sanctifying the scientific enterprise.

DESCRIPTIONS OF CONFERENCE PAPERS
1991
(PRESENTED IN ALPHABETICAL ORDER BY AUTHOR'S LAST NAME)

HENRY AHRENS
St. Joseph's College

PHILOSOPHY AND THE TECHNO-THRILLER

The newest development in popular fiction is the techno-thriller, a genre created by Tom Clancy. An in-depth study of Clancy's five novels reveals that faith in the human ability to create and operate technology has taken the place of faith in the transcendent. The rise of the techno-thriller demonstrates that Ellul, Mumford, and others are correct: Clancy's characters, and possibly Clancy himself, are convinced that technology is humanity's supreme adventure.

MARK BARBER
Department of Philosophy, St. Mary's College

GREGORY BEABOUT
Parks College of St. Louis University

AVIATION ETHICS AND SECURING SAFE SKIES:
Moral Dilemma or Technical Challenge?

In this paper, we focus on an issue which arises in aviation ethics, and we use this particular issue as a paradigm for questions and concerns which reflect the much broader scope of professional ethics. We examine problem cases in aviation ethics and discuss the dividing line between an accident which is the result of moral negligence and one which arises from yet unmet technical challenges. In light of these problem cases, we then discuss the implications of such concepts as fiduciary responsibility and negligence.

RICHARD H. BEYLER
Department of the History of Science
Harvard University

A GOD OF THE QUANTUM LEAPS?:
Jordan, Bavink and the Religious Implications
of 20th-Century Physics

The German physicist Jordan (1902-80) and science popularizer Bavink (1879-1947) both saw in the "overthrow of dogmatic materialism" by modern physics an opportunity to rationalize the legitimacy of religious belief. However, the positivist Jordan wanted simply to clear a space for belief, whereas Bavink embraced metaphysics and outlined a specific natural theology (a cosmic hierarchy of form and process). Both correlated their views with conservative to reactionary politics, consequently provoking considerable controversy.

MACKIE J. V. BLANTON
Linguistics Program, University of New Orleans

LOGOS, LOGIC, AND THE PRACTICE OF LANGUAGE

Specific observations on religion and science suggest that there must be, on our central nervous system, strong hermeneutic pressures in favor of accurate experiences. The ultimate goal of human knowing, hence, is to experience opposite points of view to achieve a unity between science and religion, in order, in turn, to experience the ultimately real or the partially real of the ultimately real. We understand one hermeneutic language, sacred or scientific, when we understand the second one.

WALTER CARVIN
Philosophy Department
Youngstown State University

BRENDAN MINOGUE
Philosophy Department
Youngstown State University

GOD AND REPRODUCTIVE ADVANTAGE

For over one hundred years, the science of evolution has been at war with many versions of Christian religion. Theologians who wage this war are often called fundamentalists. These religious theorists are usually viewed as individuals who have little in common with evolutionary theorists. But in this paper it will be argued that fundamentalists share some common assumptions with evolutionary theorists. Both parties, we will argue, proceed by asking questions that they assume to have singular, deterministic and inscrutable answers. Our aim in this paper is to spell out these similarities and argue that decent scientific explanations of species and species traits can proceed without these assumptions. We list a number of advantages associated with dropping the concept of reproductive advantage and employing only genetic hypotheses to explain the origins of species and their traits. We then distinguish science from religion and suggest that while science can do without singular deterministic and inscrutable explanations, many sensible brands of Christianity cannot.

JOHN R. CONWAY
*Interdisciplinal/Intercultural Studies
in Humanities
New England College*

HINDUISM, MONOTHEISM, AND THE SEPARATION OF RELIGION AND SCIENCE

Hinduism is not a religion but a conglomeration of approaches to aspects of Brahman, the Absolute, which may include practices that elsewhere would be allocated separately to religion, science and technology. In relation to Hinduism, monotheism can be seen as an exclusion of some paths to Brahman, in ways that led to the separation of inner, religious technologies and outer, scientific technologies, and to the exclusion of disciplines that claimed results in both spheres.

KATHY J. COOKE
Fishbein Center, University of Chicago

THE NATURE OF MAN AND RELIGIOUS BELIEF:
Charles Hodge and Charles Darwin
and Nineteenth-Century Scientific Theology

I will discuss ideas about the nature of man as held by two prominent nineteenth-century figures, Charles Hodge and Charles Darwin. In spite of their widely differing legacies, Hodge and Darwin have striking similarities in their views of man. Although Hodge was a master conservative, the implications of his view of man were not in keeping with traditional orthodoxy, and perhaps even contributed to unbelief in America.

ROBERT C. DAVIS
Department of History and Religion
Pikeville College

COSMOLOGY AND ESCHATOLOGY:
The Quest for Meaning

This paper seeks to understand the current cosmological investigation into a potentially closed or even oscillating Universe as being, in part, a search for the Universe's meaning, as well as for its mechanics. In describing this search, it is helpful to employ certain Judeo-Christian ideas concerning the purposefulness of the Created Order, particularly as expressed in the eschatology of the Bible and of more modern Judeo-Christian writings.

OLLIN J. DRENNAN
Northeast Missouri State University

SCIENCE AND RELIGION IN INTELLECTUAL HISTORY

The growth of science occurred in an intellectual world dominated by religion—primarily the Christian religion. The structure of ideas current in both science and religion today reflect the effect of the historical interplay between the two. This paper will consider that historical interplay. Differences between current religious and scientific worldviews rest upon their epistemological differences. What would a single worldview that included both worldviews be like today?

CYNTHIA GORDON
Department of Philosophy
University of California, Riverside

MEDICINE AND HALAKHAH:
The Tribulations of a Religious Bioethical System

Halakhah—the ethical-legal system associated with Orthodox Judaism—has a long history of application to medical dilemmas. The current trend within the Orthodox-halakhic world favors a very conservative, strict-constructionist approach to medical-ethical decisions, though the tradition has seen periods of creative and adaptive thought. This paper examines the difficulties encountered in the prevailing Orthodox approach to terminal care and life-support issues. These difficulties, including conflicts with emerging medical and legal norms, suggest a need for deeper exploration of fundamental Torah concepts.

DAVID J. HESS
Science and Technology Studies Department
Rensselaer Polytechnic Institute

A CULTURAL APPROACH TO
SCIENCE, RELIGION, AND POPULAR CULTURE:
Cases from Brazil and the United States

Drawing on my anthropological fieldwork among Brazilian Spiritist intellectuals, I argue that Sociological/anthropological approaches need to situate Spiritists' religion-science syntheses in a broader "ideological arena" that includes the state, the religious system, the medical profession, and (reflexively) the social sciences. I also discuss my current research on skeptics, parapsychologists, and New Agers in the U.S.

TOM M. HUGHES
Computer Science Department
Kentucky State University

RE-ESTABLISHING LEIBNIZ'S PRE-ESTABLISHED HARMONY

Leibniz's doctrine of pre-established harmony is pertinent toward unifying theological and contemporary scientific discourses, provided (1) science ultimately is the pursuit of "distinct perceptions," i.e., actions of monads when in their active state; and (2) the perplexing conceptual status of recent scientific theory (and of the foundations of mathematics and logic, as well) is due to souls, of the kind Leibniz classifies as "spirits," reaching their limits of "distinct perceptibility."

PAUL J. JOHNSON
Philosophy Department
California State University-San Bernardino

MOMENTARY CONCERN: Technology and the Obscuring
of the Religious

The paper begins by distinguishing the subjective and objective aspects of the religious in nature and then attempts to argue that the encounter with the divine in nature is fundamental to religion. Next the more obvious ways the technological cocoon separates us from nature are briefly rehearsed and I then proceed to utilize Polanyi's distinction of focal and distal awareness to suggest how technology separates us from the final natural source of religious awareness, ourselves.

WILLIAM B. JONES
Department of Philosophy and Religious Studies
Old Dominion University

APPROACHES AND OBSTACLES TO A TAXONOMY OF TECHNOLOGY AND RELIGION

In a continuing effort to establish some points of reference by means of which to organize existing knowledge and to identify promising lines of investigation, the challenge of developing a categorical scheme of the interrelations between technology and religion is addressed again herein. The results of an earlier, first step toward a taxonomy of technology and religion are reviewed, its assumptions examined, the limitations thereof noted, and suggestions for extending it considered.

IRVING A. KELTER
History Department, University of St. Thomas

PAOLO FOSCARINI'S THEOLOGICAL DEFENSE OF THE NEW ASTRONOMY:
Neglected Evidence Concerning the Condemnation of 1616

In 1616 the Roman Catholic Church issued a decree condemning absolutely the Italian *Letter . . . on the opinion of the Pythagoreans and of Copernicus concerning the mobility of the earth and the stability of the sun* (1615) written by the Carmelite monk, Paolo Antonio Foscarini. This paper analyzes a neglected work by Foscarini, the Latin Defense, in which the Carmelite theologian attempted to forestall the condemnation of Copernicus. By studying the various theological, exegetical and scientific arguments utilized by Foscarini, we can come to a better understanding of the issues involved in the famous condemnation of 1616.

KRISHNA KUMAR
Physics Department
Tennessee Technological University

REV. G. DAVID CAMPBELL
First Presbyterian Church

PREDESTINATION, FREE WILL, AND THE NEW PHYSICS

A parallel is drawn between two apparently contradictory concepts in three different contexts: Predestination and Free Will in the Christian religion; Omniscience and Karma in the Hindu religion; Predictability and Uncertainty in the new physics. Examples are given from theological studies, from physics studies, as well as from everyday life to argue that the contradiction is apparent only, that both of the seemingly contradictory concepts are essential for a deep understanding of ourselves and of our relationship with God.

PHILIP LEWIN
Liberal Studies Center, Clarkson University

SCIENCE, RELIGION, SOUL

Within the frame of modernity, science and religion exist as differentiated domains of specialization which divide cultural space between them. They share the characteristically modern form of disciplinary constitution as regimes of truth. The threat of modernity for religious sensibility follows from this constitution, consisting of its gradual delegitimation of soul, of an authentic ground of knowing and valuing situated in historically lived experience, as the person is increasingly colonized by cultural practices.

A. O. MARSHA
Department of Religion and Philosophy
Fisk University

MEDICAL TECHNOLOGY AND THE NEOCONCEPTUAL DIALECTIC OF CREATION VERSUS ABORTION

In systematically unpacking the implications of reproductive technology for creation versus abortion, the neoconceptus' right to a life emerges in sharp contradistinction to the right to life. We are led to a hugely amplified reverence for life. For even modified abortionism would rend a man "asunder from himself." I briefly conclude with an outline of a new criterion—grief—for handling counter-pressures from abortionists and others.

JOHN F. MCELLIGOTT
History Department, Eastern Illinois University

THE RECONCILIATION OF RELIGION AND SCIENCE IN AMERICAN PERIODICALS, 1830-60

Based on a large sample of American magazines, this paper describes a widespread effort to reconcile religion and science just before Darwin published. In the periodicals, science was held in the highest esteem, but it was also regarded as the basis of every attack religion endured. At bottom was a fundamental error that writers attempted to correct. Various as the sources are, the argument was completely uniform. That argument is what this paper presents.

RICHARD J. MCGOWAN
St. Joseph's College

THE THREE CULTURES, THE TRANSCENDENT, AND THE FUTURE OF HOMO SAPIENS

People such as Ellul, Mumford, and Turing long ago identified the twentieth-century as The Machine Age. Yet C. P. Snow, in 1960, identified only two cultures. I show that our culture's visual images, especially T.V. and movie images, have evolved to present a third culture, i.e., the technological culture. I suggest that the imagery leaves little room for the transcendent or any "secondary reality." Finally, I submit that the visual predominance of the technological culture calls into question the nature of homo sapiens.

EMERSON THOMAS MCMULLEN
Department of History and Philosophy of Science
Indiana University

PURPOSE, EXTRATERRESTRIAL LIFE, AND GALILEO'S TELESCOPE

An intellectual consequence growing out of the condemnation of 1277 was hypothesizing "according to the imagination." Employing the metaphysical principles of plenitude and sufficient reason, Nicholas of Cusa asserted that extraterrestrial life (ETL) exists. Later, the idea of ETL was also supported by teleological arguments. Galileo's telescopic discoveries only fueled these telic arguments for ETL. Huygens advocated planetary ETL, even though his own telescopic observations convinced him there was no life on the moon.

ALBERT B. RANDALL
Philosophy Department
Austin Peay State University

A MODERN TOWER OF BABEL: Scientific Creationism

The emergence of scientific creationism approximately twenty years ago, as an explanation of the natural world, created a controversy that has engaged not only religion and science but also philosophy, politics, education, and the law. The purpose of this paper is to examine the nature of explanation in order to distinguish the significant differences between several kinds of explanations: those of mythology, religion, history, sacred history, philosophy, science, and scientific creationism. The paper concludes that scientific creationism is a "confusion of tongues," i.e., a category mistake as an explanation.

KIM ALAINE RATHMAN
Center for Theology and the Natural Sciences
Graduate Theological Union

THE ETHICAL IMPLICATIONS OF
THE "COMMON HERITAGE" PRINCIPLE
FOR THE COMMERCIALIZATION OF OUTER SPACE

This project seeks to show how an application of contemporary Roman Catholic human rights theory, as seen in the Catholic Bishops letter on economics and the encyclicals it draws on, and the ethical works of Amartya Sen may be used (1) to adjudicate between the claims made by Third and First World countries concerning the just allocation of outer space resources, and (2) provide the ethical guidelines for an appropriate international agency capable of distributing those resources equitably.

JEFF SCHLOSS
Biology Department, Westmont College

SOCIOBIOLOGICAL ALTRUISM, EXHORTATIONS TO SACRIFICE IN THE SYNOPTICS, AND THE PAULINE NOTION OF THE FLESH: Hath Darwin Suffered a Prophet's Dishonor?

Darwinian and sociobiological naturalism are opposed by the conservative Christian theology even though their claim that biological helping behaviors are restricted to kin selection and reciprocal altruism is remarkably consistent with both Pauline and Synoptic anthropology. Thus, Christian hostility to sociobiology has been viewed as knowledge industry boundary work and/or religious anti-naturalism. However, sociological theories of religious nominalization provocatively suggest tension at this interface may reflect agreement—over truths people believe rhetorically but do not want to hear.

EDWARD L. SCHOEN
Philosophy and Religion Department
Western Kentucky University

DAVID HUME, MIRACLES AND THE VIRGIN MARY

Contrary to Hume's contention, there is no essential connection between miracles and violations of natural laws. Not only may violations of natural law be utterly nonmiraculous, miracles may occur in complete conformity with such laws. Furthermore, a proper understanding of miracles in terms of divine agency places them into an epistemic context where the growth of science does not directly threaten their possibility.

MARK SHALE
Integrative Studies Program
Kentucky State University

WILLIAM McDOUGALL AND THE REACTION TO VICTORIAN SCIENTIFIC NATURALISM

Psychologist William McDougall (1871-1938) belonged to a group of British scientists who believed the dominant scientific movement in the second-half of the nineteenth century, Victorian scientific naturalism, threatened morality and the ages-long quest of man for the spiritual. McDougall believed his theory of consciousness, conceived in part upon the energy concept and field theory in physics and experiments on vision, demonstrated the inadequacy of mechanistic materialism and promoted belief in the spiritual nature of man.

GEORGE W. SHIELDS
Philosophy Program, Kentucky State University

REFLECTIONS ON BARBOUR'S
RELIGION IN AN AGE OF SCIENCE

I shall argue that Ian Barbour has not spelled out the full complexity of issues involved in adjudicating the compatibility of process theism and natural science. While he seems correct in maintaining that process theism has an attractive fit with evolutionary biology, ecology, and certain recent interpretations of quantum physics, a number of important, germane issues are conspicuously missing from the discussion. These issues concern the compatibility of the process theistic model and (1) the existence of general relativistic singularities, (2) the thermodynamic argument for the temporal finitude of the natural universe, and (3) the Big Bang argument for the temporal finitude of the natural universe.

I will sketch an argument to the effect that the resolution of these issues requires a revision of process theism's notion of divine power.

DOUGLAS W. SHRADER
Philosophy Department, SUNY-College at Oneonta

DEATH IN A NEW AGE: MEDICAL TECHNOLOGY,
NEAR DEATH EXPERIENCES
AND THE CONCEPT OF A PERSON

The paper examines some contemporary moral dilemmas posed by the rapid advancement of medical technology, the inability of traditional religious structures to forge consensus regarding such dilemmas, and the associated widespread interest in Near Death Experiences as a possible scientific basis for belief in life after death. It will be argued that the evidence regarding NDE's is insufficient to establish immortality, but that they nonetheless provide excellent grounds for believing death to be an interesting, perhaps even intensely pleasant, experience. They may even point the way to a more refined concept of a human being: and that, it will be argued, is what is needed for the resolution of moral dilemmas stemming from technological advancement in medicine.

ROBERT H. SILLIMAN
Department of History, Emory University

PROFESSIONALISM IN THE GENESIS-GEOLOGY DEBATE OF THE EARLY 19TH CENTURY

In the first half of the nineteenth century, investigations in geology led to an account of the earth's history that apparently conflicted with the Biblical record of creation. Attracting wide public notice, the issue sparked a heated debate that engaged writers differing markedly in background, education, and expertise. In America most of the specialists, whether geologists or Bible scholars, undertook to harmonize Genesis and geology. Emerging professionalism, the paper will attempt to show, helps explain this as well as other features of the debate.

MICHELLE SCALISE SUGIYAMA
English Department
University of California at Santa Barbara

EVOLUTIONARY ANTHROPOLOGY, LITERATURE, AND "THE MORAL OF THE STORY": Is Blood Thicker than Ethics?

This paper explores the relationship between ethics and evolutionary anthropology through the medium of literature. It examines two stories which revolve around the moral dilemma of disobeying the law or betraying kin—the story of Abraham and Isaac and William Faulkner's "Barn Burning." The protagonist in each story makes a similar decision, a decision that is traditionally seen as being "right." The question posed in this paper is whether or not these decisions accord with the basic principles of evolutionary theory.

LIBA TAUB
The Adler Planetarium
Chicago, Illinois

THE PLACE OF ASTRONOMY IN ANCIENT GREEK ETHICAL PHILOSOPHY

Accepting the traditional view of the divinity of the celestial bodies, the astronomer Ptolemy further claimed that their study was an ethical endeavor. Many Hellenistic thinkers were interested in ethics, but Ptolemy's emphasis on astronomy was unusual. This view was, however, not unique within Greek philosophy. Ptolemy's writings, representing a culmination of Greek astronomy, are similarly the culmination of a neglected form of Platonic ethical theory, with its special emphasis on astronomy.

DENNIS TEMPLE
Philosophy Department, Roosevelt University

THE NEW DESIGN ARGUMENT: What Does It Prove?

The new design argument claims that the universe was "fine-tuned for life" through delicate balances of physical constants. It then claims (a) that cosmic fine-tuning needs an explanation, (b) that action of a Creator is the best explanation, and (c) that this confirms the existence of a Creator. I examine the logic of this argument from the standpoint of a theory of explanation. I argue that (a) is certainly correct, that (b) is probably correct, but that (c) is somewhat dubious.

DAVID A. VALONE
Department of Social Science
University of Chicago

ONE GOD, ONE PEOPLE: Victorian Ethnology
and the Unity of the Human Race

The question of origin and development of the human race became increasingly problematic during the course of the nineteenth century. By mid-century, the traditional explanation of the human race based on the first chapters of Genesis had been undermined by the growing evidence of the diversity of human physical and social types. In response, some turned to the emerging discipline of comparative philology to provide a new scientific explanation of human unity based on linguistic data, "domesticating" the difficulties of the savage within a conventional intellectual framework.

BRANT VOGEL
Institute of Liberal Arts, Emory University

GIORGIONE'S USE OF METEOROLOGY AND
THE EMBLEMATIC MODE OF THOUGHT

William Ashworth has drawn attention to the "emblematic world view." This epistemological paradigm treats the world as a complex of symbolic meaning held together by resemblance. Many paintings of the 16th century operate emblematically. This paper examines the apparently contradictory trend toward naturalism confluent with emblematic expression. Through the example of the Tempest, it will show how attention to the natural world operates as a part of the emblematic mode, laying the foundation for the scientific world view.

DARYL J. WENNEMANN
Department of Philosophy, St. Louis University

THE CONTEMPORANEITY OF THE NON-CONTEMPORANEOUS
OR THE VAGARIES OF
UNEVEN TECHNOLOGICAL DEVELOPMENT

This paper surveys the problem of disproportionate or uneven technological development according to Karl Mannheim's conception of the contemporaneity of the non-contemporaneous. I argue that this is the fundamental problem of technological development. Uneven technological development causes various technical and social malfunctions. This problem also informs Jacques Ellul's treatment of technique. On the basis of this analysis I am able to compare the views of Mannheim and Ellul.

DAN WETMORE
Department of Philosophy
Bowling Green State University

THE PITH OF THE PENDULUM

A seminal question in the consideration of Western religious and scientific pursuits is whether these two realms of endeavor can be meaningfully integrated. This paper is an expression of optimism on that point. Through the analogy of an object in pendulum swing, it is argued that religion and science are ultimately and necessarily conjoined. This holds, it is maintained, even given the worst case scenario that they are deemed incommensurable.

MICHAEL WUTZ
Department of English, Emory University

MALCOLM LOWRY'S *DARK AS THE GRAVE*:
Technology as Salvation

This presentation explores the opposition between Nature and the Machine in the oeuvre of Malcolm Lowry. While the world in his fiction is frequently jeopardized by the forays of technology, Lowry is also interested in the formal possibilities of technology for his fiction. As if to negotiate his opposition, Lowry probes the dual properties of machines in the service of his religious vision: they may function as engines of damnation or salvation. *Dark As The Grave* serves as a case study of this dichotomy.

IVAN L. ZABILKA
Independent Scholar, Lexington, Kentucky

CREATIONISM IS BAD SCIENCE AND BAD THEOLOGY

The purpose of this paper is to demonstrate the inadequate Creationist understanding of science through consideration of their claim that light from distant stars was created enroute, giving only the appearance of age to the universe. Secondly, the Creationist's inappropriate hermeneutic of Genesis 1 distorts the non-scientific purpose of this orally transmitted catechetical passage for which the purpose was teaching about the inappropriateness of the worship of other gods.

GREGORY J. ZOLTOWSKI
Fine Arts Department, Siena College

A WORDLESS UNION—ART AND THE PRAYER OF SILENCE

Using archetypal designations we might say that human beings have an "image-maker" within them. The artists among us act as heralds that announce the coming of this image-maker. This paper will elaborate on the phenomenon of the relationship of creator with creation, an analogical bond that results in the metamorphosis of both. Resources will include: Jung, Bateson, Berman, Neumann, Progoff, Janson, Coomaraswamy, Burke-Feldman, Edwards and Gilligan, among others.

DESCRIPTIONS OF CONFERENCE PAPERS 1992

MICHAEL ALFANO
Humanities Department, Polytechnic University

TOWARD AN ETHICS OF EMBODIMENT:
Implications for Technology

An epistemology that views "subject" and "object" as correlative and mutually constitutive will lead to an understanding of technology as a creative process in which values are present from the start and continue to exert an influence over future events. Ontologically, we relate to situations, environments, and technologies by making them a part of ourselves through an act of embodiment. The ethical implications of this thesis are exemplified in our relationships with automobiles and computers.

D. BRIAN AUSTIN
Philosophy Department, Cumberland College

RANDOMNESS, OMNISCIENCE, AND DIVINE ACTION

Natural randomness of the kind described by much of modern physics is of potential use in ameliorating some of the conceptual difficulties attendant to the notion of divine action in the world. This randomness provides the "openness" needed for a coherent motion of divine action and allows the suggestion of a greater similarity between divine and human action. Thus criticisms or divine action based on problems with contingency in the divine life can be addressed more successfully than in the past.

BRIAN CONNIFF
Department of English, The University of Dayton

AUDEN, NIEBUHR, AND MODERN RELIGIOUS POETRY

At the end of 1940, as he was struggling with his return to the Church and with the public crisis of World War I, W. H. Auden turned to the friendship and theological writings of Reinhold Niebuhr. Auden's struggle with Niebuhr's system of ethics, especially as it is developed in *Christianity and Power Politics*, provides a crucial link in his movement to religious poetry and a provocative case study in the interrelations of modern poetry, science, and theology.

ROBERT ENSIGN
Department of English, Morris Brown College

GOD THE DIVINE ENGINEER:
The Thought of Henry M. Morris
and the Institute for Creation Research

The "Scientific Creationism (SC) of Henry Morris and his associates has drawn both criticism and ridicule from mainstream philosophers of science largely on two grounds. First, SC is not science at all, but religion disguised as science. Second, though Morris and his associates consistently refer to themselves as "scientists," they are in fact engineers. Both criticisms are at least partially invalid. The first depends on how one defines "science," using the issues of Mechanism-vs-Teleology and of Theism-vs-Nontheism in methodology. The second becomes invalid when we realize that Morris perceives Creation as a vast engineering project and God as a Divine Engineer.

JOHN W. HAAS, JR.
Chemistry Department, Gordon College

JOHN WESLEY'S EIGHTEENTH-CENTURY VIEWS
ON SCIENCE AND CHRISTIANITY:
A Reexamination of the Charge of Antiscience

John Wesley (1703) is best known as an itinerant evangelist who was the father of the Methodist movement. An active participant in the English Enlightenment, he would maintain a lifelong interest in the natural sciences. His use of science to buttress his grand scheme of furthering the gospel, helping the sick and educating his constituency brought severe criticism in his day and thereafter. This paper will examine the charge of anti-science in the light of his evangelistic and social concerns.

HILTON HINDERLITER
Department of Physics
Penn State University, Kensington

THE DISPLACEMENT OF RELIGION,
FROM SIGNIFICANT PORTIONS
OF ITS HISTORIC DOMAIN,
BY SCIENCE AND TECHNOLOGY—A CONTINUING PROCESS

The relationship between religion and science/technology is explored through an analysis of cases in which science has come to address subjects formerly under the jurisdiction of religion. The most striking example has to do with ideas about the meaning and purpose of life. A particularly significant point is that religion once dictated the boundaries of science, but now science assumes the authority to declare invalid any tenet of religion with which it disagrees.

TOM M. HUGHES
Computer Science Department
Kentucky State University

CAUSES OF IMMORTALITY

A perplexing question about early patristic philosophy is why Paul was successful in communicating a doctrine, emphasizing the attainment of an active personal immortality, to audiences educated in systems of thought that do not claim this as a possibility. To answer this question, an analysis of Paul's letters is made which suggests the catalyst, underlying the spread of Pauline Christianity, is Paul revising Aristotle's natural philosophy to include a fifth cause, whereby personal immortality naturally results.

WILLIAM B. HURLBUT, M.D.
Innovative Academics Courses, Stanford University

COSMETICS AND COSMOLOGY:
African Adornment, Christianity,
and Biomedical Technology

The use of biomedical technology for purposes beyond the traditional role of healing raises difficult questions about nature, the body and the place of man as artist of his own creation. These issues are explored through the relationship between cosmetics (body adornment) and cosmology (world view) from three contrasting perspectives. The pervasive connection between medicine, cosmetics and magical and religious practices is discussed and principles are sought to guide the use of our new technology.

ALLEN E. HYE
Department of Modern Languages
Wright State University

IN THE IMAGE OF GOD? THE FRAGILITY OF HUMAN IDENTITY IN SCIENTIFIC DRAMA

Are humans indeed created in the image of God and possessed of a constant nature and firm identity? Or are they merely relative and uncertain beings whose personality and identity are determined by social, economic, and biological forces? This paper will discuss these questions as they are answered in several plays, including *Woyzeck, Gas, Inherit the Wind, A Man's Man,* and *The Ruling Class.*

HOLLIS R. JOHNSON
Astronomy Department, Indiana University

GODS AND THE NEW PHYSICS

Old and new knowledge from science challenges some ideas about God. To examine these more precisely, we consider the attributes of possible classes of Gods in the universe, including both supernatural and natural Gods. Characteristics of a "minimum God" are hypothesized. The relation of each type of God to Nature and natural laws is outlined.

WILLIAM B. JONES
Department of Philosophy and Religious Studies
Old Dominion University

THINKING ABOUT TECHNOLOGY, RELIGION, AND SCIENCE:
Toward a New Beginning

As an alternative to usual approaches to thinking about science, technology, and religion, which tend to take science as their point of reference—whether as ideal or hobgoblin, a scheme centered upon technology is proposed. The place of religion and science in such a picture is sketched. Since the kind of society and culture a people has depends upon its economic base and technological capabilities, a classification of religions emerges. Furthermore, "rational science" is exhibited as technologically conditioned.

JACQUELYN ANN K. KEGLEY
Philosophy/Religious Studies
California State University - Bakersfield

TECHNOLOGY AND NEW FORMS OF ANALYSIS:
Aesthetic and Moral

Technology is never mere neutral instrumentality, but rather is heavily value-ladened. It is a fundamental mode of human creativity and thus questions raised by aesthetic analysis can also illuminate aspects of technology. These include concepts such as "technological viruosity" and "the technological imperative." Technology is also a basic mode of human embodiment. As such it carries within it implicit assertions about the human being—what that being is and how such beings ought to be treated as well as how beings of this nature ought to be related to each other.

J. ERIC LANE
History Department
California State University - Los Angeles

MYTH AND THE MATHEMATIZATION OF NATURE

This study is an exploration of the mythological origins of two of the fundamental aspects of modern science and technology, the concept of inertia and the importance of mathematics as an analytical tool; it is an interpretation of some of the central passages of Galileo's *Two New Sciences* that establish modern mathematical physics; it is an attempt to explore the relation between the history of religions and the history of scientific ideas.

RON LEVY
History Department, The Colorado College

A CLASH OF WILLS: Theories of Voluntarism
in Early Modern Science

By exploring Robert Boyle's circumspect treatment of physical laws of nature, this study argues that law ultimately stands as a principle of divine reason rather than of divine will in Boyle's thought. A 'natural law' tradition informs Boyle's appeal to law. By honoring man's faculties of will, this tradition suggests an 'anthropological' voluntarism, one tempering the theological voluntarism compelling Boyle's epistemology. Renaissance and Reformation values coexist in Boyle's dual conceptions of voluntarism.

ANITA MANUEL
Theology and Personality Program
Emory University

SALVATION: A Dynamic Systems Approach

A dynamic systems model drawn primarily from Allen and Starr's *Hierarchy: Perspectives for Ecological Complexity* is used to critique James Lapsley's model of participation in salvatory process. Although Lapsley has attempted to replace a definition of salvation as individual escape from punishment due to sin with a socially oriented process model his model remains individualistic. A complete account of salvation must include a description of the developmental process of the environment.

JOHN N. MARTIN
Department of Philosophy
University of Cincinnati

PLOTINUS' ONE AS THE PRODUCT OF MATHEMATICAL ABSTRACTION

Philosophical explanations of the Neoplatonists' mystical reversion to the One have always been obscure. One avenue that seems to employ ideas from logic is the *via negativa*. This paper studies the roots of this idea in the notion of "abstraction" as developed in Greek mathematics and philosophy, particularly Pythagoreanism and Neoplatonism. It is argued that this negation is non-truth-functional, has a formally definable semantics, and counts as a case of scalar negation as studied in linguistics.

RONALD MAWBY
Whitney Young College
Kentucky State University

WHEN INCONSISTENCIES THREATEN: Paraconsistent Strategies in Science and Religion

Theoretical inconsistency is not uncommon either within or between science and religion. Standard logic says that accepting an inconsistent theory must be irrational. However, as scientific and religious examples show, sometimes we do not know how to remove theoretical inconsistency without robbing a theory of its cognitive value. Paraconsistent logics suggest that retaining an inconsistency while limiting its consequences can be a rational strategy in the face of inconsistence. Two such paraconsistent strategies are discussed.

JOHN F. MCELLIGOTT
History Department, Eastern Illinois University

BEFORE DARWIN: The Meaning of Evolution

This paper argues that Darwin's impact stems primarily from his deciding an issue whose terms had been well defined before he wrote. In the pre-Darwinian debate over evolution, all sides had agreed that if a theory such as his were true, then God did not exist.

JOSEPH O'CONNELL
Program in History of Science
Princeton University

RELIGIOUS IDEAS AND THE DEVELOPMENT OF ELECTRICAL STANDARDS

This paper discusses the realization, representation, and dissemination of electrical standards in Victorian England. The primary characters are J. C. Maxwell, with his explicitly religious ideas about standards, and William Thomson, with his devotion to a system of absolute units and the structured relations by which absolute values are disseminated to less accurate representations. Their system has remained in use to this day, retaining a religious language and a philosophy of metrology bearing similarities to Catholic sacramental theology.

C. GARY OLIVER
Department of Landscape Architecture
Ball State University

FIRE, AN AGENT OF ECOLOGICAL AND SPIRITUAL RENEWAL

From savaging a Brazilian rainforest to reviving an Illinois prairie, fire renews and destroys creation. When should it burn and when should it die or remain unlit? As a spiritual player fire likewise enacts opposing roles—Biblical flames level Gomorrah and ignite the Pentecostal birth of the

Christian Church. Today, when wisely governed, fire restores ecological wholeness to many plundered landscapes, and so reclaims its gift of spiritual renewal.

JEROME F. O'MALLEY
English Department, Slippery Rock University

CONTEXTS OF THE SPIRITUALISM OF SIR ARTHUR CONAN DOYLE

Sir Arthur Conan Doyle (1859-1930), the creator of Sherlock Holmes, was also the leading apostle of Spiritualism world-wide from 1917 to his death in 1930. A complete evaluation of this commitment is impossible since his private papers are closed to public scrutiny. As a response to this impasse, this study will evaluate the public writings of Doyle on Spiritualism by relating them to the cultural history of his time. This relationship makes clear that Doyle's apologetic attempts to reconcile religion and science. In fact, for him Spiritualism is a science. Doyle presented Spiritualism as the wave of the future borrowing from Auguste Comte (1798-1857) the theory of the progress of mankind through three stages. The culmination of this progress is the age of positivism or science. The scientific dimension of Spiritualism is evident from Doyle's view of the medium as an object and source for scientific data. A critique of Doyle's views from a historical and religious perspective will use Karl Barth (1886-1968), the German theologian, as a guide.

ROBERT C. PETERSEN
Department of English
Middle Tennessee State University

UNCONSCIOUS MEMORY AND BIOLOGICAL VARIATION:
Samuel Butler's *Ernest Pontifex, or the Way of All Flesh* (1903) as Response to Charles Darwin's Theory of Evolution

Samuel Butler's Ernest Pontifex, or The Way of All Flesh (1903) documents an attempt to come to terms in fiction with the evolutionary hypothesis of Charles Darwin and to revise the Darwinian heritage that looms so large in late nineteenth- and twentieth-century culture.

ERIC RAUTH
Department of Romance Languages
University of North Carolina at Greensboro

TELEOLOGY AND THE AESTHETICS
OF BIOLOGICAL FORM:
Arguments from Darwin, Kant and Gould

Darwin acknowledged a certain incommensurateness between data and design, natural form and teleology, in the metaphorical ambiguity of his term "natural selection." Kantian beauty evidences a comparably voluntarist attribution of "purposiveness without purpose" to artistic and natural forms, a paradox he resolves only be recourse to the directed functionalism of "sublimity." Gould critiques the teleology of gradualist evolution by stressing the anti-linearity of contingency and "exaptation" in speciation, terms with decidedly aesthetic implications. His punctuated evolutionism with early maximal disparity of traits, and his emphasis on the as yet unclassifiable morphological detail, highlight the classificatory rigidity of genealogical thinking in scientific as well as literary vocabularies.

BRYAN S. RENNIE
Youngstown State University

RELIGIOUS PLURALISM AND BOOTSTRAP THEORY

In suggesting that physical reality as we know it "pulls itself up by its own bootstraps" Geoffrey Chew's bootstrap theory subordinates all supposedly fundamental elements to the coherence of the whole and recognizes both "reality" and hard science to be approximate. I suggest that a valuable approach to religious pluralism which similarly subordinates questions of ontology and reality to those of coherence and significance can be derived from the thought of Mircea Eliade.

EDWARD L. SCHOEN
Department of Philosophy and Religion
Western Kentucky University

GALILEO AND THE CHURCH

For Aquinas, all science, including theological science, should be organized as a series of demonstrations from known First Principles. As God's revealed word, properly interpreted Scripture could not conflict with genuine scientific truth of any kind. Galileo shared this respect for Scripture. His conflict with the Church stemmed from his controversial understanding of proper scientific methods.

ROBERT J. SCHOLNICK
English Department, College of William and Mary

PERMEABLE BOUNDARIES:
Literature and Science in America

Based on *American Literature and Science,* a collection of original essays edited by the author that is to be published in 1992, this paper systematically examines the changing relationship between literature and science, two ways of knowing often thought to be opposed. Taking an historical perspective, it shows how such writers as Franklin, Jefferson, Poe, Emerson, Twain, and Pynchon, the novelist of the cybernetic age, made productive use of scientific concepts in their imaginative work.

ROBERT SHELTON
Science and Technology Studies
Michigan State University

SCIENCE FICTION'S COSMIC MASTERPIECE:
Olaf Stapledon's *Star Maker*

Stapledon's *Star Maker* (1937) epitomizes the grandest aspirations of speculative fiction—aspirations which invite the labels "cosmic" and "religious." My talk will argue that Stapledon, in a highly original Creation Myth, brings together the then-latest scientific theories of astrophysics with the oldest religious ideas of the spiritual. Mixing political satire, guest narrative, and philosophical contemplation, *Star Maker* modernizes the search for God (the Maker of Stars) by turning it into a journey through space-time and into the soul.

GEORGE W. SHIELDS
Philosophy Program, Kentucky State University

OF GOD, SONGBIRDS, AND SOCIOBIOLOGY

This paper critically examines some of the implications of sociobiology for religious belief and theology of nature in particular. I will focus on the work of E. O. Wilson. I shall argue that he fails to recognize the significance of the possible "over-determination" of biological phenomena. By employing

Charles Hartshorne's work on birdsong, I will show that an aesthetic as well as sociobiological perspective on animal behavior has explanatory power.

WILLIAM F. TOWNE
Department of Biology, Kutztown University

WHAT ARE BUMBLEBEES FOR?

Two answers seem seductively reasonable: bees serve mankind by producing honey, an anthropocentric answer; or they serve their ecosystems by pollinating flowers, an ecocentric one. The activities of organisms, however, support neither of these views. What bumblebees do best is make more bumblebees; this, if anything, is what they are for. Although it does not satisfactorily answer the original, implicitly teleological question, it is the only scientifically defensible answer, except perhaps this: Bumblebees just happened.

J. W. TRAPHAGAN
Department of Religious Studies
University of Pittsburgh

BEYOND RELATIVISM AND FOUNDATIONALISM:
Metaphysical Implications of Modern Physics and Christian Mysticism for Research in Ethics

In this paper, I look at the metaphysical implications of modern physics, focusing on the ideas of physicists David Bohm and Henry Margenau. I argue that if their conclusions about the nature of reality obtain, two further conclusions may be drawn. First, the argument between relativists and foundationalists concerning truth is obsolete. Second, given similarities between the ideas about reality proposed by some Christian mystics and these physicists, research into Christian mysticism may bear fruit in reconstructing ethics.

STANLEY WALLEN
Independent Scholar, Knoxville, Tennessee

THE CREATION OF THE UNIVERSE AND OUR KNOWLEDGE OF GOD:
Defining Event or Irrevelance

In recent years cosmology and particle physics have engaged in an inquiry into the earliest moments of the universe with a growing conviction that this era is essential to understanding its present state. The spectacular results that have ensued have led some to believe that we are on the threshold of an understanding not only of nature but of God as well. This paper will examine these ideas and the degree of their validity.

THOMAS G. WALSH
Integrative Studies Program
Kentucky State University

RELIGION, SCIENCE AND POSTMODERNISM:
A Weberian Analysis

Beginning with a review of the "Weber Thesis" concerning the role of religion (Calvinism) in the emergence of modern rationality and consciousness, the essay turns to examine postmodern phenomena, particularly trends in science and religion. While no attempt is made to establish any causal connection between religious developments and scientific developments, the essay does seek, with reference to the work of David Ray Griffin, to identify patterns and characteristics that reflect the shift to postmodernism. If postmodernism is to represent some grand civilizational shift of Weberian proportion, rather than a fashionable academic research program, then its features must be evident in both science and religion.

JOHN D. WHITE
Department of Philosophy, Talladega College

BELIEF SYSTEM INTERNAL INCONSISTENCY

Operative belief systems, past and present, implemented at any societal layer and in whatever numbers, do not collapse or dysfunction due to inconsistency with other belief systems; they cease to function in the long term under the weight of inconsistencies among the tenets within the system. On rare occasions the tenets are obviously inconsistent: concurrent belief in the omnipotence of God and free will, for example. Most of the time the inconsistencies are not blatant, but do present themselves subsequent to philosophical analysis. An example of this latter case is offered taken from the belief system of the Medieval Catholic Church where irregularities in music theory and music practice, had they been elucidated at the time, would have served as enucleation of a profound philosophical contradiction long before Luther.

PATRICK A. WILSON
Philosophy Department, Hampden-Sydney College

TELEOLOGY, ANTHROPOCENTRISM, AND RELIGION

An "anthropic" principle defended by Barrow and Tipler purports to account for the remarkable life-sustaining properties of the universe by reference to the special status of humans, and seems to bridge the gap between traditional religious explanations and modern scientific ones. But this principle's teleological and anthropocentric features are unintelligible outside of a religious context. The problems of specifying—and justifying the significance of—intelligent life face even a religious interpretation of the principle.

JAN WOJCIK
Philosophy Department, University of Kentucky

ROBERT BOYLE AS LAY THEOLOGIAN:
The Limits of Reason and Empirical Methodology

First, I examine Boyle's views on reason's limits where the content of revelation is concerned. Second, I show the close parallel between Boyle's views on reason's limits in the context of theology and his empirical scientific methodology. Finally, I show that Boyle's views on reason's limits sprang from his belief that God deliberately created the human mind in such a way that neither a complete understanding of theological mysteries nor a full penetration into nature's secrets is possible in this life.

ABOUT THE AUTHORS

FREDERICK FERRÉ, son of the late theologian Nels F. S. Ferré, is Research Professor of Philosophy and Chair of the Graduate Environmental Ethics Certificate Program at the University of Georgia at Athens. Professor Ferré's distinguished publishing career includes authorship of *Language, Logic and God* (1961, 1981, 1987), *Basic Modern Philosophy of Religion* (1967), and most recently, *Philosophy of Technology* (1989). Author of scores of articles and reviews, he has produced scholarly editions of William Paley's *Natural Theology* and August Comte's *Introduction to Positive Philosophy* as well as co-authored or co-edited five other volumes. He is also General Editor of the scholarly annual, *Research in Philosophy and Technology*. A past President of the American Theological Association, Dr. Ferré served for some sixteen years as Chair of the Department of Philosophy at Dickenson College, where he was elected to the Charles A. Dana Professorship in 1970. From 1983 to 1988, he was Head of the Department of Philosophy at the University of Georgia. Dr. Ferré was educated at Boston University, Vanderbilt, and St. Andrews (Scotland) where he earned the doctorate on two successive Fulbright awards.

THOR HALL is LeRoy A. Martin Distinguished Professor of Religious Studies at the University of Tennessee at Chattanooga. He holds the EX.ART. degree (Math and Physics) from Oslo University; a DIPL. THEOL. from Union Scandinavian Seminary, Gothenburg, Sweden; and the MRS and Ph.D. degrees (Systematic Theology) from Duke University (1962). He is the author of some twelve books, including *A Framework for Faith* (1970), *Anders Nygren* (1978), *Systematic Theology for Today* (1978), and *The Evolution of Christology* (1982).

STANLEY L. JAKI is the Distinguished University Professor of the History and Philosophy of Physics at Seton Hall University. Recipient of both the Lecomte du Nouy Prize and the Templeton Prize, Dr. Jaki is perhaps best known for his Gifford Lectures entitled *The Road of Science and the Ways to God* (University of Chicago Press, 1981), one of his more than twenty-five published volumes. Holding doctorates in both systematic theology (Pontifical Athenaeum of Sant' Anselmo, Rome) and physics (Fordham University), Professor Jaki was elected for a year's sojourn at the Institute for Advanced Study at Princeton University. He is a priest of the Benedictine Order and has lectured at more than seventy universities around the globe.

JACQUELYN ANN K. KEGLEY is Professor and Chair of the Department of Philosophy and Religious Studies at California State University, Bakersfield. Her numerous publications include "Technology and the Good Life" in the *Proceedings* of the International Conference on the Unity of the Sciences (1989), "History and Philosophy of Science: Necessary Partners or Merely Roommates?" in Thelma Levine, ed., *History and Anti-History in Philosophy* (1990), and a chapter on philosopher Paul Weiss in the *Library of Living Philosophers* series (forthcoming). In 1989 Dr. Kegley received the award for Outstanding Professor of the California State University system.

RON LEVY is a doctoral candidate at the University of Chicago and for the past three years has been an instructor in the Department of History at The Colorado College, Colorado Springs, Colorado. He has been the recipient of a Century Fellowship at the University of Chicago and of the Thomas J. Watson Fellowship for Overseas Study.

RONALD MAWBY is Associate Professor in the Whitney Young College, the honors program at Kentucky State University in Frankfort, Kentucky. He received his Ph.D. in Cognitive Psychology from Clark University in 1986. Dr. Mawby has been an EPSCoR Visiting Scholar (1991) at the University of Kentucky, and co-author of several papers, including "Linguistic and Logical Factors in Recognition of Indeterminacy," *Cognitive Development* (1989), and "Mapping the Cognitive Demands of Learning to Program," *Thinking* (1987). He has been the recipient of several faculty research grants allowing him to investigate paraconsistent logics.

ERNAN MCMULLIN is Director of the Program in the History and Philosophy of Science at the University of Notre Dame. Dr. McMullin is past President of the Philosophy of Science Association, the American Catholic Philosophical Association, and the Metaphysical Society of America. He is a Fellow of the American Academy of Arts and Sciences, the American Association for the Advancement of Science, and the International Academy for the History of Science. Books he has written or edited include *The Concept of Matter* (1963); *Galileo, Man of Science* (1967); *Newton on Matter and Action* (1978); *Evolution and Creation* (1985); *Construction and Constraint* (1988); *The Philosophical Consequences of Quantum Theory* (1989), which he edited with J. Cushing; and *The Social Dimensions of Science* (1991). He is currently working on a book tentatively titled *Rationality, Realism, and the Growth of Knowledge*.

EDWARD L. SCHOEN holds the Ph.D. degree from the University of Southern California, where he authored a doctoral thesis on the philosophy of W.V. Quine. He is currently Full Professor of Philosophy at Western

Kentucky University, where he received the Distinguished Professor award for outstanding performance in the area of scholarly research. The author of numerous articles and reviews in leading professional journals (including *Religious Studies, International Journal for Philosophy of Religion, The Southern Journal of Philosophy,* and *Faith and Philosophy,* among others), his major work on *Religious Explanations* (Duke University Press, 1985) has provoked discussion in recent science-religion studies and philosophy of religion circles. Elected to a number of National Endowment for the Humanities institutes, he is currently working on another book-length study which furthers the investigations begun in *Religious Explanations.*

MARK SHALE is Assistant Professor of Liberal Studies in the Whitney Young College of Leadership Studies at Kentucky State University. He received his Ph.D. in the History of Science from the University of Wisconsin, Madison in 1987. He has been an advisor and consultant to Wisconsin Public Radio and Television for the education series, "Interactions: Science, Technology, and Society," and has published articles on Maupertuis, Pavlov, Karl and August Menninger, and William McDougall.

GEORGE W. SHIELDS is Professor of Philosophy at Kentucky State University, where he directs the Philosophy Program. He received the Ph.D. from the University of Chicago, and did further study at Oxford University, participating in the 1983 Oxford/Smithsonian Seminar on Science and Belief. A recent President of the Kentucky Philosophical Association, Dr. Shields has twice been awarded lectureships at faculty training institutes by the National Endowment for the Humanities. A co-editor and co-author of the memorial *Festschrift* for Professor Eugene Peters (1987), he is the author of numerous scholarly paper presentations and publications appearing in anthologies and leading professional journals, including *The Southern Journal of Philosophy, International Journal for Philosophy of Religion, Process Studies,* and *The Journal of Religion,* among many others. In addition to philosophy of religion, his interests include mathematical logic, philosophy of science, ethics, and the history of philosophy.

DENNIS TEMPLE is Full Professor and Chair of the Department of Philosophy, and Director of the General Education Program, at Roosevelt University in Chicago, Illinois. He received the Ph.D. degree from Washington University in St. Louis. He is the author of numerous articles and reviews which have appeared in leading professional journals, including the *American Philosophical Quarterly, Philosophy of Science, Studies in the History and Philosophy of Science,* and *History of Philosophy Quarterly,* among many others. His 1990 ILS Conference paper on Hume's objections to the design argument is forthcoming in *Religious Studies.* Dr. Temple has received four invitations to NEH seminars and an invitation to an NEH institute, in areas of his philosophical interest.